Blueprints
For Basic Tax Reform

Blueprints
For Basic Tax Reform

Second Edition, Revised

David F. Bradford
and the U.S. Treasury Tax Policy Staff

TAX ANALYSTS
Arlington, Virginia
1984

Contents

Chapter 4: A MODEL TAX BASED ON CONSUMPTION

Chapter 5: QUANTITATIVE ANALYSIS

List of Tables

Chapter 6: TRANSITION CONSIDERATIONS

Preface to the Second Edition

Much has happened to the Federal income tax since the publication of *Blueprints for Basic Tax Reform* in January 1977. The tax acts of 1978 and 1981 merit the description "major," while the 1982 legislation could hardly be called "minor." But the tax system is surely no closer to being one that the majority of Americans can understand and trust. The fundamental problems to which the *Blueprints* study was addressed in 1976 are still there—they are probably worse. The reissue of *Blueprints* by Tax Analysts reflects the view that it remains highly pertinent to dealing with those problems.

For some time now copies of *Blueprints* have been obtainable from government sources only in microfiche form, or at the substantial cost of photocopying. Tax Analysts' object in sponsoring republication is to make *Blueprints* easily and inexpensively available to policymakers, students, researchers, and interested laymen.

Although newly set up for printing, and in a revised format, this edition is essentially identical to the original. I have undertaken a light editing of the text to improve its clarity. I have not, however, attempted to up-date either the statistical or the legal materials. Readers of the second edition may therefore find it useful to have some sense of how the events of the intervening years affect the study's continuing relevance. Let me begin with what has happened to the law.

Changes in the Law

In general outline the income tax on individuals and corporations looks much the same in 1984 as it did in 1976. I would single out two changes as representing important departures in the principles underlying the tax. For efficiency and equity *Blueprints* urged that a reduced rate of tax apply to the earnings of a second worker in a married couple. A provision to that effect was enacted in 1978. *Blueprints* also stressed the desirability of making relative tax burdens independent of the rate of inflation. This involves both appropriate choice of rules for defining the tax base, and indexation of the structure of exemptions and rate brackets. The Economic Recovery Tax Act of 1981 introduced indexation of exemptions and brackets of the individual income tax, effective 1985. Index-ation of the base itself is yet to come.

In addition to these fundamental changes, new legislation has lowered the top marginal rate on the individual income tax from 70 to 50 percent, and reduced the remaining marginal rates by 23 percent. Corporate rates have been reduced slightly. The exclusion of long-term capital gains has been increased from 50 to 60 percent. Depreciation allowances have been accelerated, and the rules for classifying assets have been extensively changed. There has been a significant expansion of tax-sheltered savings oppor-tunities, especially via Individual Retirement Accounts.

These changes do not add up to a significant alteration in the structure of the system. Most of *Blueprints* can be read with very little correction for the evolution of the law.

The Quantitative Data

The quantitative data in Chapter 5 might seem more vulnerable to the passage of time. Most obviously, the estimates refer to a snapshot of the U.S. taxpaying public as of 1976, instead of 1984. While details of the distributions of tax payments are therefore less useful than up-dated figures would be, the broad outlines of the story are surely not radically different today. (As this is written the Treasury is at work on preparing a data set allowing comparable estimates to those in *Blueprints* to be made for the present.)

A rough correction can be made easily for the effect of inflation on the value of money. Increasing dollar magnitudes by 75 percent will give readers a feel for their meaning in terms of 1984 purchasing power. This would translate the effective tax rates shown in Tables 6 and 14 of Chapter 5, for example, to those shown in Table 1 below. Similarly, the exemptions and rates under the two model reform plans described by *Blueprints* are expressed in 1984 dollars in Table 2 below.

The effect the changes in the law would have on the 1976 taxpaying population is difficult to estimate, primarily because of the complexity of attributing to individuals the reduction in the corporation income tax. We can, however, be reasonably sure there has been a reduction in the effective tax rate at the top of the distribution, crossing over to an increase in effective tax rates at the bottom of the distribution. The schedule of exemptions and rates comparable to Table 2, but designed to match 1984 liabilities, would have a lower top rate and probably lower exemptions.

Table 1

Effective Rates of Combined Individual
and Corporation Income Tax

Comprehensive income base class	Effective tax rate 1976 law	Cash flow base class	Effective tax rate 1976 law
($000 (1984))	(percent)	($000 (1984))	(percent)
Less than 0	-0.6	Less than 0	0
0-9	1.7	0-9	2.2
9-18	6.4	9-18	7.4
18-26	9.9	18-26	11.8
26-35	12.7	26-35	14.8
35-53	15.4	35-53	18.0
53-88	19.8	53-88	23.6
88-175	25.2	88-175	30.7
175 or more	32.4	175 or more	36.0

Table 2

Blueprints Rate Structures*

Comprehensive Income Tax		Cash Flow Tax	
Basic exemption: $2,800 per return plus $1,750 for each taxpayer and dependent.		Basic exemption: $2,625 per return plus $1,400 for each taxpayer and dependent.	
Comprehensive income bracket	Marginal tax rate	Cash flow bracket	Marginal tax rate
(dollars)	(percent)	(dollars)	(percent)
Joint returns:		**Joint returns:**	
0-8,050	8	0-9,100	10
8,050-70,000	25	9,100-52,500	28
over 70,000	38	over 52,500	40
Single returns:		**Single returns:**	
0-4,900	8	0-5,600	10
4,900-70,000	22.5	5,600-52,500	26
over 70,000	38	over 52,500	40

*Adjusted for inflation from 1976 to 1984. These rates, together with special rules for secondary workers, were designed to yield approximately the same distribution of tax burdens as was generated by 1976 law.

Evolution of Ideas

The ideas in *Blueprints* have also been subject to discussion and criticism since 1977. It is beyond my limitations of time and space to attempt anything like a survey of the directly related published literature. However, four works deserve mention for their likely usefulness to readers of the second edition.

Useful References

In the United Kingdom, a committee sponsored by the Institute for Fiscal Studies, and under the chairmanship of Nobel Laureate, Professor James E. Meade, was carrying out a review of the British tax and transfer system at about the same time as the U.S. Treasury was at work on *Blueprints*. The Meade Committee report, entitled *The Structure and Reform of Direct Taxation*, and published in 1978 by Allen and Unwin of London, is most relevant to the U.S. situation. Subsequently a conference was held at the Brookings Institution in Washington on the central question of the choice between consumption and income as the guiding principle of the tax system. The proceedings, edited by Joseph A. Pechman, were published by Brookings in 1980 as *What Should Be Taxed: Income or Expenditure?* The third and fourth works are two reports by the Special Committee on Simplification of the Section of Taxation of the American Bar Association. Both discuss the potential for simplifying the tax law inherent in the *Blueprints* reform models. "Evaluation of the Proposed Model Comprehensive Income Tax," appeared in the Spring, 1979, issue of *The Tax Lawyer*, pp. 563-686. "Complexity and the Personal Consumption Tax," analyzing *Blueprints'* Cash Flow Tax proposal, appeared in the Summer, 1981, issue of the same journal, pp. 415-442.

Both the discussion of the issues and the experience of the intervening years prompt me to offer one point of clarification and to record two changes of view with respect to *Blueprints*. The clarification concerns the treatment of gifts and bequests as discussed in Chapter 2. The changes in viewpoint concern two important provisions of the Comprehensive Income Tax proposal of Chapter 3.

Treatment of Gifts and Bequests

Focusing on the differences between income and consumption, Chapter 2 considers the fundamental question of what ought to be the basis for taxation. The discussion is cast partly in terms of a simple system of accounts, by which a person's tax base would be calculated. In this way, such matters as the appropriate treatment of medical expenses or interest payments can be clearly analyzed. The tax consequences of gift and bequest transactions was one issue addressed, as of particular interest to tax policymakers.

Blueprints distinguishes two concepts of income and consumption, according to the accounting for gifts and bequests. No deduction is allowed for gifts or bequests given in reaching "ability-to-pay" income or consumption; "standard-of-living" income or consumption is obtained by deducting gifts and bequests given. What is not made clear in the text, and has occasioned some mistaken criticism, is that gifts and bequests *received* are understood as *included* in the calculation of all four possible tax bases, "ability-to-pay" and "standard-of-living" income and consumption.

Inflation and Interest Rates

I have mentioned that *Blueprints* recommended the adoption of rules making tax burdens insensitive to the rate of inflation. Thus, for example, under the Comprehensive Income Tax, the recommended basis for calculation of capital gains is the purchase price of the asset multiplied by the proportional change in the price level since the date of acquisition. Interest rates are also known to be sensitive to the rate of inflation. In the absence of tax considerations, an interest rate of two percent with no inflation is equivalent for both borrowers and lenders to an interest rate of 12 percent when prices are rising at 10 percent per year. The extra 10 percentage points on the interest rate is sometimes called the "inflation premium." In effect, it is a payment from the borrower to the lender to compensate for the loss in value of the loan principal during the year.

Under a proper income tax, such a payment would not give rise to any increase in the tax base of the lender or any deduction by the borrower. Thus an inflation correction to interest receipts and payments is called for.

On grounds of simplicity, however, *Blueprints* recommended against any adjustment, arguing that market forces were capable of providing an automatic correction. The assumed correction would be in the form of changes in the market interest rate to accommodate *both* the inflation premium *and* the taxes due on that premium. In our example, an increase in the interest rate from 2 percent with no inflation to 22 percent with 10 percent inflation would confront taxpayers in the 50 percent bracket with exactly the same real after-tax interest rate of 1 percent (50 percent of 2 with no inflation compared to 50 percent of 22, less the 10 percent inflation rate).

There are two problems with the *Blueprints* solution. First, empirically, interest rates do not adjust to anything like the degree suggested by the simple argument just made. At most, interest rates increase by one percentage point for each percentage point in the inflation rate. Second, and perhaps more important, differences in marginal tax rate within the taxpaying population mean that there is no single interest adjustment that will give the proper result.

Again to take our example, if the interest rate were to rise to 22 percent with the jump in inflation to 10 percent, thereby leaving unchanged the real net borrowing and lending terms for 50 percent bracket taxpayers, the real return obtained by tax-exempt lenders (pension funds, for example) would increase from 2 percent to 12 percent (22 percent interest less 10 percent inflation). The resulting distortions in financial incentives might be of secondary importance in a world of very low inflation rates, but they become very great indeed when inflation rates of 5 to 10 percent are in question. Table 3 gives some simple calculations for a not unreasonable case in which the interest rate is assumed to vary point for point with inflation. It will be seen that minor differences across tax brackets in the after-tax price of future purchasing power become huge differences with 10 percent inflation. I conclude that an explicit adjustment to interest payments and receipts is essential to an income tax in an economy susceptible to the inflation rates experienced in the last few years.

Table 3

Illustration of the Effect of Inflation on the Price (via Borrowing and Lending) of a Dollar Purchasing Power 25 Years Hence

Individual tax rate on interest	No inflation or inflation plus adjustment of interest for tax purposes	10 percent annual inflation and no adjustment
(percent)	(dollars)	(dollars)
0	.61	.61
15	.65	.95
30	.70	1.50
50	.78	2.77

Entries show the present amount one would have to set aside at compound interest to obtain one dollar (in present purchasing power) 25 years hence. In the illustration the interest rate with no inflation is assumed to be 2 percent; with inflation at 10 percent the interest rate is assumed to be 12 percent.

Unlimited Deduction of Capital Losses

Under an income tax a perennial problem is the taxation of accruing change in the value of assets held. It is well known to tax scholars that the special rules relating to capital gains, an aspect of the accruing value problem, account for much of the complexity of the existing Code. Unfortunately, practical systems seem bound to base the measurement of capital gains on realization transactions, typically sale or exchange of the asset. This gives rise to the possibility of deferral, even when no special rates of tax are involved. *Blueprints* reluctantly adopted the realization basis for taxing capital gains (albeit with adjustment of the basis for inflation). Arguing that the proposed integration of corporation and individual income taxes eliminated the worst part of the problem, and in the interest of simplicity, *Blueprints* recommended taxation of gains in full, and allowance in full for any capital losses.

It is now clear to me, as it was not in 1976, that allowing unlimited capital losses is fatally defective. A policy of holding gains and realizing losses could be arranged essentially to eliminate a taxpayer's liability. There is no neat solution to this problem, but unless a system of imputing interest charges to deferred liability is adopted, or a genuine accrual accounting system is worked out, deductibility of net capital losses must be sharply limited.

Acknowledgments

Let me close by reminding readers that this volume represents the joint effort of many individuals. While I take pride in being identified as its principal author, I cannot sufficiently emphasize the contributions of the Treasury tax staff, and of others outside the Treasury, as enumerated in the Acknowledgments to the first edition.

To that list should now be added Executive Director Thomas F. Field and Production Manager Cindy Chegwidden of Tax Analysts. Tom enthusiastically supported the republication of *Blueprints*, and Cindy implemented the decision with admirable skill. Several other members of the *Tax Notes*/Tax Analysts staff deserve mention as well, most notably design and layout artists Paul Doster and Kathy Regan and typographers Linda Killen, Bill Brewer, and Harvey Johnson. Rick Bauer's creative work resulted in the cover design. Finally, I should like to thank again Dan Feenberg, whose contribution to the original study was acknowledged there. Now on the staff of the National Bureau of Economic Research, Dan generously devoted many hours to a review of the data set used in the quantitative analysis presented in Chapter 5.

David F. Bradford

Foreword

In December 1975, in a speech to the Tax Foundation, I called for a fundamental overhaul of the U.S. tax system. I felt that I was speaking for millions of Americans who were fed up with the current tax system and wanted it replaced with one they could understand and trust. I noted that we need to return to the basic principles upon which our income tax system was founded and the three cornerstones of its structure—equity, efficiency and simplicity. I said we need to wipe the slate clean of personal tax preferences, special deductions and credits, exclusions from income and the like, and impose a single, simple progressive tax on all individuals. In the months that have passed since that speech, I have received overwhelming evidence that this is indeed the way the American people feel.

It is time to start over from scratch and develop a new tax system in the United States. It must be a system that is designed on purpose, based on a clear and consistent set of principles, which everyone in the United States can understand.

During the past year, at the same time my staff and I were working with the Congress on the Tax Reform Act of 1976, we were also engaged in a major study, which we called the "Basic Tax Reform" study. We began by examining the concept of "income" and what it can and should mean as the base for Federal taxation. We looked at all the transactions and circumstances that produce what we commonly think of as "income," and we also considered "income" from the standpoint of its uses—its value to those receiving it.

We then tried to develop an ideal income base that took into account all possible forms of income but that equally considered practical realities and the overriding importance of a simple tax system. Our "real-world" implementation reflects many compromises and modifications that we have discussed explicitly in the study so that everyone can evaluate our judgments and our conclusions.

Our report—Blueprints for Basic Tax Reform—presents the results of this year-long study. It gets down to the fundamentals.

This report presents two specific model tax systems. The first is a plan for broadening the base of the income tax. It calls for integration of the corporate and personal income taxes, taxation of capital gains at full rates after allowing an adjustment for inflation, and taxing many other items that presently are not taxed. In place of the existing complex rate structure, with rates ranging from 14 to 70 percent, the model plan has only three rate brackets, ranging from 8 percent to 38 percent.

The second model is based on consumption and is called a cash flow tax. It differs from an income tax in excluding savings, although the withdrawal of savings for consumption of goods and services would be taxed. This model also has three tax brackets with rates from 10 to 40 percent. Because the present income tax system has many important similarities to the cash flow tax, the change to this model would not be as great as it might seem.

After years of seeking to reform the tax system, I am convinced that tinkering is no longer the answer. We must design an entirely new tax system, adopt it as an integrated whole, with a much broader tax base but with much lower and simpler rates so that it will be widely accepted and so that all can share its advantages. This report is a start toward this objective. It demonstrates clearly that we can construct a fair, efficient progressive tax system in the United States.

Responsibility for preparation of this study was taken by Assistant Secretary for Tax Policy Charles M. Walker. Deputy Assistant Secretary William M. Goldstein provided important counsel. Primary work on this project was undertaken by Deputy Assistant Secretary David F. Bradford. Mr. Bradford and the staff of the Office of Tax Analysis are due special recognition for their professional expertise and special thanks for their devotion to this task.

William E. Simon

Washington, D.C.
January 1977

Acknowledgments

It is hard to imagine a project more appealing to a public finance economist than directing the professional staff of the United States Department of the Treasury in a study of income tax reform. A year ago Secretary William E. Simon asked Assistant Secretary Charles M. Walker to prepare a plan to simplify the tax system. As Deputy Assistant Secretary and Director of the Office of Tax Analysis, I was asked to lead this effort. With the publication of "Blueprints for Basic Tax Reform," the main objective of the project is accomplished, and it is my pleasure now to acknowledge the superb efforts of those who did so much of the work.

The pages of the report are the product of a tremendous cooperative effort, much of it applied during evenings and weekends, by many dedicated people. An especially important role was played by Harvey Galper, Associate Director of the Office of Tax Analysis. His experience and acumen as a tax analyst contributed directly to the project and his sense of humor and enormous capacity for work contributed indirectly by ensuring the smooth functioning of the Office. It was a delight to work with him.

Other principal associates in drafting the report were Larry L. Dildine and Eric J. Toder of the Office of Tax Analysis and Charles M. Whedbee, on loan from the Internal Revenue Service. Their analytical skills are reflected throughout the report.

Nelson McClung took principal responsibility for assembling the data base for the study, supported by J. Scott Turner, with Roy Wyscarver manning the computer simulations. Gary Robbins kept the project moving toward a sequence of unmeetable deadlines. Ron Garbin and the Office of Computer Science, Office of the Secretary, provided programming support.

The early groundwork for the study was developed with the assistance of Seymour Fiekowsky, Nelson McClung, Hudson Milner, and Ralph Bristol of the Office of Tax Analysis, and Richard Koffey, now Deputy Tax Legislative Counsel.

Many others, inside and outside the Department of the Treasury, contributed to the work. These include Peter Cook, John Copeland, Daniel Feenberg, David Flynn, Geraldine Gerardi, Gary Hufbauer, Michael Kaufman, Thomas King, Allen Lerman, Howard Nester,

Gabriel Rudney, Jay Scheck, Eugene Steuerle, Walter Stromquist, and John Wilman, all members of the Office of Tax Policy Staff. Joseph Foote of Washington, D.C., Peter Mieszkowski of the University of Houston, Harvey Rosen of Princeton University, Richard Barr of Southern Methodist University, and Ann Bergsman of Hendrickson Corporation brought their special knowledge to bear on the problems we confronted. Others outside the Treasury who assisted in various ways include William Andrews, Martin Bailey, Edwin Cohen, Martin Feldstein, Frederic Hickman, Daniel Halperin, Bernard Saffran, Emil Sunley, Nicholas Tideman, and Alvin Warren.

Finally, for their unsurpassed skill, never ending patience and cheerfulness, deepest thanks to Rosalind Carter and Kathi Cambell who typed and typed and typed and....

David F. Bradford
Deputy Assistant Secretary
for Tax Policy (Tax Analysis)

Washington, D.C.
January 1977

Introduction

The income tax experienced one transformation nearly fifty years ago, from a tax chiefly on those with substantial incomes to a mass tax. It may be facing another transformation now, into a "comprehensive" income tax with far fewer deductions, exclusions and the like, and with a much less progressive rate scale, and possible elimination of most of the corporate income tax. It might even be replaced, or supplemented by, a progressive tax on consumption. But are such changes really practicable?

Until the Second World War, the income tax in most countries consisted largely of a tax on investment income and high-level compensation. To finance the war, the tax was extended to labor income generally. This expansion was made possible by a device we now take for granted, namely withholding of tax on wages and salaries.

The fact that some eminent authorities, including the then U.S. Commissioner of Internal Revenue, protested that such withholding would be administratively quite impracticable should give heart to tax reformers of today. We should start, I believe, with the presumption that a progressive-rate consumption tax is indeed feasible, and that so too is the comprehensive income tax, including all forms of integration of the corporate and individual taxes, not excluding periodic accrual accounting for capital gains and losses.

In effect, tax historians can reassure legislators and administrators that experience shows we are capable of implementing sweeping changes that must at first seem formidable. If this sounds too easy—the bleachers shouting to the team—I submit that the history of tax administration and of tax compliance, at least in certain countries, indicates that the possibilities are usually greater than they at first appear.

In fact, a rather more difficult task has already been accomplished, though with little public recognition. The Internal Revenue Code, as it emerged from the mixing machines of ERTA, TEFRA, and their predecessors, might well have been adjudged impossible to operate under self-assessment. Yet somehow the Internal Revenue Service has made Form 1040 and its schedules and subsidiary forms a masterpiece of workability, considering the jungle of code provisions on which they are based.

The indirect tax field offers similar examples of impossibilities becoming realities. When Germany and France introduced the "cascade" turnover tax near the end of the First World War, that tax seemed difficult enough to implement. During the next two decades little attention was paid to suggestions that the grave distortions caused by the cascade feature—e.g., pressures toward vertical integration of business firms—could be obviated by something termed a value-added tax. Today, of course, one has to hunt to find a cascade tax, and VAT is the mainstay of indirect taxation in European and many other revenue systems.

Again, let us look at the retail sales tax. When Mississippi in 1932 and New York State in 1933 enacted the first permanent taxes based largely on retail sales, they had virtually no precedents to go by; the European general sales taxes offered little guidance for retail-level taxation at substantial rates. Yet this type of tax proved quite workable, even, in later years, at much higher rates.

In tax reform, then, history teaches us that boldness pays. Taxpayers may well suffer less under radical reform than under a blizzard of piecemeal changes. Occasional failures (for example, the consumption tax in India and Sri Lanka (then Ceylon) do not upset the general conclusion, at least for the United States. Here, the deluge of uncoordinated changes that has been known as tax reform has led many taxpayers and their accountants and legal counsel to the verge of despair as they try to understand and comply. The Code has become so complex that a taxpayer's decision on a particular point (to do or not to do, to opt or not) may have unforseen ramifications in remote sections of the Code that may negate all the benefits anticipated.

Blueprints renders a notable service in focusing so carefully on two possible reforms: a comprehensive three-bracket income tax on individuals and a progressive consumption tax. We are stimulated to intensive thought on the two, facilitated by the orderly and dispassionate arrangement and tone of this document, which will surely become a classic in tax analysis.

At the same time, a third option probably deserves equally careful consideration: a return to the individual income tax more or less as it existed before the wave of tax preferences of the past two or three decades, and, as in *Blueprints*, virtual repeal of the corporate income tax. A few of the recent innovations might be kept, e.g., the I.R.A. The rate schedule would be more progressive than that in *Blueprints*. Undistributed corporate profits would be reached by a triennial accrual treatment of capital gains and losses (I would add, of all kinds). Errors in the once-in-three-years valuations would be self-correcting upon realization (though of course with differences in timing), yet there would be much less need to determine at just what point realization occurs, thus simplifying the Code by defining realization in less stupifying detail. Corporate profits would be taxed directly only as they accrued to foreign holders.

In any event, we must be prepared to accept a reform that does not yield complete purity: a pure income tax, a pure consumption tax. Too many disparate views are held too tenaciouisly to allow a pure outcome. A tax reform must be a consensus reform if it is to be workable. The consensus need not degenerate into a package of wildly inconsistent features, but it almost has to lead to an outcome somewhere between those two pure types of tax. *Blueprints* notes that the present tax is a mixture of the two, perhaps more like a consumption tax in many respects. I would not infer that this is necessarily undesirable. If society wants tò encourage saving for retirement by low and middle income groups, the income tax seems usable for this limited purpose. What must be resisted is the inclination to riddle the income tax with rewards for almost every conceivable social or economic action deemed somehow desirable. Certainly the alternative of a direct subsidy must be studied carefully before turning to the income tax. (A research project that would compare cash subsidy with tax expenditure for every existing subsidy and tax expenditure, one by one, is long overdue; the answers would almost surely not favor the subsidy in every single case, but presumably would in most of them.)

The basic evil remains that of continual change. Each year the taxpayer finds the forms and schedules to be unfamiliar, they differ so from those of the preceding year. If only the income tax law and regulations could be left unchanged for say five years!

This in turn sounds an important alarm for the broadly oriented tax reformer. The new tax—comprehensive three-bracket individual income tax or consumption tax—must be carefully thought out in considerable detail. The points on which differences of judgement and possible friction will arise must be debated at length. Only then can a statute and its regulations be drawn up that Congress will be willing to accept with a self-limiting provision or understanding that no changes at all will be made for say the first five years. The taxpayer must be allowed to become easy with the wholly new tax forms and schedules.

In these deliberations, and in the five years ensuing, the hardest task will be to resist the temptation to improve the world, or at least one constituent's economic position, by insertion of seemingly minor exclusions, exemptions, credits, options and other tax moles that eventually can destroy any levy. Here is it difficult to be as sanguine as with respect to the inherent administrative feasibility of a radically new tax. It may be that our system of government, together with the astonishing expansion of tax expertise (e.g., every member of the Finance and Ways and Means Committees now has at least one tax aide) will never let a tax alone.

Direct-tax reforms of the types analyzed in *Blueprints* are already in the air, here and elsewhere.[1] *Blueprints*, with its clarity of exposition and rigorous logic, remains an indispensable source for anyone interested in these tax developments.

Carl S. Shoup

---

[1]For a critique of the 1982 *First Report of the Commission on Taxation*, in Ireland, entitled *Direct Taxation*, which advocates a combination of flat-rate comprehensive income tax and progressive-rate consumption tax, see A.R. Prest, "Taxation in Ireland," *British Tax Review*, 1983, No. 3, pp. 353-363.

CHAPTER 1

Summary

OVERVIEW

There has been increasingly widespread dissatisfaction in the United States with the Federal tax system. Numerous special features of the current law, adopted over the years, have led to extreme complexity and have raised questions about the law's basic fairness. Many provisions of the code are, in effect, subsidies to certain types of taxpayers, or to particular interests, for some forms of investment and consumption. These subsidies are rarely justified explicitly and, in some cases, may even be unintentional. In many instances, they alter the pattern of economic activity in ways that lower the value of total economic output. Further, although the Federal tax system by and large relates tax burdens to individual ability to pay, the tax code does not reflect any consistent philosophy about the objectives of the system.

Previous efforts at tax reform have not attempted a thorough rethinking of the entire tax structure. As a result, reform legislation over the past 25 years has consisted of a series of patchwork palliatives, leading to a tax system increasingly difficult to understand. Indeed, the Tax Reform Act of 1969 has been referred to as the "Lawyers and Accountants Relief Act," and the Tax Reform Act of 1976 deserves this sobriquet no less. The confusion and complexity in the tax code led Secretary of the Treasury William E. Simon to suggest that the Nation should "have a tax system which looks like someone designed it on purpose."

The first part of this report is devoted to clarifying the goals of the tax system, attempting to give specific content to the universally recognized objectives of equity, efficiency, and simplicity. Based on this analysis, two alternative conceptions of an ideal tax system are adopted to form the basis for practical reform plans. The report presents two model plans, comprehending both the individual and corporate income taxes, which demonstrate that the tax system *can* be made more equitable, easier to understand and justify, and more conducive to the efficient operation of the private economy.

1

Both plans have the general effect of broadening the tax base—the measure of income to which personal exemptions and tax rates are applied. This is the result of including in the base items excluded from tax under current law. This permits a simpler code in that elaborate rules are no longer required for defining items of tax preference or for protecting against the abuse of such preferences. Under either plan, the revenues currently collected from individual and corporate taxpayers could be raised with a substantially lower rate structure. In turn a lower rate structure would mitigate the distorting effects of taxes on economic decisions.

The alternative proposals for tax reform are: (1) an income base tax, called a Comprehensive Income Tax, and (2) a consumption base tax, called a Cash Flow Tax. Both proposals seek to treat individual items in the tax code in ways that would achieve consistency with an ideal base, departing from the ideal only when necessary for administrative feasibility, simplicity, or compelling economic or other policy reasons. When concessions are suggested, they are identified as such and justification is provided.

The differences between the proposals derive from their underlying concepts of the tax base. The Comprehensive Income Tax proposal is based on a broad concept of income that is defined in terms of the uses of an individual's receipts. According to this definition, an individual's income can be allocated either to consumption or to increasing his wealth (net worth). Because all increments to wealth constitute income, this approach is sometimes called an accretion concept. The Cash Flow Tax assesses tax burdens on the basis of consumption, excluding from the tax base all positive and negative changes in net worth.

Both proposals deal with the major areas in which changes from the current tax code merit consideration. In all cases where there are ambiguities about defining consumption or change in net worth as components of income, or where the benefits achieved by exclusions or deductions from income under the current law appear to merit continued consideration, specific policy judgments are made for the purpose of presenting complete proposals. The report identifies the features of each proposal that are essential to the definition of the ideal tax base, distinguishing them from elements that can be handled differently and still remain consistent with a reasonable definition of either the comprehensive income or consumption tax base. The table at the end of this chapter compares the major features of the model tax reform plans with the current tax system.

This study shows that it is feasible to have a broadly based tax that departs in major ways from the current tax law. In providing specific alternative plans, the report sets out a guide for future legislation aimed at sweeping tax reform. It also points out some of the major policy issues that remain to be resolved. In presenting a plan for a tax system based on the consumption concept, the report points toward a promising alternative approach to tax reform that is not as different from our present system as it might seem and that, if consistently implemented, should provide major advantages in fairness, simplicity, and economic efficiency.

COMPREHENSIVE INCOME TAX

Proposals to adopt a more comprehensive definition of income in the tax base have received the most attention from tax reform advocates.

As previously stated, income may be viewed as the sum of consumption and change in net worth in a given time period. Although income is thus defined conceptually in terms of *uses* of resources, it is not practical to measure an individual's annual income by adding up all of his individual purchases of consumer goods and the change in value of all the items on his balance sheet. Rather, the measurement of income is accomplished by using the accounting notion that the sum of receipts from all sources within a given time period must equal the sum of all uses. To compute income, it is necessary simply to subtract from sources expenditures that represent neither consumption nor additions to net worth. These expenditures include the cost of operating a business (payment of salaries, rent, interest, etc.), or the direct cost of earning labor income (union dues, work clothing, etc.). They may include other specified expenditures, such as interest, charitable contributions, State and local income and sales taxes, and large nondiscretionary medical expenditures.

Because of exclusions, deductions, and shortcomings in income measurement rules, the tax base under current law departs from this comprehensive concept of income. For example, State and local bond interest and one-half of realized capital gains are not included in the tax base. On the other hand, corporate dividends are included in the tax base twice, once at the corporate level and once at the individual level. In some cases, rules for tax depreciation allow deductions in excess of actual changes in asset values. When this occurs, business income is understated, and the taxpayer has increase in net worth that goes untaxed.

In setting out a practical plan to achieve equity, simplicity, and efficiency in the tax system, the model Comprehensive Income Tax follows a broad concept of accretion income as a guide. The major features of the model Comprehensive Income Tax are summarized below.

Integration of the Corporation
and Individual Income Taxes

A separate tax on corporations is not consistent with an ideal comprehensive income tax base. Corporations do not "consume" or have a standard of living in the sense that individuals do; all corporate income ultimately can be accounted for either as consumption by individuals or as an increase in the value of claims of individuals who own corporate shares. Thus, corporations do not pay taxes in the sense of bearing the burden of taxation. People pay taxes, and corporate tax payments are drawn from resources belonging to people that would otherwise be available to them for present or future consumption.

It is difficult, however, to determine which people bear the burden of corporate tax payments. In a free enterprise system goods are not produced unless their prices will cover the costs of rewarding those who supply the services of labor and capital required in their output as well as any taxes imposed. The corporation income tax thus results in some combination of higher relative prices of the products of corporations and lower rewards to the providers of productive services, and it is in this way that the burden of the tax is determined. In spite of many attempts, economists have not succeeded in making reliable estimates of these effects, although a substantial body of opinion holds that the corporation income tax is borne by all capital owners in the form of lower prices for the services of capital.

The two major advantages of integrating the corporate and personal taxes are that (1) it would eliminate the incentive to accumulate income within corporations by ending the double taxation of dividends, (2) it would enable the effective tax rate on income earned within corporations to be related to the circumstances of individual taxpayers.

Under the model Comprehensive Income Tax, the integration of corporate income with the other income of shareholders is accomplished by providing rules to allocate all corporate income, whether distributed or not, to individual shareholders. Corporate distributions to shareholders are regarded simply as a change in the composition of investment portfolios—that is, a portion of each shareholder's equity claims is converted to cash—and have no tax consequences. Under this "full integration" plan, corporation income is fully taxed at the rates appropriate to each shareholder.

For this reason, the model plan eliminates the corporation income tax. The possibility of having corporations withhold taxes on behalf of shareholders, in order to alleviate problems arising when tax liabilities exceed corporate cash distributions, is examined. It is emphasized that full integration is proposed in the context of a plan that attempts to tax equally income from all sources. "Dividend" integration such as that proposed by the Ford Administration in 1975, which represents, in itself, a desirable change in the absence of comprehensive reform, may also be considered as a transition to the model treatment of corporate income.

Treatment of Capital Gains and Losses

Under the broadest concept of an income tax base, capital gains that represent an increase in real wealth would be taxed even though not realized by sale or exchange of the asset. Similarly, capital losses, whether realized or not, would be subtracted in full from all sources of income in computing the tax base. The proposal moves in that direction by adopting the integration concept. Full integration provides a practical method for taxing increases in asset values arising from corporate retained earnings, a major source of capital gains in the current system. Capital gains realized upon sale or exchange of assets are taxed fully under the model plan *after* allowing a step-up in basis for inflation. Because maximum tax rates would be considerably lower if a comprehensive tax base were adopted, there is far less reason for special treatment of capital gains to achieve rough averaging effects in a progressive rate structure. Realized capital losses are fully deductible against ordinary income in the model system.

Thus, the proposal, while ending the current provision for exclusion of one-half of capital gains from the base, will also end the taxation of purely inflationary gains and eliminate current limits on deductibility of realized capital losses. Compared with present law, taxation of capital gains would be lower during periods of rapid inflation and possibly somewhat higher during periods of relative price stability. The proposal does not recommend taxation of gains as accrued (that is, prior to realization) because the administrative cost of annual asset valuations is prohibitive and because otherwise taxpayers might face problems in making cash tax payments when no cash had been realized. The corporate integration proposal would enable the largest part of individual income previously reflected in realized capital gains to be taxed as accrued by eliminating the corporate tax and taxing corporate income directly to the shareholders, whether or not it was distributed. This is a fair and workable solution.

Depreciation Rules

The proposal defines some general principles for measuring depreciation of assets for tax purposes. It is recommended that a systematic approach to tax depreciation, perhaps one modeled after the Asset Depreciation Range System, be made mandatory for machinery and equipment and structures. A set of accounting procedures would be prescribed that would provide certainty to the taxpayer that his depreciation allowances would be accepted by the tax collector and would reasonably approximate actual declines in the value of these depreciable assets. Cost depletion is recommended in place of percentage depletion for mineral deposits, as a better measure of the income arising from these properties.

State and Local Bond Interest

The proposal suggests that interest from State and local bonds be treated like all other interest receipts in the computation of the tax base, on the grounds that those receipts can be used for consumption or increases in net worth. Transition problems relating to existing bond holdings are recognized. The implicit tax burden in ownership of State and local bonds resulting from their lower interest yield is identified and evaluated. The report mentions alternative, less costly ways of providing the same subsidy to state and local governments as is presently provided by the interest exemption.

Imputed Income from Consumer Durables

Under the broadest form of income base, the imputed return in the form of the rental value of consumption services from ownership of consumer durables would be taxed. The exclusion of this form of income from tax provides an important benefit to home owners. They have invested part of their net worth in their home, rather than investment assets, but the value of the use of their home (the income it produces) is not taxed. This is particularly true when, as under our present system, interest on home mortgages is deductible from other income. This proposal does *not* recommend taxation of the imputed value of the use of homes and consumer durables because of difficulties of measurement. However, it is recommended that the deductibility of local taxes on noncommercial property, including owner-occupied homes, be reconsidered, on the grounds that this amounts to exclusion of *more* than the income that would be imputed to such assets.

Itemized Deductions

The report considers options for the treatment of major deductions, including deductions for medical expenses (which could be replaced with a catastrophic insurance program), charitable contributions (for which the deduction could be eliminated or retained without compromising the basic integrity of either the Comprehensive Income or Cash Flow Tax), State and local income taxes (which would remain deductible) and sales taxes (not deductible) and casualty losses (not deductible). Decisions as to whether, and in what form, major personal deductions should be maintained depend on whether or not these expenditures should be viewed as consumption and on whether or not particular types of activities ought to continue to be encouraged through the tax system. The report presents specific proposals for treatment of major deductions but it is noted that other rules are also consistent with the concept of a comprehensive income base. The deduction of interest is maintained, as is, in modified form, the deduction of child care expenses. The report recommends elimination of the standard deduction, which will be replaced in part by more generous personal exemptions.

Retirement Income and Unemployment Compensation

Under a conceptually pure income tax, both contributions to retirement pensions and the interest earned on such contributions would be included in the base. However, a roughly equivalent result is achieved by taxing earnings on pension funds as they accrue and retirement benefits as received and allowing employer *and* employee contributions to pensions to be deducted from the tax base. This procedure is preferable because it minimizes problems of income averaging. Rules for making different types of pension accounts conform to this principle are outlined in the report. It is proposed that deduction of both employee and employer contributions to Social Security be allowed and that all social security retirement benefits be included in the tax base. The report also recommends that unemployment compensation payments be included in the tax base.

Liberal personal exemptions recommended will insure that persons with very low incomes are not taxed on social security benefits or unemployment compensation.

Choice of a Filing Unit and Exemptions for Family Size

The decision on the appropriate filing unit represents a compromise between objectives that are mutually exclusive under a progressive tax: a system in which families of equal size and income pay equal taxes and a system in which the total tax liability of two individuals is not altered when they marry. The report recommends continuation of family filing, with separate structures of exemptions and rates for married couples, single individuals, and unmarried heads of household. To reduce the work disincentive caused by taxation of secondary earners at marginal rates determined by the income of a spouse, the plan proposes that only 75 percent of the first $10,000 of earnings of secondary workers be included in the tax base. Alternative treatments of the filing unit consistent with the general principles of a comprehensive income base are presented.

The report discusses the issues in the choice between exemptions and tax credits as adjustments for family size, and recommends a per-member exemption instead of a credit. However, it is noted that various methods of adjusting for family size, including use of credits, are fully consistent with the comprehensive income base.

The report shows how adoption of the recommended changes in the tax base would change tax rates. With an exemption of $1,000 per taxpayer and an additional $1,600 per tax return, *it is possible under the Comprehensive Income Tax to raise the same revenue with roughly the same distribution of the tax burden by income class as under the present income tax,* using only three rate brackets, ranging from 8 percent in the lowest bracket, to 25 percent for middle income taxpayers, to 38 percent for upper income taxpayers. Alternatively, it is possible to raise the same revenue under the Comprehensive Income Tax with a flat rate of slightly over 14 percent on all income if there are no exemptions and with a flat rate of slightly under 20 percent with exemptions of $1,500 per taxpayer.

In summary, the Comprehensive Income Tax proposal is a complete plan for a major rebuilding of the tax system that eliminates many of the inconsistencies in the present tax code. The plan clearly demonstrates the feasibility of major improvements in the simplicity, efficiency, and fairness of the income tax.

CASH FLOW, CONSUMPTION BASE TAX

Consumption is less widely advocated than income in discussions of tax reform, but it deserves serious consideration as an alternative ideal for the tax base. A consumption tax differs from an income tax in excluding savings from the tax base. In practical terms, this means that net savings, as well as gifts made, are subtracted from gross receipts to compute the tax base. *Withdrawals* from savings, and gifts and bequests received but not added to net savings, are *included* in gross receipts to compute the tax base.

Advantages of a Consumption Base

The report shows that a version of a consumption base tax, called the Cash Flow Tax, has a number of advantages over a comprehensive income tax on simplicity grounds. The Cash Flow Tax avoids the most difficult problems of measurement under a comprehensive income tax—such as depreciation rules, inflation adjustments, and allocation of undistributed corporate income—because all forms of saving would be excluded from the tax base.

In addition, the report demonstrates that the Cash Flow Tax is more equitable because it treats alike all individuals who begin their working years with equal wealth and the same present value of future labor earnings. They are treated differently under an income tax, depending on the time pattern of their earnings and the way they choose to allocate consumption expenditures among time periods.

By eliminating disincentives to savings, the Cash Flow Tax would encourage capital formation, leading to higher growth rates, more capital per worker and higher before-tax wages.

How a Consumption Base Could be Taxed

According to one method of designing a consumption tax, the taxpayer would include in his tax base all monetary receipts in a given time period, including withdrawals from past savings and gifts and bequests received, and exclude from his tax base current savings, gifts made, and certain itemized expenditures also allowed as deductions under the comprehensive income tax. Thus, the full proceeds of asset sales would be taxed if used for consumption rather than for purchase of other assets (including such "purchases" as deposits in savings accounts). Inclusion of asset sales and deduction of asset purchases from the tax base make it possible for the tax base to measure an individual's annual consumption without actually tallying up his purchases of consumption goods and services.

A second method of computing the base for a tax based on consumption is to exempt all capital income from tax. Dividends, interest, capital gains, and profit from a personal business would be excluded from an individual's tax base. Interest receipts would be excluded from the base, and interest payments on loans would not be deducted. Purchases of productive assets would not be deductible, because the returns from them would not be in the base.

These alternative treatments of assets lead to a tax base with the same present value. Deferral of tax in the present leads to payment of the same tax plus interest when the asset is sold for consumption. However, the payment of taxes occurs later under the method

which allows a savings deduction than under the method which
allows an interest exemption.

Similarities to the Present Tax Base

The report points out that the current tax system is closer to a
consumption tax than to a comprehensive income tax in its treatment of many forms of the income from capital. In particular, one
important type of saving for many Americans—employer contributions to retirement annuities (or contributions of individuals to
Keogh Plans and IRAs)—is treated under the current law almost
exactly the same way it would be treated under a consumption tax
which allows a deduction for savings. A second major type of
household saving—acquisition of a home—receives the alternative,
yield-exclusion, treatment. Similarly, many of the present system's
uncoordinated exclusions of capital income from tax approximate
the second approach to a consumption base tax. Thus, the model
Cash Flow Tax is not as complete a change from the present tax
system as it might seem.

Treatment of Investments in the Model Plan

In the model Cash Flow Tax individuals may choose between the
two essentially equivalent ways of treating investments. Purchases
of assets are eligible for deduction only if made through "qualified
accounts." Each year, net contributions to qualified accounts
would be computed and subtracted from the tax base. If withdrawals exceed contributions in any year, the difference would be
added to the tax base. Thus, the proceeds from an investment
made through a qualified account are subject to tax *only when
withdrawn*.

Savings not deposited in a qualified account are ineligible for
deduction, but the interest and capital gains from investments
financed by such saving are not included in the tax base. There is
no need to monitor the flow of investments or the investment income earned outside of qualified accounts because they have no
place in the calculation of tax.

The report spells out the consequences of allowing a taxpayer to
choose between alternative ways of being taxed on income from
assets, providing specific examples of how the tax would work. It is
shown how allowing two alternative treatments for both assets and
loans provides a simple averaging device that would enable taxpayers to avoid the inequities associated with applying a progressive rate system to individuals with different annual variation
in the level of consumption. The report also shows how allowing
alternative treatment of assets and loans simplifies the measurement of the tax base.

Other Features of the Cash Flow Tax

Under the proposal, all consumer durables (such as automobiles and homes) are treated as assets purchased outside of a qualified account. No deductions are allowed for the purchase of a consumer durable, and receipts from the sale of a consumer durable are not included in the tax base.

Gifts are treated differently under the Cash Flow Tax than under both the comprehensive income tax and the current tax system. In the Cash Flow Tax proposal, gifts and inheritances received are included in the tax base, while gifts given are deducted. Under present income tax law and under the model Comprehensive Income Tax the treatment is reversed, with gifts received excluded from the donee's tax base but no deduction allowed for an individual who makes a gift. It is assumed that in both systems there would continue to be a separate tax on transfers of assets by gift or bequest, such as the present estate and gift tax.

The proposal describes in detail how specific items of capital income—dividends, interest, capital gains, income from personal business, and accumulation of retirement pensions—are treated. The corporate income tax is eliminated because there is no longer a need to tax undistributed corporate income. Purchases of corporate stocks through qualified accounts are tax deductible, while all withdrawals from qualified accounts are included in the tax base. Sale proceeds of corporate stock, dividends, and interest, if remaining in the qualified account, are not taxed.

The Cash Flow Tax, like the Comprehensive Income Tax, would move towards neutrality in the tax treatment of different kinds of investments. In doing so, both proposals would have the effect of encouraging the best use of available capital. In addition the Cash Flow Tax would eliminate the discouragement to capital formation inherent in the concept of a tax on income.

The Filing Unit and Tax Rates

The Cash Flow Tax proposal treats definition of the filing unit, exemptions for family size, and deductions of personal consumption items the same way as the Comprehensive Income Tax proposal. The differences between the two proposals are in the treatment of items which represent a change in net worth, or income from capital, and in the treatment of gifts and inheritances.

Under the Cash Flow Tax, an exemption of $800 per person and $1,500 per return together with three rate brackets—10 percent, 28 percent, and 40 percent—would allow present tax revenues to be raised while maintaining the same vertical distribution of tax burdens.

TRANSITION PROBLEMS

Reforming the existing tax system poses a different set of problems than designing a new tax system from scratch. Although the report concentrates on the design of approximations to ideal tax systems, the problems of transition have also been examined and possible solutions embodied in specific proposals.

Transition to a new set of tax rules poses two separate, but related problems. First, changes in rules for taxing income from capital will lead to changes in the relative value of assets. Problems of fairness would exist if investors who had purchased a particular type of asset in light of the present tax system were subjected to losses by sudden major changes in tax policy. Similarly, changes in tax policy may provide some investors with windfall gains. Second, changes in the tax law raise questions of what to do about income earned before the effective date, but not yet subject to tax. For example, the comprehensive income tax, which proposes full inclusion of capital gains in the base (subject to an inflation adjustment), requires a transition rule for taxing capital gains accumulated before, but realized after, the effective date.

The report describes two methods for moderating the wealth effects of tax reform—"grandfathering," or exempting existing assets from the new tax provisions, and phasing-in of the new rules. Specific proposals for use of these instruments for projected changes in the tax code are presented. The report also outlines specific transition proposals for handling income earned before the effective date, but not yet taxed.

HOW AN INDIVIDUAL WOULD CALCULATE TAX LIABILITY UNDER THE REFORM PLANS

Elements Common To Both Plans

The method of calculating tax liabilities under the model tax systems would be similar to the method in use today. Taxpayers would fill out a form like the Form 1040, indicating family status and number of exemptions. There would not be a standard deduction under either plan. Taxpayers who had eligible deductions would choose to itemize; to reduce the number of itemizers, deductions would be subject to floor amounts.

The tax base would be calculated on the form, and the tax rate schedule appropriate to the filing unit (i.e., single, married, head of household) would be applied to compute tax liability. Taxes owed and refunds due, would depend on the difference between tax liability and taxes withheld as reported on W-2 statements or estimated tax paid.

The wages and salaries of the primary wage earner would remain the biggest item in the tax base of most households and would be entered into the calculation of income the same way as under the current system. The first $10,000 of wages and salaries of *secondary* wage earners would be multiplied by .75 before being added to the tax base. The rules for calculating some deductions (e.g., child care) would be changed, and other deductions (e.g., property and gasoline taxes) would be eliminated.

The Comprehensive Income Tax

Under the Comprehensive Income Tax, some additional items would be added to the computation of tax. Corporations would supply to all stockholders a statement of the amount of profit attributed to that stockholder in the previous year, and an adjustment to basis that would rise with earnings and fall with distributions. Similar statements of attributed earnings would be supplied to taxpayers by pension funds and insurance companies. In addition to the income reported in these statements, taxpayers would report income from interest on State and local bonds, unemployment compensation, and social security retirement benefits.

All capital gains (or losses) would be entered in full in the computation of taxable income. The basis for corporate shares would be increased by corporate income taxed but not distributed to them. In computing gains from sale or exchange, the taxpayer would be allowed to adjust the basis of assets sold for inflation. A table of allowable percentage basis adjustments would be provided in the tax form. The taxpayer would use statements received from corporations to adjust the basis of corporate shares upward for any past attributed corporate profits and downward for dividends or other distributions received.

The Cash Flow Tax

The major change under the Cash Flow Tax is that the taxpayer would receive yearly statements of net withdrawals or deposits from all qualified accounts. If deposits exceeded withdrawals, the difference between deposits and withdrawals would be subtracted from the tax base. If withdrawals exceeded deposits, the difference would be added to the tax base.

Interest, dividends, and capital gains realized on investments made outside of qualified accounts would not be reported on the tax form and would not be included in taxable income. The rationale for this is that the tax would have been pre-paid, because no deduction was allowed at the time of purchase.

Gifts and inheritances received would be included in the tax base (but if deposited in a qualified account would have an offsetting deduction). A deduction would be allowed for gifts and bequests given. The identity of the recipient of deductible gifts would be reported on the donor's return.

CHAPTER-BY-CHAPTER OUTLINE OF
THE REMAINDER OF THE REPORT

Chapter 2 — What Is To Be the Tax Base?

Chapter 2 reviews the main issues in choosing an appropriate tax base (the sum to which the structure of exemptions and rates is applied) and presents the case for considering a cash flow tax based on consumption as an alternative to a reformed comprehensive income tax. General issues of equity in design of a tax system are discussed, and the concepts of consumption and income are explained. It is shown that the current tax system contains elements of both a consumption base and a comprehensive income base. Thus, it is shown how the adoption of a consumption or cash flow tax would not be as great a change from the present system as it might seem. The alternative tax bases are compared on grounds of equity, simplicity, and effects on economic efficiency.

Chapter 3 — A Model Tax Based On Income

A model income tax, called the Comprehensive Income Tax, is presented in chapter 3. The major innovations in the plan relate to integration of the corporation and individual income taxes, and to tax treatment of capital gains, State and local bond interest, income accumulated in pensions and life insurance funds, retirement income, and unemployment compensation. Changes in many personal deductions are suggested. Recommendations for changes in the filing unit, adjustment for family size, and taxation of secondary wage earners are set forth. International considerations in income taxation are discussed briefly. The chapter concludes with a description of a sample form for tax calculation under the Comprehensive Income Tax proposal.

Chapter 4 — A Model Tax Based On Consumption

In chapter 4, a model tax system based on consumption is presented. Called the Cash Flow Tax, its major innovation is that savings may be deducted from the tax base. The use of qualified accounts to measure the flow of saving and consumption is proposed. The equivalence between deductibility of saving and exclusion of capital earnings from tax is explained, and alternative treatments of assets reflecting this equivalence are presented. Treatment of specific items under the model Cash Flow Tax is compared with treatment of corresponding items under the Comprehensive Income Tax. Arguments against the Cash Flow Tax on grounds of progressivity and effects on wealth distribution are evaluated. The use of a supplementary wealth transfer tax to provide greater progressivity is explored. The chapter concludes with a description of a sample tax form under the Cash Flow Tax proposal.

Chapter 5 — Quantitative Analyses

Chapter 5 presents simulations of the effects of the proposed reforms on the tax liabilities of different groups of taxpayers. The chapter demonstrates that the vertical structure of tax burdens under the present income tax system may be broadly duplicated with a more generous set of exemptions and a rate schedule which is more moderate and much simpler so long as the tax base is greatly broadened as proposed under either the Comprehensive Income Tax (chapter 3) or the Cash Flow Tax (chapter 4).

Chapter 6 — Transition Considerations

Chapter 6 proposes transition rules to accompany adoption of the model tax plans. Problems which may arise in *changing* tax laws are explained, and instruments to ameliorate adjustment problems, including exempting existing assets from changes and phasing in new rules, are described and evaluated. Specific proposals are presented for transition to both a Comprehensive Income base and a Cash Flow base that cover the timing of the application of new rules to specific proposed changes in the tax code.

Table 1
Summary Comparison of Model Tax Plans

Item	Current tax	Comprehensive Income Tax	Cash Flow Tax
Corporate income			
a. Retained earnings	Separately taxed to corporations	Attributed to individuals as income and included in tax base	No tax until consumed
b. Dividends	Separately taxed to corporations, included in individual tax base with $100 exemption	Not taxed separately	No tax until consumed
Capital gains	50% of long-term gains included when realized; alternative tax available	Fully included in tax base on realization; no partial exclusion	No tax until consumed
Capital losses	50% of long-term losses deductible against included portion of long-term gains and $1,000 of ordinary income; carryover of losses allowed	Fully deductible from tax base on realization	No tax offset unless consumption is reduced
Depreciation	Complex set of depreciation rules for different types of equipment and structures	Reformed rules for depreciation; depreciation to approximate actual decline in economic value on a systematic basis by industry classes	Permits expensing of all business outlays, capital or current
State and local bond interest	Excluded from tax base	Included in tax base	Excluded from tax base until consumed
Other interest received	Included in tax base	Included in tax base	Excluded from tax base until consumed

Table 1

Summary Comparison of Model Tax Plans
(Continued)

Item	Current tax	Comprehensive Income Tax	Cash Flow Tax
Proceeds of loans	Excluded from tax base	Excluded from tax base	Inclusion in tax base optional
Interest paid on loans	Deducted from tax base	Deducted from tax base	Deducted from tax base if proceeds of loan included in base
Principal repayments on loans	Not deducted from tax base	Not deducted from tax base	Deducted from tax base if proceeds of loan included in base
Rental value of owner-occupied homes	Excluded from tax base	Excluded from tax base	Implicitly included in tax base because purchase treated as consumption
State or local property, sales and gasoline taxes (non-business)	Deducted from tax base	Not deducted from tax base	Not deducted from tax base
Medical expenses[1]	Expenses over 3% of adjusted gross income deducted from tax base	No deduction; possible credit for expenses over 10% of income*	No deduction; possible credit for expenses over 10% of consumption*
Charitable contributions[2]	Deducted from tax	Not deducted from tax base*	Not deducted from tax base*
Casualty losses	Uninsured losses deducted from tax base	Not deducted from tax base	Not deducted from tax base
State and local income taxes	Deducted from tax base	Deducted from tax base*	Deducted from tax base*
Child care expenses[3]	Limited tax deduction	Revised tax deduction*	Revised tax deduction*

Table 1
Summary Comparison of Model Tax Plans
(Continued)

Item	Current tax	Comprehensive Income Tax	Cash Flow Tax
Contributions to retirement pensions	Employer contributions untaxed; employee contributions taxed	All contributions excluded from tax	All contributions excluded from tax
Interest earnings on pension funds	Excluded from tax	Attributed to employer or to individuals and taxed in full as accrued	Excluded from tax
Retirement benefits from pension funds	Included in tax base except for return of employee contribution	Included in tax base	Included in tax base unless saved
Social security contributions	Employer contributions untaxed; employee contributions taxed	All contributions excluded from tax	All contributions excluded from tax
Social security retirement income and unemployment compensation	Excluded from tax base	Included in tax base	Included in tax base unless saved
Wage and salary income[4]	Included in tax base	Included in tax base for primary earner; for secondary earners, 75% of wages under $10,000 and all wages over $10,000 included*	Included in tax base for primary earner; for secondary earners, 75% of wages under $10,000 and all wages over $10,000 included*; savings out of wages deductible
Deposits in qualified investment accounts	No tax consequences	No tax consequences	Deducted from tax base

Table 1
Summary Comparison of Model Tax Plans
(Continued)

Item	Current tax	Comprehensive Income Tax	Cash Flow Tax
Withdrawals from quali- fied investment accounts	No tax consequences	No tax consequences	Included in tax base
Standard deduction	Available to non-itemizers only; $1,600 or 16% of adjusted gross income up to $2,400 for single taxpayer, $1,900 or 16% of adjusted gross income up to $2,800 for married couple filing jointly	No standard deduction; $1,600 per return exemption	No standard deduction; $1,500 per return exemption
Personal exemptions	$750 per individual; extra exemptions for aged and blind	$1,000 per individual	$800 per individual

Source: Office of the Secretary of the Treasury, Office of Tax Analysis
*Indicates alternative treatments possible.
¹Medical deduction optional under model tax plans. Alternative ways of structuring deduction or credit possible.
²Charitable deduction optional under model tax plans. Other alternatives possible, including limited credit.
³Child care deduction and its form and limits optional under model tax plans.
⁴Treatment of secondary earners optional under model tax plans.

CHAPTER **2**

What Is To Be The Tax Base?

INTRODUCTION

The dominant complaint made about the present tax system is that it does not tax all income alike. This complaint reflects concern about equity: taxpayers with the same level of income bear different tax burdens. It reflects concern about efficiency: taxation at rates that differ by industry or by type of financial arrangement leads to misallocation of resources. Finally, it reflects concern about simplicity: the enormously complex tangle of provisions the taxpayer confronts in ordering his affairs and calculating his tax leads to differential rates of taxation.

The usual approach to the complaint that all income is not taxed alike is to attempt to make income as defined by tax law correspond more closely to the "real thing." The problem with this approach is the difficulty of identifying the "real thing." As with other abstractions, there are numerous ways to look at the concept of income, some of which may be better or worse according to context.

Laymen find it hard to believe that there are major problems in defining income. They are used to thinking in terms of cash wages and salaries, which are easily identified and clearly income. In fact, wages and salaries account for the great bulk of income—however defined—in the U.S. economy; other items like interest and dividends are also easily identified. So it may be fairly said that most of the dollars identified as income in the total economy will be the same under any definition of income.

But as one approaches the edges of the concept of income, there is a substantial grey area. It is small compared with the bulk of income, but this grey area (capital gains, for example) is the focus of much controversy. There is an extensive literature on the subject, beginning before the turn of the century and continuing to the present, with no consensus except that particular definitions may be more practical in certain circumstances than in others.

Many of the major problems in defining income concern expectations or rights with respect to the receipt of payments in the future—does an individual have income when the expectation or right arises, or only when the money comes in? Is the promise to pay a pension to be counted as income when made, although the amounts will be paid 20 years hence? Is a contract to earn $60,000 a year for the next five years to be discounted and counted as income in the year the contract is made? Is the appreciation in the market value of an outstanding bond resulting from a decline in the general market rate of interest to be counted as income now, even though that appreciation will disappear if interest rates rise in the future? Is the increase in the present value of a share in a business attributable to favorable prospects of the business earning more in future years to be counted as income now or in the future years when the earnings actually materialize?

Differences in view with respect to the definition of income cut across political philosophies. Although many "liberal" economists argue for an expansive definition of income, the extreme view that income cannot be defined adequately to constitute a satisfactory tax base has been advanced by the eminent British socialist economist, Nicholas Kaldor, who argues for a consumption tax. At another extreme, one of the most all-inclusive definitions of income was formulated by Professor Henry Simons, a conservative economist long affiliated with the University of Chicago.

Professor Simons' definition—usually referred to as the "Haig-Simons definition" or the "accretion" concept of income—is perhaps most commonly used in discussions about income taxes. Professor Simons himself was careful to say that the definition was not suitable for all purposes and would not, without modification, describe a satisfactory tax base. Most analysts would agree. However, the definition is useful for analytical purposes. It represents a kind of outer limit that helps identify items that are potential candidates for inclusion or exclusion in any income tax base. In the discussions that follow, it should be understood that the Haig-Simons or accretion definition is used and discussed in that way, and that no blanket endorsement of that definition of income is intended.

Indeed, the accretion concept of income has many shortcomings as a tax base. Several of them are serious, and attempts to deal with them account for much complexity in the present tax code. Among these shortcomings are severe measurement problems. Many items that are required for the calculation of net income must be imputed—either guessed at or determined by applying relatively arbitrary rules (as in the case of depreciation). Because such rules are never perfect, they are the subject of continual controversy. A particular problem with certain current rules is their inability to measure income correctly in periods of inflation.

An especially serious drawback of an accretion income base is that it leads to what is sometimes called the double taxation of savings: savings are accumulated after payment of taxes and the yield earned on those savings is then taxed again. This has been recognized as a problem in the existing tax law, and many techniques have been introduced to make the tax system more neutral with respect to savings. The investment tax credit, accelerated depreciation, special tax rates for capital gains, and the exclusion of contributions to and accruing earnings on employer-sponsored pension plans are examples of devices in current law that offset the taxation of savings that is characteristic of an accretion income base. Significantly, this last example is also viewed as desirable for reasons of equity.

All these techniques have the same practical effect as exempting from tax the income from the investment. *To this extent, this is equivalent to converting the base from accretion income to consumption.*

The present tax system thus may be regarded as having a mixture of consumption and accretion income bases. In view of this, a question that arises is whether the proper objective of tax reform should be to move *more* explicitly toward a consumption base rather than toward a purer accretion base. The issue is considered in this chapter.

The analysis suggests that the consumption tax has many important advantages as compared with an income tax and accordingly should be seriously considered in designing a reformed tax system. In some respects, a broad-based consumption tax is more equitable than a broad-based income tax. It is also easier to design and implement and has fewer harmful disincentive effects on private economic activity. In many important ways, a broad-based consumption tax more closely approximates the current tax system than does a broad-based income tax and would constitute *less* of a change.

The remainder of this chapter compares consumption and income taxes with respect to various criteria. The chapter includes:

- A discussion of some general issues relating to equity;
- An explanation of the concepts of consumption and income, including a discussion of some definitional problems;
- A comparison of the treatment of personal savings under the current tax system with the treatment of savings under a consumption tax and a broad-based income tax;
- A discussion of the merits of the alternative tax bases on criteria of equity;
- A comparison of the alternative tax bases for simplicity; and

- A discussion of the economic efficiency effects of tax policies
  and a comparison of the efficiency losses under a consumption
  tax and an income tax.

TWO PRELIMINARY MATTERS OF EQUITY

As has already been suggested, the specification of a tax code has
the effect of defining the conditions under which two taxpayers are
regarded as having the same circumstances, so that they should
properly bear the same tax burden. This section considers two
aspects of such a comparison that have important implications for
tax design: first, over what period of time are the circumstances
(and tax burdens) of two taxpayers to be compared; and, second,
what are the *units*—individuals or families—between which comparisons are to be drawn.

Equity Over What Time Period?

Most tax systems make liabilities to remit payments depend
upon events during a relatively short accounting period. In many
cases, this is a matter of practical necessity rather than principle.
That is, tax liabilities must be calculated periodically on the basis
of current information. Generally, there is nothing sacred about
the accounting period—be it a week, a month or a year—as far as
defining the period over which taxpayer circumstances are to be
compared. Indeed, it is usually regarded as regrettable that
practical procedures do not allow the calculation of liabilities to
take a much longer view. Averaging and carryover provisions
represent (inadequate) attempts to resolve inequities that arise in
this respect.

An example from another program will illustrate. Under many
welfare programs the accounting period is one month. A family
earning just at the eligibility level at an even rate for the year will
receive nothing. A family earning the same amount during the
year, but earning it all during the first three months will appear to
have *no* earnings during the remaining nine months. That family
will then be eligible for *full* benefits for nine months, in spite of
being no worse off than the first family in the perspective of a
year's experience.

It is assumed in this study that the period over which such
comparisons are made should be as long as possible. Ideally, two
taxpayers should be compared on the basis of a whole *lifetime* of
circumstances, and this is taken here to be a general goal of tax
system design: lifetime tax burden should depend upon lifetime
circumstances.

It is important to note that lifetime tax burden depends not only on the sum of all tax liabilities over a taxpaying unit's lifetime, but also on their timing. Deferral of a portion of tax liability is a form of reduction in tax burden because interest can be earned on the deferred tax payments. For example, if investors can expect a 10-percent annual rate of return on riskless assets, a tax liability of $110 a year from now is equivalent to a tax liability of $100 today because $100, if untaxed and invested, will gross to $110 in value in one year's time. A common way of expressing this is to say that the *present value* of a tax liability of $110 one year in the future is $100. When comparing the lifetime tax burdens of two taxpayers, we are, in fact, comparing the present value of the sum of current and future tax liabilities viewed from the vantage of some particular point in the life of the two taxpayers (e.g., at birth, or at the beginning of working years, or at age 18).

Is the Family or the Individual the Appropriate Unit?

What taxpaying unit is the subject of this comparison of situations? When it is asked whether one taxpayer is in the same situation as another, is the taxpayer an individual or a family? The sharing of both consumption and wealth within families supports continuation of present law in regarding the family as the unit of comparison.

On the other hand, a family is not a simple institution, with a predictable lifetime, and a constant identity. Quite apart from the problem of distinguishing varying degrees of formality in family structure (e.g., is the second cousin living in the guest room part of the family?), the family necessarily is a changing unit, with births, deaths, marriages, and divorces continually altering family composition.

In this study, differences in family association have been regarded as relevant to that comparison of lifetime situation by which relative tax burdens are to be assigned to different individuals. The practical consequence of this will be that the tax liability of a father, for example, will depend in part upon consideration of the situation of the whole family.

INCOME AND CONSUMPTION

A tax base is not a quantity like water in a closed hydraulic system, wherein the total remains constant regardless of how it is directed by valves and pumps. Rather, it is an aggregation of transactions, usually voluntary. The transactions that take place will depend in part upon how they are treated by the tax system.

The choice of a tax base is a choice about how to tax certain transactions.

An operational tax requires and is in effect defined by a set of accounting rules that specifies the use of actual and implicit transactions in reaching the tax base, that is the total to which a tax schedule is applied to determine the taxpayer's liability. The Internal Revenue Code prescribes an "income" tax, with "income" defined by the elaborate body of statutory and administrative tax law that has evolved. But this definition is criticized by many observers, who believe that tax burdens should be related to a broader tax base, i.e., to a wider set of transactions.

As was pointed out above, the concept of income generally used in discussion of tax reform has been called an accretion concept. It is supposed to measure the command over resources acquired by the taxpayer during the accounting period, that command having been either exercised in the form of consumption or held as potential for future consumption in the form of an addition to the taxpayer's wealth. Hence, the apparently paradoxical practice of defining "income" by an "outlay" or "uses" concept—consumption plus change in net worth.

Everyday usage on the other hand tends to associate income with the sources side of the accounts. Thus, one speaks of income "from labor," such as wages, or income "from capital," or "from proprietorships," such as interest and profits. Because sources and uses must be equal in a double entry accounting system, the result should be the same whichever side is taken for purposes of measurement, provided that *all* uses are regarded as appropriate for inclusion in the tax base.

Definitions of Income and Consumption

In this section, a rudimentary classification of transactions is developed to define income and consumption. The accounts considered first are those of a wage earner whose only sources of funds are his wages and his accumulated balance in a savings account.

In the simplest case, the possible applications he can make of these funds may be divided into the purchase of goods and services for his immediate use and additions to or subtractions from his accumulation of savings. Thus, an account of his situation for the year might be the following:

SOURCES	USES
Wages	Rent
Interest	Clothing
	Food
	Recreation
Balance in savings account at beginning of period	Balance in savings account at end of period

The two sides of this account are, of course, required to balance. Of the uses, the first four are generally lumped under the concept of consumption, the last constituting the net worth of the household. Thus, the accounts may be schematically written as:

SOURCES	USES
Wages	Consumption
Interest	
Net worth at beginning of period	Net worth at end of period

The concept of income concerns the *addition* or *accretion* to sources and the application of that accretion during the accounting period. This can be found simply by subtracting the accumulated savings (net worth) at the beginning of the period from both sides, to give:

ADDITION TO SOURCES	USES OF ADDITION TO SOURCES
Wages	Consumption
Interest	Savings (equals increase in net worth over the period)*

*Note savings may be negative.

Income may be *defined* as the *sum of consumption and increase in net worth*. Note carefully that a *uses* definition is adopted as a measure of differences in individual circumstances. This approach to the concept of income has substantial advantages as a device for organizing thinking on particular policy issues, even though it will no doubt be unfamiliar to many readers, who naturally think of income as something that "comes in" rather than as something that is used. With this uses definition of income, the situation of the illustrative individual may be represented by:

ADDITION TO SOURCES	USES OF ADDITION TO SOURCES
Wages Interest	Income

The last version of the accounts makes clear the way in which information about sources is used to determine the individual's income. To calculate his income for the year, this individual obviously would not add up his outlays for rent, clothing, food, recreation, and increase in savings account balance. Rather, he would simply add together his wages and interest and take advantage of the accounting identity between this sum and income.

This classification of uses into consumption and increase in net worth is not sufficient, however, to accommodate distinctions commonly made by tax policy. It will be helpful, therefore, to refine the accounts to the following:

ADDITION TO SOURCES	USES OF ADDITION TO SOURCES
Wages Interest	Consumption Cost of earnings Certain other outlays Increase in net worth

An individual's outlays for special work clothes needed for his profession requires the category "cost of earnings." These outlays are netted out in defining income. Note that the decision about which outlays to include in this category is a *social* or *political* one. Thus, in present law, outlays for specialized work clothes are deductible, but commuting expenses are not. There is no un-ambiguous standard to which one can appeal to determine whether such outlays are consumption, and hence a part of income, or work expenses, and hence out of income.

Similarly, a judgment may be made that some outlays, while not costs of earning a living, are also not properly classified as consumption. The category of "other outlays" is introduced for want of a better label for such transactions. For example, in everyday usage, State income taxes would not be an application of funds appropriately labeled "personal consumption," much less "increase in net worth." (They might be allocated to the "cost of earnings" category.) Thus, using the definition of income as the sum of consumption and the increase in net worth, we now have:

ADDITION TO SOURCES	USES OF ADDITION TO SOURCES
Earnings (Wages + Interest)	Income (Consumption + Increase in net worth) Cost of earnings Certain other outlays

Again, to *calculate* income it is generally convenient to work from the left-hand, sources side of the accounting relationship described above. In this case,

Income   =   Earnings
                                minus
                         Cost of earnings
                                minus
                         Certain other outlays.

Similarly, and of great importance in understanding this study, consumption may be calculated by starting with sources data:

Consumption   =   Earnings
                                minus
                         Cost of earnings
                                minus
                         Certain other outlays
                                minus
                         Increase in net worth.

To address an issue often raised in tax policy discussions, one further addition to the accounting scheme is needed at this point: the item "gifts and bequests." This is a use of funds that some would regard as consumption by the donor, but in the following schematic account the term consumption refers to the narrower notion of goods and services of direct benefit to the individual in question. The accounts now have the following structure:

ADDITION TO SOURCES	USES OF ADDITION TO SOURCES
Wages Interest Gifts and bequests received	Consumption Gifts and bequests given Cost of earnings Certain other outlays Increase in net worth.

It must be decided whether gifts and bequests given are to be
regarded as income, that is, as a component of the total by which
taxpayers are to be compared for assigning burdens. The term
"ability-to-pay" is used to describe the income or consumption
concept that considers consumption to be the sum of consumption
narrowly conceived, plus gifts and bequests given. Because it is
within the taxpayer's ability to choose among these uses, it may
be argued both uses measure taxpaying potential equally. It
should be emphasized that the label "ability-to-pay" is intended to
be suggestive only. There is no agreed upon measure of the idea of
a taxpayer's ability to pay. Because of this, quotation marks will be
used when the term "ability-to-pay" is used in its role as a label for
an income or consumption concept.

"Ability-to-pay" income or consumption would be calculated as
follows by starting on the sources side:

"Ability-to-pay" income   =   Earnings
                                       plus
                                   Gifts and bequests received
                                       minus
                                   Cost of earnings
                                       minus
                                   Certain other outlays.

"Ability-to-pay" consumption =   Earnings
                                       plus
                                   Gifts and bequests received
                                       minus
                                   Cost of earnings
                                       minus
                                   Certain other outlays
                                       minus
                                   Increase in net worth.

The difference between consumption and income is savings or the
increase in net worth over the period. Thus, equivalently:

"Ability-to-pay" consumption =   "Ability-to-pay" income
                                       minus
                                   Increase in net worth.

Finally, there is the pair of income and consumption concepts
that excludes gifts and bequests given from the category of uses by
which tax burdens are to be apportioned. These are given the label
"standard-of-living" because they are confined to outlays for the
taxpayer's direct benefit. As with the term "ability-to-pay," this

label is intended to be suggestive only. The "ability-to-pay" and "standard-of-living" concepts are related as follows:

"Standard-of-living" income = "Ability-to-pay" income
minus
Gifts and bequests given.

"Standard-of-living" = "Standard-of-living" income
consumption   minus
Increase in net worth.

This discussion leads to a four-way classification of tax bases:

	Gifts given included	Gifts given excluded
Increase in net worth included	"Ability-to-pay" income	"Standard-of-living" income
Increase in net worth excluded	"Ability-to-pay" consumption	"Standard-of-living" consumption

THE PRESENT TAX BASE

Is the Present Base Consumption or Income?

While the present income tax system does not reflect any consistent definition of the tax base, it has surprisingly many features of a "standard-of-living" consumption base.

The idea of consumption as a tax base sounds strange and even radical to many people. Nonetheless there are many similarities between a consumption base tax and the current tax system. Adoption of a broad-based consumption tax might actually result in less of a departure from current tax treatment of savings than adoption of a broad-based income tax.

The current tax system exempts many forms of savings from tax. In particular, the two items that account for the bulk of savings for most Americans, pensions and home ownership, are treated by the present tax code in a way that is more similar to the consumption model than to the comprehensive income model.

Retirement savings financed by employer contributions to pension plans (or made via a "Keogh" or "Individual Retirement Account" (IRA)) are currently treated as they would be under a consumption tax. Under the current system, savings in employer-funded pension plans are not included in the tax base, but retirement benefits from those plans, which are available for consumption in retirement years, are included. Employee contributions to pension plans are treated somewhat less liberally. The original contribution is included in the tax base when made, but the portion of retirement income representing interest earnings on the original contributions is not taxed until these earnings are received as retirement payments. If the tax on those interest earnings were paid as the earnings accrued, treatment of employee contributions to pension plans would be the same as that under a comprehensive income tax. However, the tax on interest earnings in pension funds is lower than under a comprehensive income base because the tax is deferred. If no tax were paid on the interest earnings portion of retirement pay, then the present value of tax liability would be exactly the same as the present value of tax liability under a consumption tax. Thus, the current treatment of employee contributions incorporates elements of both the comprehensive income model and the consumption model but, because of the quantitative importance of tax deferral on pension fund earnings, the treatment is closer to the consumption model.

The current tax treatment of home ownership is very similar to the tax treatment of home ownership under a consumption tax. Under present law, a home is purchased out of tax-paid income (is not deductible), and the value of the use of the home is not taxed as current income. Under a consumption tax, two alternative treatments are possible. Either the initial purchase price of the house would be included in the tax base (i.e., not deductible in calculating the tax base) and the flow of returns in the form of housing services would be ignored for tax purposes, or the initial purchase price would be deductible and an imputation would be made for the value of the flow of returns, which would be included in the tax base.

In equilibrium, the market value of any asset is equal to the net present value of the flow of future returns, either in the form of monetary profits or value of consumption services. For example, the market value of a house should equal the present value of all future rental services (the gross rent that would have to be paid to a landlord for equivalent housing) minus the present value of future operating costs (including depreciation, operating costs, property taxes, repairs, etc.). Thus, in both cases, the present value of the tax base would be the same. For example, if an individual purchased a $40,000 house, the present value of his future tax base for that item of consumption would be $40,000 regardless of how he chose to be taxed. Because the initial purchase price is easier to observe than the imputed service flow, it would be most practical, under a consumption tax, to include the purchase of a house in the tax base and exclude net imputed returns. In that case, capital gains from sale of a house would not be taxable.

In the current tax system, as in the consumption tax system, the down payment and principal payments for an owner-occupied residence are included in the tax base, and the imputed net rental income in the form of housing services is excluded from tax. Capital gains from housing sales are taxable at preferential capital gains rates upon realization (which allows considerable tax deferral if the house is held for a long period), and no capital gains tax is levied if the seller is over 65 or if the gain is used to purchase another house.

In contrast, under a comprehensive income base, the entire return on the investment in housing, received in the form of net value of housing services, would be subject to tax and, in addition, the purchase price would not be deductible from the tax base.

Many special provisions of the tax law approximate a consumption tax in the lifetime tax treatment of savings. For example, allowing immediate deduction for tax purposes of the purchase price of an item that will be used up over a period of years (i.e., immediate expensing of capital investments) is equivalent to consumption tax treatment of investment income because it allows the full deduction of savings; thus, accelerated depreciation approximates the consumption tax approach. While depreciation provisions under the present law are haphazard, a consumption base tax would allow the immediate deduction of saving to *all* savers.

In conclusion, taxation of a significant portion of savings under the current system more closely resembles the consumption model than the comprehensive income model. For owner-occupied housing, a large fraction of pension plans, and some other investments, the tax base closely approximates either the present value of imputed consumption benefits or the present value of consumption financed by proceeds of the investment.

Is the Tax System Presently on an "Ability-to-Pay" or a "Standard-of-Living" Basis?

Three possibilities may be considered for the income tax treatment of a gift from one taxpaying unit to another: (1) the gift might be deducted from uses in calculating the tax base of the donor and included in sources in calculating the base of the donee; (2) it might be left in the base of the donor *and also* included in the base of the donee; or (3) it might be left in the base of the donor but excluded from the base of the donee.

The first of these treatments is that implied by a "standard-of-living" basis for determining relative tax burdens. The second treatment expresses an "ability-to-pay" view. The third treatment is that of the present income tax (excluding the estate and gift tax) law, at least with respect to property with no unrealized appreciation at the time the gift is made.

The *first* and *third* treatments are similar in that there is no separate tax on the transfer of wealth from one taxpaying unit to another. The tax burdens under those two options may differ with a progressive tax structure, however. Under the third treatment, aggregate tax liability is unaffected by the gift, but under the first, it will rise or fall depending on whether or not the marginal tax bracket of the donee is higher than the marginal tax bracket of the donor. Under the second treatment, with the gift or bequest in the tax base of both the donor and the donee, the consumption or change in net worth financed by the gift is, in effect, taxed twice. It is taxed as consumption by the donor, and then taxed again as consumption or an increase in net worth of the donee.

To illustrate the alternative treatments of wealth transfers, consider the case of taxpayers A and B, who start life with no wealth and who are alike except that A decides to accumulate an estate. Their sons, A' and B', respectively, consume their available resources and die with zero wealth. Thus, A has lower consumption than B; A' (who consumed what his father saved) has higher consumption than B'. Under a "standard-of-living" approach, the pair A-A' should bear roughly the same tax burden as the pair B-B'. This is so because the higher consumption of A' is simply that which his father, A, did not consume. Under an "ability-to-pay" approach, the combination A-A' should bear more tax than B-B'. A and B have the same ability to pay, but because A chooses to exercise his ability to pay by making a gift to his son, A' has a greater ability to pay than B', by virtue of the gift received.

Neglecting the effect of progressivity, present income tax law taxes the combination A-A' the same as it does the combination B-B' (whether or not A and A' are related). In this respect, present income tax law incorporates a "standard-of-living" basis. The way this is accomplished, however, is "backward." That is, instead of taxing A on his "standard-of-living" income and then taxing A' on his "standard-of-living" income, present law taxes A on his consumption plus increase in net worth *plus* the gift given (i.e., the gift is not deductible in calculating the income tax due from A), while A' is taxed on the value of his consumption plus increase in net worth *minus* the value of the gift received (i.e., the receipt of the gift is not included in calculating the tax due from A').

This procedure clearly mismeasures the income of A'. It mismeasures the income of A, as well, if a "standard-of-living" concept of income is used. The income of A' is understated (gift received is not included) and that of A is overstated (gift given is not excluded). However (continuing to neglect the effect of progressivity), the impact of the tax system on A and A′ is the same as if the treatment were the other way around, at least as far as intentional gifts are concerned. Suppose, for example, that A wants to enable A′ to have an extra $750 worth of consumption. Under present law, A simply gives A′ $750 cash and A′ consumes it. Under a "standard-of-living" concept of income (assuming A and A′ are both in the 25 percent rate bracket), A would give A′ $1,000. After paying taxes of $250, A′ would have $750 to consume. At the same time, A would deduct $1,000 from his tax base, saving $250 and making the net cost of his gift $750.

Although the effects of progressivity would alter this somewhat, it is not clear that the differences in rates between giver and receiver are likely to be large if a lifetime view is taken. Naturally, under present law, an adult donor will tend to have a higher marginal rate of income tax than a child donee. It is for this reason that present income tax law treatment of gift and bequest transactions may come closer than the more intuitively obvious one— excluding to donor, including to donee—to measuring "standard-of-living" income correctly. Certain administrative aspects also favor the present treatment of gifts and bequests for income tax purposes.

In summary, whether by accident or design, present income tax law incorporates a rough sort of "standard-of-living" view of the concept of income because it does not include an extra tax on wealth transfers as an integral part of the income tax. Such treatment approximates a provision where a gift given is included in the income of the donee and excluded from the income of the donor, even though the mechanics of calculating the tax are on the opposite basis.

It is, then, mainly the estate and gift tax that introduces the "ability-to-pay" element into the tax system, because it results in a gift or bequest being taxed twice to the donor, once under the income tax and again under the transfer tax. The value implicitly expressed is that taxes should generally be assessed on a "standard-of-living" basis, except in the case of individuals whose ability to pay is very large, *and* whose standard of living is low relative to ability to pay (i.e., those who refrain from consuming in order to make gifts and bequests).

ALTERNATIVE BASES: EQUITY CONSIDERATIONS

The previous section considered what tax base is implicit in present law. In a sense, the answer itself is an equity judgment, because equity traditionally has played an important role in the tax legislation process. This section considers the relative equity claims of a "consumption" as compared with an "income" basis, *of either* "ability-to-pay" or "standard-of-living" type, and the "ability-to-pay" or "standard-of-living" version of *either* consumption or income.

Consumption or Income: Which is the Better Base?

The choice between consumption and income as the basis for assessing tax burdens involves more than a simple subjective judgment as to whether, of two individuals having different incomes in a given period but who are identical in all respects in all other periods, the one with the higher income should pay the higher tax. Examples of tax burdens considered within a life-cycle framework suggest that a consumption base deserves careful attention if the primary consideration is fairness, whether one takes an ability-to-pay or a standard-of-living view.

Many observers simply consider income and consumption to be alternative reasonable ways to measure well-being; often, income is regarded as somewhat superior because it is a better measure of ability to pay. However, in a life-cycle context, income and consumption are *not* independent of each other. Of two individuals with equal earning abilities at the beginning of their lives, the one with *higher* consumption early in life is the one who will have a *lower* lifetime income. This is true because saving is not only a way of using wealth, but also a way of producing income. Thus, the person who saves early in life will have a higher lifetime income in present-value terms. Although his initial endowment of financial wealth and of future earning power *is* independent of the way he chooses to use it, his lifetime income is not independent of his consumption/savings decisions.

The examples presented below show that a consumption base would be more likely to maintain the same relative rankings of individuals ranked by endowment than an income base, if "endowment" is defined as an individual's wealth, in marketable and nonmarketable forms, at the beginning of his working years. Wealth so defined consists of the total monetary value of financial and physical assets on hand, the present value of future labor earnings and transfers, less the cost of earning income and less the present value of the "certain other outlays" discussed in the accounting framework above. If endowment is regarded as a good measure of ability to pay over a lifetime, this implies that *a consumption base is superior to an income base as a measure of lifetime ability to pay.*

If individuals consume all of their initial endowment during their lifetime (that is, leave no bequest), a consumption tax is exactly equivalent to an initial endowment tax. However, an income tax treats individuals with the same endowment differently, if they have either a different pattern of consumption over their lifetime or a different pattern of earnings.

Consider first two individuals with no initial financial or physical wealth, no bequest, the same pattern of labor earnings, and different patterns of consumption. Intuition suggests that, unless these individuals differ in some respect other than how they choose to use their available resources (e.g., with respect to medical expenses or family status), they should bear the same tax burden, measured by the present value of lifetime taxes. The tax system should not bear more heavily on the individual who chooses to purchase better food than on the one who chooses to buy higher quality clothing. Nor should it bear more heavily on the individual who chooses to apply his endowment of labor abilities to purchase of consumption late in life (by saving early in life) than it does on the one who consumes early in life.

While an income tax does not discriminate between the two taxpayers in the case where the two taxpayers consume different commodities, it does in the case where they choose to consume in different time periods in their lives. An income tax imposes a heavier burden on the individual who prefers to save for later consumption than on the one who consumes early, and the amount of difference may be significant. The reason is the double taxation of savings under an income tax. The "use" of funds for savings is taxed, and then the yield from savings is taxed again. The result is that the individual who chooses to save early for later consumption is taxed more heavily than one who consumes early.

Note that under an income tax the tax burden may be reduced by *borrowing* for early consumption, since, just as interest received is included, interest paid is deducted in calculating income.

Now, suppose that the two individuals have different time paths of labor earnings but that the two paths have the same present discounted value. For example, individual A may earn $10,000 per year in a given 2-year period, while individual B works for twice as many hours and earns $19,524 in the first of the 2 years, but earns nothing in the second. (The figure of $19,524 is the total of $10,000 plus the amount that would have to be invested at a 5-percent rate of return to make $10,000 available one year later.) Each individual prefers to consume the same amount in both periods, and in the absence of tax, each would consume the same amount, $10,000 per year. Intuition suggests these two individuals should bear the same tax burden. However, under an income tax (even at a flat rate, i.e., not progressive), they would pay different taxes, with B paying more than A. The reason, again, is the double taxation of B's savings. The differences may be very large if a long time period is involved. An income tax imposes a higher burden on the individual who receives labor income earlier even though both have the same initial endowments in present-value terms and the same consumption paths in the absence of tax.

"Standard-of-Living" or "Ability-to-Pay": Which Criterion?

Although for the vast majority of individuals, bequests and gifts of cash and valuable property constitute a negligible portion of sources and an equally negligible portion of uses of funds, the tax treatment of these transactions will have significant consequences for a minority of wealthy individuals and, therefore, for the perceived fairness of the tax system.

The equity judgment embodied in present law is that large transfers should be subject to a substantial progressive tax under the estate and gift tax laws and that relatively small transfers need not be taxed. For income tax purposes, amounts given are taxed to the donor and are not taxed to the donee. This has general appeal. The usual reaction to the idea that gifts given should also be included in the tax base of the donee is that this would be an unfair double taxation.

As has been pointed out, the circumstances under which large transfers occur are the relatively large wealth and low consumption of the donor. The imposition of a substantial transfer tax (estate and gift tax) is consistent with a common argument for this tax; namely, that it is desirable to prevent extreme accumulations of wealth. If this is, indeed, the equity objective, it suggests that the Code's present allowance of relatively large exemptions and imposition of high rates on very large transfers is sensible.

Summing Up: The Equity Comparison of Consumption and Income Bases

As a general matter, the important conclusions to be drawn from the foregoing discussion are:
- Either an income or a consumption tax may be designed to fulfill "ability-to-pay" or "standard-of-living" objectives. The difference is not between these two types of tax, but rather between a tax in which gifts given are considered part of the tax base of either donor or donee or, instead, part of the tax bases of both donor and donee. In the latter case, the tax embodies an "ability-to-pay" approach; in the former, the tax follows from a "standard-of-living" approach. The present in-

come tax system expresses a "standard-of-living" basis of comparison, while the present estate and gift tax system combines with income tax to give an "ability-to-pay" approach in certain cases.

- The difference between a consumption base and an income base of either the "standard-of-living" or the "ability-to-pay" type is between one that depends upon the timing of consumption and earnings (and gifts, in the case of an "ability-to-pay" tax) during an individual's lifetime and one that does not. The income tax discriminates against people who earn early in life or prefer to consume late in life. That is, if a tax must raise a given amount of revenue, the income tax makes early earners and late consumers worse off than late earners and early consumers. A consumption tax is neutral between these two patterns.

- A consumption tax amounts to a tax on lifetime endowment. It may be viewed as an ideal wealth tax, that is, a tax that makes an assessment on lifetime wealth. An income tax will tend to assess tax burdens in a way presumably correlated with lifetime wealth, but because it depends upon matters of timing, the correspondence is nowhere near as close as would be the case under a consumption base tax.

- As previously noted, present law introduces an "ability-to-pay" element into the tax system through the estate and gift provisions. The same device is equally compatible with either an income base or a consumption base tax. As will be discussed in Chapter 4, in some respects an estate and gift tax system fits more logically with a consumption base system, which allows deduction of gifts by the donor and requires inclusion by the donee.

ALTERNATIVE TAX BASES: SIMPLICITY CONSIDERATIONS

Of central importance in determining the complexity of a tax system—to the taxpayer in complying and to the tax collector in auditing compliance—is the ease with which the required transaction information can be assembled and the objective nature of the data. Three desirable characteristics are readily identifiable:

- Transactions should be objectively observable—as in the case of the transaction of a wage payment. Such transactions are called "cash" transactions in this report. "Imputed" transactions, i.e., values arrived at by guesses or rules of thumb—as in the case of depreciation—should be kept to a minimum.

- The period over which records need to be kept should be as short as practicable.
- The Code should be understandable.

Consumption or Income Preferable on Grounds of Simplicity?

With respect to simplicity criteria, the consumption base has many advantages, as can be seen on examination of the accounting relationships. At this stage, both the concept of consumption and the concept of increase in net worth must be complicated by adding imputed elements to the simple example.

The portion of consumption calculable from cash transactions includes cash outlays for goods and services and transfers to others (optional, depending upon the choice between "standard-of-living" and "ability-to-pay" versions). In addition, an individual usually obtains directly the equivalent of certain consumption services that he could purchase in the marketplace. The most important of these are the services from durable goods, such as owner-occupied houses, and household-produced services, such as child care, recreation, etc.

The change in net worth over a given time period, the other component of income, is calculable in part by cash transactions. These include such items as net deposits in savings accounts. Imputed elements, however, are extensive and lead to some of the most irksome aspects of income tax law. Among these are the change in value of assets held over the period, including the reduction in value due to wear and tear, obsolescence, etc. (depreciation); increases in value of assets due to the nearing of a future payoff, retained earnings in corporate shares held, changed expectations about the future, or changed valuation of the future (accruing capital gains); and other instances of accruing value of claims to the future (such as pension rights, and life insurance).

Thus, both consumption and the change in net worth can be expressed as the sum of items calculable from cash transactions within the accounting period and items that must be imputed. The cash items are easy to measure, but imputed items are a source of difficulty. Because the imputed consumption elements are needed for a comprehensive income *or* consumption base, consider first some of the more significant imputed elements of the change in net worth, representing necessary *additions* to complexity if an income base is used.

Four problems commonly encountered in measuring change in net worth are depreciation, inflation adjustment, treatment of corporate retained earnings, and treatment of unrealized capital gains on nonmarketed assets.

Measurement Problems

Depreciation. Depreciation rules are necessary under an income base to account for the change in value of productive assets due to wear and tear, obsolescence, and increases in maintenance and repair costs with age. Because productive assets often are not exchanged for long periods of time, imputations of their annual change in market value must be made.

Inevitably, depreciation rules for tax accounting, as in the present Code, can only approximate the actual rate of decline in the value of capital assets. Because changes in depreciation rules can benefit identifiable taxpayers, such rules become the object of political pressure groups and are sometimes used as instruments of economic policy, causing the tax base to depart even further from a true accretion concept. Thus, accelerated depreciation, at rates much faster than economic depreciation, has been allowed in some industries as a deliberate subsidy (e.g., mineral industries, real estate, and some farming). To the extent that the relationship between tax depreciation and economic depreciation varies among industries and types of capital, returns to capital investment in different industries and on different types of equipment are taxed at different effective rates. Differences in the tax treatment of capital income among industries create distortions in the allocation of resources across products and services and in the use of different types of capital in production.

Unrealized depreciation of an asset is neither added to nor subtracted from the consumption base. Thus, the time path of depreciation imputed to assets does not affect the tax base of asset owners. Adoption of a consumption base tax would automatically eliminate current tax shelters that operate by allowing depreciation in excess of economic depreciation in some industries. Alternative tax subsidies to the same industries, if adopted, would have to be much more explicit and would be easier to measure. The accidental taxation of returns to capital in different industries at different rates that arises under the current system because of imperfect knowledge of true economic depreciation rates would not occur.

Inflation Adjustment. During a period of rapid inflation, the current income tax includes inflationary gains along with real gains in the tax base. For example, an individual who buys an asset for $100 at the beginning of a year and sells it for $110 one year later has not had any increase in the purchasing power of his assets if the inflation rate is also 10 percent. Yet, under the current system he would include at least part of any gain on the sale of the asset in the sources side of his tax calculation.

An ideal income base would have to adjust for losses on existing assets, including deposits in savings banks and checking accounts, resulting from inflation. Such adjustments would pose challenging administrative problems for assets held for long periods of time. The current tax system effects a rough compromise in its treatment of "long-term capital gains" by requiring that only half of such gains be included in taxable income and by allowing no inflation deduction. (However, this treatment has been substantially modified by the minimum tax and by denial of maximum tax benefits for "earned income" if the taxpayer also has capital gains.) Dividends and interest income are taxed at the same rate as labor income even though the underlying assets may be losing real value.

A second type of inflationary problem under the current tax system is that rising nominal incomes move taxpayers into higher marginal tax brackets, and thus increase the average tax rate even when real income is not growing. Inflation will automatically raise the average tax rate in any tax system with a graduated rate structure, whether based on income, consumption, or the current partial-income base. A possible solution is some type of indexing plan, such as automatic upward adjustment of exemption levels. Because this problem does not affect the relative distribution of the tax base among individuals, it is not an issue in choosing between a consumption and an income base.

Under a consumption tax, inflation would not lead to difficulties in measuring the relative tax base among individuals because consumption in any year would be measured automatically in current dollars. A decline in the value of assets in any year because of inflation would be neither a positive nor a negative entry in the consumption base.

Treatment of Corporate Income. Given the difficulty of taxing gains in asset values as they accrue, the present corporate income tax serves the practical function of preventing individuals from reducing their taxes by accumulating income within corporations. Naturally, this is but a rough approximation of the appropriate taxation of this income and the difficulty of identifying incidence and allocation effects of this tax is well known. Under a fully consistent income tax concept, as outlined below in chapter 3, "corporation income" would be attributed to individual stockholders. This integration of the corporation and personal income taxes is desirable for a progressive income tax system because the variation among individuals in marginal tax rates makes it impossible for a uniform tax on corporate income, combined with exclusion of dividends and capital gains, to assess all individual owners at the appropriate rate. Although feasible and desirable in an income tax system, full corporate integration is sometimes regarded as posing too many challenging administrative problems. A partial integration plan that allowed corporations to deduct dividend payments and/or allowed shareholders to "gross up" dividends by an amount reflecting the corporation income tax, taking a credit for the same amount in their individual income tax calculation, would eliminate the problem of "double taxation" of corporate dividends. This could be done without introducing significant complexity into the tax Code, but the problem of how to treat corporate retained earnings would remain unresolved.

Treatment of corporate income under a consistent consumption tax is simpler than under a comprehensive income tax. The corporation profits tax as such would be eliminated. Individuals would normally include in their tax base all dividends received and the value of all sales of corporate shares, and they would deduct the value of all shares purchased. There would be no need to treat receipts from sales of shares differently than other sources or to attribute undistributed corporate profits to individual shareholders.

Treatment of Unrealized Asset Value Changes. The increase in net worth due to any changes in value of assets, whether realized or not, would be included in the accretion concept of income. An individual who sells a stock at the end of the year for $100 more than the purchase price at the beginning of the year and an individual who holds a parcel of land that increases in value by $100 during the same time interval both experience the same increase in net worth. However, unrealized asset value changes are often difficult to determine, especially if an asset has unique characteristics and has not been exchanged recently on an open market. Further, there is a question as to what is meant by the value of an asset for which the market is very thin and whether changes in the value of such assets should be viewed in the same way as an equal dollar flow of labor, interest, or dividend income. For example, if the value of an individual's house rises, he is unlikely to find it convenient to realize the gain by selling it immediately. Any tax obligation, however, must ordinarily be paid in cash.

Similar questions arise with respect to the treatment of increases in the present value of a person's potential income from selling his human services in the labor market. It is not practical to measure either the increase in an individual's wealth from a rise in the demand for his labor or the depreciation of the present value of future labor earnings with age. Present law makes no attempt to recognize such value changes nor would they be captured in the comprehensive income tax proposal presented in chapter 3.

Under a consumption tax, unrealized changes in asset value would not need to be measured because consumption from such assets does not occur unless either cash flow is generated by the asset or the asset is converted into a monetary value by sale.

The Problem of Averaging. Finally, the problem of income averaging can be minimized with techniques of cash flow management. Averaging is desirable under an income tax because, with a progressive rate structure, an individual with an uneven income stream will have a higher tax base than an individual with the same average income in equal annual installments. Equity would seem to require that two individuals pay the same tax when they have the same lifetime endowment, regardless of the regularity of the pattern in which earnings are received (or expended).

The consumption tax may be viewed as a tax in the initial time period on the present value of an individual's lifetime consumption expenditures. Deferral of consumption by saving at positive interest rates raises total lifetime consumption but leaves unchanged the present value of both lifetime consumption and the tax base.

Although the annual cash flow measure of the consumption tax correctly measures the present value of lifetime consumption, averaging problems may arise if annual cash flow varies from year to year. The major averaging problem results from large irregular expenditures, such as the purchase of consumer durables. As described in chapter 4, there are two alternative ways of dealing with loans and investment assets in measuring the tax base. Both methods yield the same expected present value of the tax base over time but enable an individual to alter the timing of his recorded consumption expenditures. The availability of an alternative treatment of loans and assets enables individuals to even out their recorded pattern of consumption for tax purposes and represents a simple and effective averaging device under a consumption tax.

The same type of automatic averaging cannot be introduced under an income tax because an income tax is *not* a tax on the present value of lifetime consumption. Under an accretion income tax, the present value of the tax base rises when consumption is deferred, if interest earnings are positive, because the income used for saving is taxed *in the year it is earned* and then the interest is taxed again. Thus, allowing deferral of tax liability under an income tax permits a departure from the accretion concept, lowering the present value of tax liability.

The discussion above suggests that, contrary to popular belief, a consumption-based tax might be easier to implement, using annual accounting data in an appropriate and consistent fashion, than an income-based tax.

"Standard-of-Living" or "Ability-to-Pay"
Preferable on Simplicity Grounds?

The choice between an "ability-to-pay" and a "standard-of-living" approach under the consumption or income tax has significant implications for simplicity of administration. It is relatively easy to insure that the amount of a gift is counted in the tax base of either the donor or the donee. Under present law, gifts (other than charitable gifts) are not deductible from the tax base of the donor. If gifts were deductible, the donor could be required to identify the donee. A requirement that both donor and donee be taxed, as would be implied by an "ability-to-pay" approach, would introduce a great temptation to evade. Taxing both sides would require that the gift not be deductible by the donor and that it be included in the tax base of the donee. Particularly for relatively small gifts and gifts in-kind, auditing compliance with this rule, where no evidence is provided in another person's tax return of having made the gift, could be a formidable problem. For much the same reason, compliance with the existing gift tax law is believed to be somewhat haphazard.

The issue of gifts in-kind is important. It is difficult to establish whether a gift has been given in these cases (e.g., loan of a car or a vacation home). Again, if the gift need only be taxed to one of the parties to the transaction, failing to report a gift simply means it is taxed to the giver and not the recipient.

Gifts in-kind are significant in another sense. Gifts and bequests can be considered a minor matter to most people only if the terms are taken to refer to transfers of cash and valuable property. If account were taken of the transfers within families that take the form of supporting children until their adulthood, often including large educational outlays, inheritance would certainly be seen to constitute a large fraction of the true wealth of many individuals. Any discussion of gifts and bequests should take into account that the parent who pays for his child's college education makes a gift no less than the parent who makes a gift of the family farm or of cash, even though this equivalence is not recognized in present tax law.

Where large gifts of cash and property are involved, it seems likely that enforcement of a double tax on transfers will be less costly than when gifts are small. This has proved to be the case under current law.

EFFICIENCY ISSUES IN A CHOICE BETWEEN
AN INCOME AND A CONSUMPTION BASE

In public discussions, the efficiency of a tax system is often viewed as depending on its cost of administration and the degree of taxpayer compliance. While these features are important, one other characteristic bears significantly on the efficiency of a tax system: As a general principle, *the tax system should minimize the extent to which individuals alter their economic behavior so as to avoid paying tax.* In other words, it is usually undesirable for taxes to influence individuals' economic decisions, for example, to work or save. There may, of course, be exceptions where tax policies are used deliberately to encourage or discourage certain types of activities (for example, tax incentives for installation of pollution equipment or high excise taxes on consumption of liquor and tobacco).

Both an ideal consumption tax and an ideal income tax, though neutral among commodities purchased and produced, do have important incentive effects that are unintended by-products of the need to raise revenue. Specifically, individuals can reduce their tax liability under either tax to the extent it is possible to conduct economic activities outside of the marketplace. For example, if an individual pays a mechanic to repair his automobile, the labor charge will enter into the measurement of consumption or income and will be taxed under either type of tax. On the other hand, if the individual repairs his own automobile, the labor cost will not be accompanied by a measurable transaction and will not be subject to tax. Phrased more generally, both an income and a consumption tax distort the choice between labor and leisure, where leisure is defined to include all activities, both recreational and productive, that are conducted outside the process of market exchange.

While both consumption and income taxes distort the choice between market and nonmarket activities, only an income tax distorts the choice between present and future consumption.

Under an income tax, the before-tax rate of return on investments exceeds the after-tax interest rate received by those who save to finance them. The existence of a positive market interest rate reflects the fact that society, by sacrificing a dollar's worth of consumption today and allocating the dollar's worth of resources to the production of capital goods, can increase output and consumption by more than one dollar next year. Under an income tax, the potential increase in output tomorrow to be gained by sacrificing a dollar's worth of output today exceeds the return to an individual, in increased future consumption, to be derived from saving. In effect, the resources available to an individual for future consumption are double-taxed; first, when they are earned as current income and second, when interest is earned on savings. The present value of an individual's tax burden may be reduced by shifting consumption from future periods to the present.

A consumption tax, on the other hand, is neutral with respect to the choice to consume in different periods because current saving is exempted from the base. The expected present value of taxes paid is not affected by the time pattern of consumption. A switch from an income tax to an equal-yield consumption tax would thus tend to increase the fraction of national output saved and invested, and thereby raise future output and consumption.

The fact that a tax is neutral with respect to the savings-consumption decision is not, of course, decisive in its favor even on efficiency grounds. No taxes are neutral with respect to all choices. Thus, for example, it has already been pointed out that neither the income nor the consumption tax is neutral in the labor/leisure choice; that is, both reduce the incentive to work in the market-place. Economic theorists have developed measures of the amount of damage done by nonneutrality in various forms. Although it is not possible on the basis of such research to make a definite case for one tax base over the other on efficiency grounds, when reasonable guesses are made about the way people react to various taxes it appears that the efficiency loss resulting from a consumption tax would be considerably smaller than that from an equal yield income tax.

The possible efficiency gains that would result from adopting a consumption base tax system relate closely to the frequently expressed concern about a deficient rate of capital formation in the United States. Switching from an income to a consumption base tax would remove a distortion that discourages capital formation by U.S. citizens, leading to a higher U.S. growth rate in the short run, and a permanently higher capital/output ratio in the long run.

SUMMING UP

The previous discussions have attempted to provide a systematic approach to the concept of income as composed of certain *uses* of resources by individuals. The current income tax law lacks such a unifying concept. Indeed, as has been suggested here, income as implicitly defined in current law deviates from a consistent definition of accretion income especially in that it excludes a major part of income used for savings (often in the form of accruing rights to future benefits). Eliminating savings from the tax base changes an income tax to a tax on consumption.

This chapter has considered whether there is any sound reason for considering substitution of a consumption base for the present makeshift and incomplete income base. It has been suggested that there is much to be said for this on grounds of equity; such a base would not have the drawback, characteristic of an income tax, of favoring those who consume early rather than late in life, and of taxing more heavily those whose earnings occur early rather than late in life. The argument has been made that the choice is *not* between a tax favoring the rich (who save) and the poor (who do not), as some misconceive the consumption tax, and a tax favoring the poor over the rich by the use of progressive rates, as some view the income tax. The choice is between an income tax that, *at each level of endowment*, favors early consumers and late earners over late consumers and early earners and a consumption tax that is *neutral* between these two types of individuals. The relative burdens of rich and poor are determined by the degree of progressivity of the tax. *Either tax is amenable to any degree of progressivity of rates.*

A distinction has been drawn between a tax based on the uses of resources for the taxpayer's own benefit and one based on these uses plus the resources he gives away to others. The shorthand term adopted for the former is the "standard-of-living" approach to assigning tax burdens; for the latter, it is the "ability-to-pay" approach. It has been suggested that either a consumption or an income tax could be designed to fit either concept. Examination of current practice suggests that the basic tax—the present income tax—is, broadly speaking, of the "standard-of-living" type. An "ability-to-pay" element is introduced by special taxes on gifts and estates.

The next two chapters consider two different approaches to reform of the tax system. Chapter 3 contains a plan for a comprehensive income tax, and chapter 4 contains a plan for a very different tax, called a cash flow tax, which is essentially equivalent to a consumption tax. In both cases, a "standard-of-living" approach is adopted, under the assumption that a transfer tax of some sort, perhaps the existing estate and gift tax, would continue to be desirable as a complement.

CHAPTER **3**

A Model Tax Based On Income

OVERVIEW

This chapter presents a model tax system, called the Comprehensive Income Tax, based, as nearly as practicable, on a consistent definition of "standard-of-living" income as set forth in the previous chapter. The exceptions to strict conformity with the conceptual income definition are noted. These exceptions occur when rival considerations of efficiency or simplicity seem to overrule the underlying principle that all income should be taxed alike. In addition, those cases where the concept of income is not readily translated into explicit rules are noted and discussed. In every case, a specific model tax treatment, sometimes with optional treatments, is defined and highlighted.

Purpose of the Model Tax

The purpose of the model tax is to provide a concrete basis for the discussion of fundamental tax reform and also to define a standard for the quantitative analysis presented in chapter 5. For each major issue of income tax policy, the model tax reflects a judgment of the preferred treatment. It is not claimed, however, that the model tax provides the unequivocally right answer to all the difficult issues of measurement, definition, and behavioral effects raised. The chapter does not, therefore, only advocate a particular set of provisions; it also presents discussions of alternative treatments.

Base-Broadening Objective

Alternative treatments are suggested when a change from the model tax provision clearly would not violate the basic principle that an income tax should be based on a practical measure of income, consistently defined. In some cases, alternative accounting methods or alternative means of applying tax rates may be used; and there may also be some uncertainties in the interpretation of the income concept itself. Because a low-rate, broad-based tax promises a general improvement in incentives, and because there are costs associated with recordkeeping and administration, there is a presumption against deductions, exemptions, and credits throughout the model tax. In particular instances, this presumption may be reversed in favor of an alternative treatment without offending the basic principle of income measurement.

Organization of Chapter 3

The first issues taken up in the chapter concern rules for a definition of income suitable as a tax base. Such rules are derived for three broad sources of household income—employee compensation, government transfer payments, and business income. The first of these is treated in the next section. The third section considers the tax treatment of government transfer payments, and the fourth section deals with problems of accounting for income from businesses. The next four sections of the chapter discuss some specific issues in the taxation of income derived from the ownership of capital. In each of these sections, the model tax is compared with the existing federal income taxes. Next are three sections that treat issues in the definition of taxable income from all sources. These are the major personal deductions under the existing tax. Here, each of these items—medical expenses, state and local taxes, charitable contributions, and casualty losses—is considered as an issue of income measurement and economic efficiency. Following these is a brief discussion of the problems and principles of international income tax coordination. Finally, the questions of the proper unit for reporting taxable income and of appropriate adjustments for family size and other circumstances are considered. The chapter concludes with a sample model income tax form that serves as a summary of the model tax provisions.

EMPLOYEE COMPENSATION

The customary starting point for systems of income accounting is to observe the terms under which individuals agree to provide labor services to employers. In the simplest case, described in the previous chapter, the employee is paid an annual wage that is equal to his consumption plus change in net worth. However, in practice, complications usually will arise. On the one hand, the employee may have expenses associated with employment that should not be regarded as consumption. On the other hand, he may receive benefits that have an objective market value, which, in effect, represent an addition to his stated wage.

The model Comprehensive Income Tax attempts to measure the value to the employee of all the financial terms of his employment. In general, the accounting for employee compensation is (1) wage and salary receipts, less (2) necessary employment expenses, plus (3) the value of fringe benefits. The remainder of this section discusses the measurement problems presented by items (2) and (3).

Expenses of Employment

Model Tax Treatment. *The model Comprehensive Income Tax would allow deduction from wage and salary receipts for expenses required as a condition of a particular job,* such as the purchase of uniforms and tools, union dues, unreimbursed travel, and the like. *No deduction would be allowed for expenditures associated with the choice of an occupation, place of employment, or place of residence,* even though each of these is related to employment. The latter rule would continue the present treatment of education and commuting expenses, but would disallow moving expenses.

Inevitably, such rules are somewhat arbitrary. For example, whether commuting expenses are deemed costs of employment or consumption expenditures will depend upon whether the work trip is regarded principally as a part of one's choice of residence, i.e., the consumption of housing services, or as a part of the job choice. The guidelines followed here are that expenses should be deductible only if they vary little among individuals with the same job and are specific to the current performance of that job. As at present, regulations would be required to set reasonable limits for those expenses that may be subject to excessive variation, e.g., travel.

A Simplification Option. An option that would simplify individual recordkeeping and tax administration would be to allow deduction for employee business expenses only in excess of a specified amount. If this floor were substantially higher than expenses for the typical taxpayer, most employees would no longer need to keep detailed expense records for tax purposes. The principal disadvantage of this limitation of deductions is that it would tend to discourage somewhat the relative supply of labor to those occupations or activities that have relatively large expenses. Over time, such supply adjustments could be expected to provide compensating increases in wages to those whose taxes are increased by this provision, but the inefficiency of tax-induced occupation changes would remain.

Employer-Provided Pensions

A substantial share of the compensation of employees is in the form of the annual increase in the value of rights to future compensation upon retirement. This increase adds to the net worth of the employee, so that an annual estimate of the accretion of these rights is income under our definition. The model tax treatment is intended as a uniform, practical means to estimate the income for tax purposes for different types of private pension plans.

The model Comprehensive Income Tax would continue to exclude employer contributions to pension plans from the employee's tax base and to tax benefits when received. In addition, *employee contributions would be deductible in the years paid.* However, *the earnings of pension plans would be taxed as they accrued.* Liability for tax on pension plan earnings would be either upon the employer, if no assignment of rights were made to employees as the earnings accrue, or upon the employee to whom these earnings are allocated by the plan.

Types of Pension Plans. Employer-provided pension plans come in two forms—defined-contribution and defined-benefit. The first form is essentially a mutual fund to which the employer deposits contributions on behalf of his employees. Each employee owns a percentage of the assets, and each employee's account increases by the investment earnings on his share of the assets. Upon retirement, his account balance may be distributed to him as a lump sum payment or may be used to purchase an annuity. The income of any individual from such a plan is simply the contribution made by the employer on his behalf plus his share of the total earnings as they accrue.

Most pensions are of the second type, defined-benefit pensions. This is something of a misnomer because the benefit is not fully defined until retirement. It usually depends on the employee's average wage over the years of employment, the outcome of contract negotiations, etc. The employee's benefits may not vest for a number of years, so that the value to him, and the cost to his employer of his participation is an expectation that depends on the chance of his continued employment. By a strict definition of income, the annual change in the present value of expected future benefits constitutes income from the plan, since this is conceptually an annual increase in the net worth of the employee. In general, it is not possible to determine the accrued value of future benefits in such a plan without many arbitrary assumptions about the employee's future employment prospects, marital status at retirement, and similar issues.

A Practical Measurement System. As an alternative to estimating pension income as an accrual of value to the employee, the
model plan would approximate such treatment through the current taxation of plan earnings and full taxation of actual benefits.
If done correctly, this would be equivalent to the taxation of the
increase in present value of expected future benefit as such
increases accrue.

The following example illustrates the equivalence between taxation of accrued pension earnings and taxation of both pension plan
earnings and benefits received.

> Mr. Jones' employer contributes $160 to his pension plan at
> the beginning of this year. Over the year, the contribution
> will earn 10 percent. Mr. Jones retires at the beginning of
> next year, taking his pension—the contribution plus earn-
> ings—in one payment. Mr. Jones' tax rate in both periods is 25
> percent.

Method 1. Under a system of taxation of pensions as accrued,
Mr. Jones would include the contribution in his taxable income
and owe a tax of $40. The earnings of $12 on the remaining $120
would incur an additional tax liability of $3, leaving net earnings
of $9. (Note that Mr. Jones could restore the pension fund to $160
only by drawing down his other savings, with a presumably equal
rate of return, by the amount of the tax.) Upon retirement, Mr.
Jones would receive a tax-prepaid pension distribution of $120
plus $9, or $129.

Method 2. The model tax treatment would subject only the
earnings of the fund—10 percent of $160—to tax in the first year.
This tax of $4 would leave net earnings of $12. Mr. Jones would
then receive $172 upon retirement, but would owe tax on this full
amount. The tax in this case would be $43, so that the remainder
[$172 - $43=$129] would be identical to that resulting from use of
method 1, and Mr. Jones should be indifferent between the two
treatments.

The method of including actual benefits has the advantage of
avoiding the necessity to allocate prospective benefits among
nonvested participants. Investment earnings would, however, have
ambiguous ownership for the reasons mentioned above. Consequently, it would be necessary to assess a tax on the employer for
that share of earnings not assigned to particular employees.

Present Law. Under present law, if an employer-provided
pension plan is legally "qualified," retirement benefits are taxable
to the employee only when received, not as accrued, even though

contributions are deductible to the employer as they are made. The plan's investment income is tax exempt. Certain individuals are also allowed tax benefits similar to qualified pension plans under separate laws. These laws allow a limited amount of the retirement saving to be deducted from income, its yield to be tax free, and its withdrawals taxable as personal income. This treatment allows an interest-free postponement of tax liability that would not exist under the model tax. Postponement introduces nonneutral tax treatment among forms of saving and investment, encourages a concentration of wealth in pension funds, and reduces the available tax base.

Social Security

Social security retirement benefits (OASI) present other problems. They are financed by a payroll tax on the first $15,300 (in 1976) of annual earnings, half of which is paid by the employer and half by the employee. The half paid by the employee is included in his tax base under the current income tax; the tax paid by the employer is not, although it is a deductible expense to the employer. Social security benefits are tax free when paid.

For an individual employee, the amount of annual accrual of prospective social security benefits is ambiguous. Actual benefits, by contrast, are readily measurable and certain. Furthermore, because participation in Social Security is mandatory, failure to tax accruals does not present the same tax neutrality problem encountered with private pensions; that is, there is no incentive to convert savings to tax-deferred forms. *Consequently, the model tax base would allow deduction of employee contributions by the individual and continue to allow deduction of employer contributions by the employer, but OASI benefit payments would be subject to tax.* Very low-income retired persons would be shielded from taxation by provision of a personal exemption and an additional family allowance.

Employer-Paid Health and Casualty Insurance

Issues in the tax treatment of health and casualty insurance are discussed separately below in the sections on medical expenses and casualty losses. In the case of employer-paid premiums for insurance unrelated to occupational hazards, the model tax adopts the same treatment that is recommended for individual purchase. *The taxpayer would include as taxable employee compensation the value of the premiums paid on his behalf. Proceeds would not be included in income. The same model tax treatment would apply to the health insurance (Medicare) component of Social Security.*

Disability Insurance

Private Plans. Under present law, employees are not required to include employer-paid disability insurance premiums in income, and, subject to a number of conditions, disability grants do not have to be included in the individual's income tax base. *Under the proposed system, premiums paid into such disability plans by employers would not be taxable to employers, and employees would be allowed to deduct their own contributions, but the benefits would be taxable.*

Conceptually, the premiums paid by the employer do increase the net worth of the employee by the expected value of benefits. Whether benefits are actually paid or not, this increase in net worth is income by our definition. However, when benefits are taxable, as they would be under the model plan, the expected value of tax is approximately equal to the tax liability under a current accrual taxation system. The model tax treatment is preferred because valuing the worth of the future interests would pose insurmountable administrative difficulties.

Social Security Disability Insurance. *The model tax would provide exactly the same treatment for the disability insurance portion of Social Security (DI) that is given for private plans.* Accrual taxation is impractical because the annual value of accruing DI benefits is even less certain than for private plans.

Life Insurance

Term Life Insurance. There is no similar difficulty of valuation in employer provision of term life insurance. The annual value to the employee is equal to the premium paid on his behalf. Therefore, under the model tax, *term life insurance premium payments made by the employer would be included in income to the employee; benefits would not be included in income.* This parallels the present treatment of an individual's own purchase of term insurance, and that treatment would be continued.

Whole Life Insurance. Whole life insurance involves some additional considerations. A whole life policy represents a combination of insurance plus an option to buy further insurance. When one buys a whole life policy, or when it is purchased on his behalf, that policy may be viewed as one year's insurance plus an option to buy insurance for the next and subsequent years at a certain prescribed annual premium. That option value is recognized in the form of the "cash surrender value" of the policy. It represents the value, as determined by the company's actuaries, of buying back from the insured his option to continue to purchase on attractive terms. Naturally, the value of this option tends to increase over time, and it is this growth in value that represents the income associated with the policy. Dividends paid on life insurance are, in effect, only an adjustment in the premium paid— a price reduction.

The total annual income associated with a whole life insurance policy is equal to the increase in its cash surrender value plus the value of the term insurance for that year (the term insurance premium) less the whole life premium, net of dividend. *Under the Comprehensive Income Tax, insurance companies would inform each policyholder annually of this income, which would be included in the policyholder's income.* This treatment is recommended whether the premium is paid by the individual or by his employer. *In addition, the contribution of the employer to the annual payment of the premium would be included in income, as with term insurance.*

Unemployment Compensation

Under present law, both the Federal Unemployment Tax Act (FUTA) taxes to finance the public unemployment compensation system and the unemployment compensation benefits are excluded from the income of covered employees. Following the recommended treatment of disability insurance, which has similar characteristics, the model Comprehensive Income Tax would exclude *payroll taxes from income as at present, but, unlike the present law, unemployment compensation benefits would be included in taxable income.*

This treatment has two basic justifications. First, it conforms with the basic equity principle of subjecting all income to the same tax. Employed individuals would not be subject to differentially higher tax than those of equal income who derive their income from unemployment benefits. Second, by taxing earnings and unemployment benefits alike, this treatment would reduce the disincentive to seek alternative or interim employment during the period of eligibility for unemployment benefits. Again, the personal exemption and family allowance would prevent the tax from reaching very low-income persons who are receiving such benefits.

PUBLIC TRANSFER PAYMENTS

A large element of the income of many households is provided by payments or subsidies from government that are not related to contributions by, or on behalf of, the recipients. These transfer payments are presently excluded from the calculation of income for federal taxes, despite their clear inclusion in a comprehensive definition of income.

Model Tax Treatment

The logic of including transfers in a tax base varies among transfer programs. A distinction may be made between those grants that are unrelated to the current financial circumstances of recipients, e.g., veterans' education benefits, and those that depend upon a stringent test of means, such as Aid to Families with Dependent Children. A second useful distinction is between cash grants that are readily measurable in value and publicly provided or subsidized services. The amount of income provided by these "in-kind" benefits, such as public housing, is not readily measurable.

The model income tax would include in income all cash transfer payments from government, whether determined by a test of means or not. Such payments include veterans' disability and survivor benefits, veterans' pensions, Aid to Families with Dependent Children, Supplemental Security Income, general assistance, workmen's compensation, black lung benefits, and the subsidy element of Food Stamps.[1] *The model tax would not require reporting the value of government-provided or subsidized services.* Hence, there would be no extra tax associated with the benefits of such programs as Medicaid, veterans' health care, and public housing.

Rationale for Taxing Transfer Payments

Horizontal Equity. The principal argument for taxing transfer payments is horizontal equity. Under present law, families that are subject to tax from earnings or from taxable pensions may face the same financial circumstances before tax as others that receive transfer income. If an adequate level of exemption is provided in the design of a tax rate structure, these families would have no tax in either case. But for those whose incomes exceed the exemption level, the present treatment discriminates against the earning family. This is both an inequity and an element of work disincentive.

Those transfer payments that are not contingent on a strict means test are especially likely to supplement family incomes that are above the level of present or proposed exemptions. These programs are the various veterans' benefits, workmen's compensation, and black lung benefits.

The taxation of benefits from any government transfer program would effectively reduce benefits below the level that Congress originally intended, and restoration of these levels may require readjustment of the rates of taxation. However, with a progressive rate tax, the benefits to individuals would be scaled somewhat to family circumstances and, in addition, the tax consequences of earnings and grants would be equalized.

Vertical Equity. The means-tested programs—Aid to Families with Dependent Children, Supplemental Security Income, general assistance, Food Stamps, Medicaid, and public housing—have rules to determine eligibility and to scale the value of benefits according to income and wealth of the recipient family. However, these rules may be based on measures of well-being that are different from those appropriate for an income tax. The rules also vary by region, and certain grants may supplement each other or be supplemented by other forms of assistance. Consequently, it is possible that families with similar financial circumstances before transfers will diverge widely after transfer payments are added. To the extent that some recipient households have total incomes that exceed the tax exemption level, inclusion of these grants in the tax base would reduce this divergence. Taxation of grants is no substitute for thorough welfare reform, but it may be regarded as a step toward reducing overlap of the various programs and of reducing regional differences in payment levels.

Valuing In-Kind Subsidies

Those programs of assistance to families that provide particular commodities or services, such as housing and medical care, present difficult administrative problems of income evaluation. One objective approximation of the income to households from these services is the cost of providing them. This is the principle employed to value pension contributions, for example. But in the case of in-kind transfers, costs are not readily allocable to particular beneficiaries. Consider how difficult it would be to allocate costs among patients in veterans' hospitals, for example. Furthermore, because a recipient's choices regarding these services are restricted, the cost of the services may be substantially larger than the consumption (i.e., income) value to the beneficiary. The recipient family would almost certainly prefer an amount in cash equal to the cost of provision. Because of these uncertainties and because of the attendant costs of tax administration and reporting, the in-kind programs might reasonably be excluded from the tax base.

BUSINESS INCOME ACCOUNTING

Basic Accounting for Capital Income

What is meant here by "business income" is that part of the annual consumption or change in net worth of the taxpayer that derives from the *ownership of property* employed in private sector production. In the ordinary language of income sources, this income includes those elements called interest, rent, dividends, corporate retained earnings, proprietorship and partnership profits, and capital gains, each appropriately reduced by costs. Unfortunately, there is no generally accepted set of accounting definitions for all of these ordinary terms. An important objective of the model income tax is to outline an accounting system for property income that is at once administrable and in close conformance with a comprehensive definition of income.

It is apparent from the definition that income is an attribute of families and individuals, not of business organizations. Furthermore, it is useful analytically to think of income in terms of uses of resources, rather than receipts of claims. Nonetheless, accounting for income is most easily approached by beginning with receipts of individual business activities (or firms), then specifying adjustments for costs, and, finally, allocating income earned in each business among its claimants. The sum of such claims for all activities in which a taxpaying unit has an interest is that taxpayer's business income for purposes of the model tax.

In broad outline, accounting for business income proceeds as follows. Begin with *gross receipts* from the sale of goods and services during the accounting year and *subtract purchases* of currently used goods and services *from other firms*. Next, *subtract* the share of income from the activity that is compensation to suppliers of labor services, generically called *wages*. Next, *subtract* a *capital consumption allowance*, which estimates the loss in value during the year of capital assets employed in production. The *remainder* is *net capital income*, or, simply, business income. Finally, *subtract interest* paid or accruing to suppliers of debt finance. The *remainder* is income to suppliers of equity finance, or *profit*. A business activity thus generates all three sources of income to households—wages, interest, and profit.

Major problems in defining rules of income measurement for tax purposes include (1) issues of timing associated with a fixed accounting period, such as inventory valuation; (2) estimation of capital consumption, i.e., depreciation and depletion rules; and (3) imputations for nonmarket transactions, e.g., self-constructed capital assets. In each of these cases, there are no explicit market transactions within the accounting period to provide the appropriate valuations. Rules for constructing such valuations are necessarily somewhat arbitrary, but the rules described here are intended to be as faithful as possible to the concept of income.

Capital Consumption Allowances

Rules for capital consumption allowances should not be regarded as arbitrary allowances for the "recovery of capital costs." Rather, they are a measure of one aspect of annual capital cost; namely, the reduction in value of productive capital occasioned by use, deterioration, or obsolescence. Rules for estimating this cost should be subject to continuous revision to reflect new evidence on actual experience and changing technology.

Depreciation of Machinery and Equipment. *For machinery and equipment, the model tax would require that depreciation be estimated by means of a system similar, in some respects, to the existing Asset Depreciation Range (ADR) system but with annual adjustment of basis for increases in the general price level.* The essential features of this system are (1) classification of all assets by type of activity, (2) mandatory vintage accounting, (3) a guideline annual repair allowance, (4) a specified annual depreciation *rate* (or permissible range) to be applied to the undepreciated balance (together with a date on which any remaining basis may be deducted) and (5) annual adjustment of basis in each account by a measure of the change in price levels. The inflation adjustment would be a factor equal to the ratio of the price level in the previous year to the current price level, each measured by a general price index. Notice that the recommended depreciation rules would establish a constant relative rate of depreciation as the "normal" depreciation method instead of straight-line depreciation, and it would disallow all other methods.

Depreciation of Structures. *Depreciation of structures would be treated in a way similar to that for equipment except that prescribed depreciation rates may be made to vary over the life of a structure.* For example, depreciation of x percent per year may be allowed for the first 5 years of an apartment building, y percent for the next 5 years, and so on. However, in no case would total depreciation deductions be allowed to exceed the original basis, after annual adjustment for inflation. Gains and losses would be recognized when exchanges or demolitions occur. Depreciation and repair allowance rates for exchanged properties always would be determined by the age of the structure, not by time in the hands of the new owner. Expenditures for structural additions and modifications that exceed a guideline repair allowance would be depreciated as new structures.

Depletion of Mineral Property. For mineral property, capital assets include the value of the unexploited deposits in addition to depreciable production equipment. The value of the mineral deposit depends upon its accessibility as well as the amount and quality of the mineral itself. This value may change as development proceeds, and this change in value is a component of income. The value of the deposit will be subsequently reduced, i.e., depleted, as the mineral is extracted. To measure income accurately, a depletion allowance should then be provided that is equal to the annual reduction in the value of the deposit.

Unfortunately, the value of a mineral deposit becomes known with certainty only as the mineral is extracted and sold. Its value at discovery becomes fully known only after the deposit has been fully exploited. Yet, the value on which to base a tax depletion allowance and an annual depletion schedule must be estimated from the beginning of production. Uncertainty about the amount of mineral present, the costs of extraction and marketing, and future prices of the product make estimation of annual capital consumption particularly difficult in the case of minerals. The uncertainties are especially great for fluid minerals.

An objective market estimate of the initial value of a mineral deposit prior to the onset of production is the total of expenditures for acquisition and development, other than for depreciable assets. *The model tax would require that all preproduction expenses be capitalized. All such expenditures, except for depreciable assets, would be recovered according to "cost depletion" allowances computed on the basis of initial production rates combined with guideline decline rates derived from average experience.* The treatment would be similar to the model tax treatment of depreciation for structures. After each five years of experience, or upon exchange of property ownership, the value of the deposit would be re-estimated and corrections made to subsequent annual allowances. But, as with depreciation, total deductions are not to exceed the (inflation-adjusted) cost basis. All postproduction expenditures, except for depreciable assets, also must be capitalized and recovered by cost depletion according to the rules in effect for that year.

Self-Constructed Assets

Capital assets that are constructed for use by the builder, rather than for sale, are an example of a case in which a market transaction normally used in the measurement of income is missing. The selling price for a building, machine, or piece of transportation equipment constructed by one firm for sale to another helps to determine the income of the seller and, simultaneously, establishes the basis for estimating future tax depreciation and capital gain of the buyer. Income to the seller will be determined by subtracting his costs from the selling price, so that (with proper accounting for inventories over the construction period) all income generated in the construction process will have been subject to tax as accrued. However, when a construction firm builds an office building, or a shipping company a ship, for its own use or rental, no explicit transfer price is attached to that asset. If any costs associated with construction of the building or ship can be deducted currently for tax purposes, or if any incomes arising from construction can be ignored, current income is understated and a deferral of tax is accomplished.

Unrecognized income is derived from inventories of unfinished buildings, for example. An independent contractor who produces a building for sale must realize sufficient revenue from the proceeds of that sale to compensate suppliers of all capital, including capital in the form of the inventory of unfinished structures during the construction period. But, for self-constructed assets, incomes accruing to suppliers of equity during construction are not recognized for tax purposes because there is no sale. Under current law, certain construction costs, such as taxes and fees paid to governments, may be deducted as current expenses. The result of these lapses of proper income measurement is a tax incentive for self-construction and for vertical integration of production that would otherwise be uneconomic. The present treatment also encourages various arrangements to defer income taxes by providing the legal appearance of integration. These arrangements are popularly known as tax shelters.

To provide tax treatment equivalent to that of assets constructed for sale, *the model tax would require that all payments for goods and services associated with construction of capital goods not for sale (including property taxes and other fees to government, depreciation of own equipment, but not interest paid) be segregated into a special account. During the construction period, a guideline rate of return would be imputed to the average value of this account and added to the income tax base of the builder and also to the depreciable basis of the assets.*[2] When such assets are placed in service, they would be depreciated according to the regular rules.

Other Business Income Accounting Problems

A number of other problems of inventory valuation must be faced in order to specify a fully operational Comprehensive Income Tax. Also, special rules would be required for several specific industries, in addition to minerals, to improve the measurement of income as compared to the present law. For example, agriculture, banking, and professional sports have presented special difficulties. This section has not spelled out all of these special rules, but has attempted to suggest that improvement of business income measurement for tax purposes is possible and desirable.

INTEGRATION OF THE INDIVIDUAL AND CORPORATION INCOME TAXES

Strictly speaking, the uses concept of income—consumption plus change in net worth—is an attribute of individuals or families, not of business organizations. Corporations do not consume, nor do they have a "standard of living." The term corporate income is shorthand for the contribution of the corporate entity to the income of its stockholders.

The Corporation Income Tax

Under existing law, income earned in corporations is taxed differently from other income. All corporate earnings are subject to the corporate income tax, and dividend distributions are also taxed separately as income to shareholders. Undistributed earnings are taxed to shareholders only as they raise the value of the common stock and only when the shareholder sells his stock. The resulting gains upon sale are taxed under the special capital gains provisions of the individual income tax. Thus, the tax on retained earnings generally is not at all closely related to the shareholder's individual tax bracket.

Subchapter S Corporations. An exception to these general rules exists for corporations that are taxed under subchapter S of the Internal Revenue Code. If a corporation has 10 (in some cases 15) or fewer shareholders and meets certain other requirements, it may elect to be taxed in a manner similar to a partnership. The income of the entity is attributed directly to the owners, so that there is no corporate income tax and retained earnings are immediately and fully subject to the individual income tax. For earnings of these corporations, then, complete integration of the corporate and individual income taxes already exists.

Inefficiency of the Corporation Income Tax

The separate taxation of income earned in corporations is responsible for a number of serious economic distortions. It raises the overall rate of taxation on earnings from capital and so produces a bias against saving and investment. It inhibits the flow of saving to corporate equities relative to other forms of investment. Finally, the separate corporate tax encourages the use of debt, relative to equity, for corporate finance.

The existing differential treatment of dividends and undistributed earnings also results in distortions. Distribution of earnings is discouraged, thus keeping corporate investment decisions from the direct test of the capital market and discouraging lower-bracket taxpayers from ownership of stock.

Owners of closely held corporations are favored relative to those that are publicly held. Owner-managers may avoid the double taxation of dividends by accounting for earnings as salaries rather than as dividends, and they may avoid high personal tax rates by retention of earnings in the corporation with eventual realization as capital gains. Provisions of the law intended to minimize these types of tax avoidance add greatly to the complexity of the law and to costs of administration.

A Model Integration Plan

In the model tax system, the corporate income tax would be eliminated, and the effect of subchapter S corporation treatment would be extended to all corporations. There are alternative methods of approximating this result. Because the direct attribution of corporate income to shareholders most nearly matches the concept of an integrated tax, a particular set of rules for direct attribution is prescribed as the model tax plan. However, there are potential administrative problems with this approach. These problems will be noted and alternative approaches described.

The model tax treatment of corporate profits may be summarized by the following four rules:

1. The holder of each share of stock on the first day of the corporation's accounting year (the "tax record date") would be designated the "shareholder of record."
2. Each shareholder of record would add to his tax base his share of the corporation's income annually. If the corporation had a loss for the year, the shareholder would subtract his share of loss.
3. The basis of the shareholder of record in his stock would be increased by his share of income and decreased by his share of loss.
4. Any shareholder's basis in his stock would be reduced, but not to below zero, by cash dividends paid to him or by the fair market value of property distributed to him. Once the shareholder's basis had been reduced to zero, the value of any further distributions would be included in income. (A distribution after the basis had been reduced to zero would indicate the shareholder had, in the past, income that was not reported.)

Designation of a shareholder of record to whom to allocate income earned in the corporation is necessary for large corporations with publicly traded stock. This treatment is designed to avoid recordkeeping problems associated with transfers of stock ownership within the tax year and to avoid "trafficking" in losses between taxpayers with different marginal rates.

Importance of the Record Date. Suppose that the record date were at the end of the taxable year when reliable estimates of the amount of corporate earnings or losses would be known. Shortly before the record date, shareholders with high marginal rates could bid away shares from shareholders with relatively low marginal rates whose corporations are expected to show a loss.

The losses for the year then would be attributed to the new shareholders for whom the offset of losses against other income results in the greatest reduction in tax liability. Thus, a late-year record date would have the effect of reducing the intended progressivity of the income tax and would bring about stock trading that is solely tax motivated.

The earlier in the tax year that the record date were placed the more the shareholder's expected tax liability would become just another element in the prediction of future returns from ownership of stock in the corporation, as is now the case under the corporation income tax. If the record date were the first day of the tax year, the tax consequences of current corporate earnings or losses already accrued in the corporation could not be transferred to another taxpayer.

Treatment of the Full-Year Shareholder. Under the model tax scheme, a shareholder who holds his stock for the entire taxable year would be taxed on the full amount of income for the year (or would deduct the full amount of loss). Any gain from sale of the stock in a future year would be calculated for tax purposes by subtracting from sale proceeds the amount of his original basis plus the undistributed earnings upon which he has been subject to tax. His corporation would provide him with a statement at the end of each taxable year that informed him of his share of corporate earnings. He then could increase his basis by that amount of earnings less the sum of distributions received during the year. For full-year stockholders, then, basis would be increased by their share of taxable earnings and reduced by the amount of any distributions.

It should be noted that, under this treatment, dividends would not be considered income to the shareholder, but would be just a partial liquidation of his portfolio. Income would accrue to him as the corporation earned it, rather than as the corporation distributed it. Hence, dividend distributions would merely reduce the shareholder's basis, so that subsequent gains (or losses) realized on the sale of his stock would be calculated correctly.

Treatment of a Shareholder Who Sells During the Year. A shareholder of record who sells his stock before the end of the tax year would not have to wait to receive an end-of-year statement in order to calculate his tax. He simply would calculate the difference between the sale proceeds and his basis as of the date of sale. The adjustment to basis of the shareholder's stock to which he would be entitled at the time of the corporation's annual accounting would always just offset the amount of corporate income or loss that he would normally have to report as the shareholder of record. Therefore, the income of a shareholder who sold his shares would be determined fully at the time of sale, and he would have no need for the end-of-year statement.

A numerical example may be useful in explaining the equivalence of treatment of whole-year and part-year stockholders. Suppose that, as of the record date (January 1), shareholder X has a basis of $100 in his one share of stock. By June 20, the corporation has earned $10 per share, and X sells his stock for $110 to Y. The shareholder would thus realize a gain of $10 on the sale, and this would be reported as income.

To illustrate that subsequent corporate earnings would be irrelevant to the former shareholder's calculation of income for taxes, suppose the corporation earns a further $15 after the date of sale, so that as the shareholder of record X receives a report attributing $25 of income to him, entitling him to a $25 basis increase (on shares he no longer owns). One might insist that X take into his tax base the full $25 and recalculate his gain from sale. In this event, the increase in basis from $100 to $125 would convert his gain of $10 from sale to a loss of $15 (adjusted basis = $125; sale price = $110). The $15 loss, netted against $25 of corporate income attributed to him as the shareholder of record, yields $10 as his income to be reported for tax, the same outcome as a simple calculation of his gain at the time of sale. The equivalence between these two approaches may not be complete, however, if the date of sale and the corporate accounting occur in different taxable years. Nonetheless, in the case cited, the model plan appears superior in the simplicity of its calculations, in allowing the taxpayer to know immediately the tax consequences of his transactions, and in its better approximation to taxing income as it is accrued.

In the event there had been a dividend distribution to X of the $10 of earnings before he sold, this distribution would be reflected in the value of the stock, which would now command a market price of $100 on June 20. The amount of the dividend also would reduce his basis to $90, so that his gain for tax purposes would be $10, just as before. The dividend per se has no tax consequences. At the end of the year he again would be allocated $25 of corporation income, but, as before, an offsetting increase in basis. Thus, he will not report any income other than his gain on the sale of the share on June 20.

Note that the same result would obtain in this case if the shareholder included the dividend in income but did not reduce his basis. There would then be $10 attributable to the dividend and no gain on the sale. This treatment of dividends in the income calculation gives correct results for the shareholder who disposes of his shares. However, it would attribute income to a purchaser receiving dividends before the next record date even though such distributions would represent merely a change in portfolio composition. This approach (all distributions are taken into the tax base with only retained earnings allocated to record date shareholders and giving rise to basis adjustments) might, nevertheless be considered an alternative to the treatment of the model plan because it is more familiar and would involve fewer basis adjustments and hence a reduced recordkeeping burden. The substance of the full integration proposal would be preserved in this alternative treatment.

The proposed full integration system would make it possible to tax income according to the circumstances of families who earn it, regardless of whether income derives from labor or capital services, regardless of the legal form in which capital is employed, and regardless of whether income earned in corporations is retained or distributed. To the extent that retained earnings increase the value of corporate stock, this system would have the effect of taxing capital gains from ownership of corporate stock as they accrued, thereby eliminating a major source of controversy and complexity in the present law.

Administrative Problems of Model Tax Integration

The Liquidity Problem. Some problems of administration of the system just described would remain. One such problem is that income would be attributed to corporate shareholders whether or not it actually was distributed. To the extent the corporation retained its earnings, the shareholders would incur a current tax liability that must be paid in cash, even though their increases in net worth would not be immediately available to them in the form of cash. Taxpayers with relatively small current cash incomes might then be induced to trade for stocks that had higher rates of dividend payout to assure themselves sufficient cash flow to pay the tax.

Imposition of a withholding tax at the corporate level would help to reduce this liquidity problem and perhaps also reduce the cost of enforcement of timely collections of the tax.

One method of withholding that is compatible with the model tax method for assigning tax liabilities is to require corporations to remit an estimated flat-rate withholding tax at regular intervals during the tax year. This tax would be withheld on behalf of stockholders of record. Stockholders of record would report their total incomes, including all attributed earnings, but also would be allowed a credit for their share of taxes withheld. Taxpayers who hold a stock throughout the entire year would receive one additional piece of tax information from the corporation—the amount of their share of tax withheld throughout the year—and would subtract the tax withheld as a credit against their individual liability.

This withholding system would complicate somewhat the taxation of part-year stockholders. As explained above, the taxable income of the corporation attributed to stockholders could be determined fully at the time of sale as the sum of dividends received during the year and excess of sale price over basis that existed on the record date. However, if withholding were always attributed to the shareholder of record, he would be required to wait until corporate income for the year had been determined to know the amount of his tax credit for withholding during the full tax year. The selling price of the stock may be expected to reflect the estimated value of this prospective credit in the same way that share prices reflect estimates of future profits. But, in this case, the seller who was a stockholder of record would retain an interest in the future earnings of the corporation, because the earnings would determine tax credit entitlement to the end of the tax year. At the price of this drawback, such corporate-level withholding would insure sufficient liquidity to pay the tax, except in cases where the combination of distributions and withheld taxes is less than the amount of tax due from the shareholder of record.

Audit Adjustment Problem. Another administrative problem could arise because of audit adjustments to corporate income, which may extend well beyond the taxable year. This would appear to require reopening the returns of shareholders of earlier record dates, possibly long after shares have been sold. In the present system, changes in corporate income and tax liability arising from the audit process are borne by shareholders at the time of the adjustment. Precisely this principle would apply in the model plan. Changes in income discovered in audit, including possible interest or other penalties, would be treated like all other income and attributed to shareholders in the year the issue is resolved. Naturally, shares exchanged before such resolution but after the matter is publicly known would reflect the anticipated outcome.

Deferral Problem. There are also some equity considerations. A deferral of tax on a portion of corporate income may occur in a year when shares are purchased. The buyer would not be required to report income earned after the date of purchase but before the end of the taxable year. All earnings in the year of sale that were not reflected in the purchase price would escape tax until the buyer sells the stock.

The 1975 Administration Proposal for Integration

In the context of a thorough revision of the income tax, integration of the corporate and personal tax takes on particular importance. The model tax plan has provisions designed to assure that the various forms of business income bear the same tax, as nearly as possible. If incomes from ownership of corporate equities are subject to greater, or lesser, tax relative to incomes from unincorporated business, pension funds, or bonds, the economic distortions would be concentrated on the corporate sector. For this reason, a specific plan for attributing to stockholders the whole earnings of corporations has been presented here in some detail.

A significant movement in the direction of removing the distortions caused by the separate corporation income tax would be accomplished by the dividend integration plan proposed by the Administration in 1975. That proposal may be regarded as both an improvement in the present code, in the absence of comprehensive tax reform, and as a major step in the transition to a full integration of the income taxes, such as the model tax.

CAPITAL GAINS AND LOSSES

Capital gains appear to be different from most other sources of income because realization of gains involves two distinct transactions—the acquisition and the disposition of property—and each transaction occurs at a different time. This difference raises several issues of income measurement and taxation under an income tax.

Accrual Versus Realization

The first issue is whether income (or loss) ought to be reported annually on the basis of changes in market values of assets—the accrual concept—or only when realized. The annual change in market value of one's assets constitutes a change in net worth and, therefore, constitutes income under the "uses" definition. If tax consequences may be postponed until later disposition of an asset, there is a deferral of taxes, which represents a loss to the government and a gain to the taxpayer. The value of this gain is the amount of interest on the deferred taxes for the period of deferral. Distinct from, but closely related to, the issue of deferral is the issue of the appropriate marginal tax rate to be applied to capital gains. If capital gains are to be subject to tax only when realized, there may be a substantial difference between the applicable marginal tax rate during the period of accrual and that faced by the taxpayer upon realization. Also, the extent to which adjustment should be made for general price inflation over the holding period of an asset must be considered. Finally, the desirability of simplicity in the tax system, ease of administration, and public acceptability are important considerations.

The range of possible tax treatments for capital gains can be summarized in an array that ranges from the taxation of accrued gains at ordinary rates to the complete exclusion of capital gains from income subject to taxation. Alternatives within the range may be modified to allow for (a) income averaging to minimize extra taxes resulting from the bunching of capital gains and (b) adjustments to reflect changes in the general price level.

Present Treatment of Capital Gains

Present treatment for individuals is to tax gains when realized, at preferential rates, with no penalty for deferral. There are a number of special provisions. When those assets defined in the code as "capital assets" have been held for 6 months or more,[3] gains from their realization are considered "long-term" and receive special tax treatment in two respects: one-half of capital gains is excluded from taxable income, and individuals have the option of calculating the tax at the rate of 25 percent on the first $50,000 of capital gains. There are complex restrictions on the netting out of short- and long-term gains and losses, and a ceiling of $1,000[4] is imposed on the amount of net capital losses that may be used to offset ordinary income in any 1 year, with unlimited carryforward of such losses. Also, there are provisions in the minimum tax for tax preferences that limit the extent to which the capital gains provisions can be used to reduce taxes below ordinary rates and that deny the use of the 50-percent maximum tax on earned income by the amount of such preferences. Limited averaging over a 5-year period is allowed for capital gains as well as for most other types of income.

There are many other capital gains provisions in the tax law that (1) define what items may be considered capital assets, (2) specify when they are to be considered realized, (3) provide for recapture of artificial accounting gains, and (4) make special provisions for timber and certain agricultural receipts. There also are special provisions that allow deferral of capital gains tax on the sale or exchange of personal residences. Much of the complexity of the tax code derives from the necessity of spelling out just when income can and cannot receive capital gains treatment.

Model Tax Treatment of Capital Gains

Under the model income tax, *capital gains would be subject to full taxation upon realization at ordinary rates after (1) adjustment to basis of corporate stock for retained earnings (as explained in the integration proposal) and (2) adjustment to basis for general price inflation.* Capital losses could be subtracted in full from positive elements of income to determine the base of tax, but there would be no refund for losses that reduce taxable incomes below zero. Adjustment for inflation would be accomplished by multiplying the cost basis of the asset by the ratio of the consumer price index in the year of purchase to the same index in the year of sale. These ratios would be provided in the form of a table accompanying the capital gains schedule. Table 1 is an example of such a table. (Note that for the last 3 years, the ratios are given monthly. This is to discourage December 31 purchases coupled with January 1 sales.) No inflation adjustment would be allowed for intra-year purchases and sales.

Table 1

Inflation Adjustment Factors
(Consumer Price Index based on December, 1975)

1930	3.326	1940	3.960	1950	2.307	1960	1.875	1970	1.430
1931	3.647	1941	3.771	1951	2.138	1961	1.856	1971	1.371
1932	4.066	1942	3.408	1952	2.092	1962	1.836	1972	1.327
1933	4.286	1943	3.210	1953	2.076	1963	1.814		
1934	4.147	1944	3.156	1954	2.066	1964	1.790		
1935	4.046	1945	3.085	1955	2.074	1965	1.760		
1936	4.007	1946	2.843	1956	2.043	1966	1.711		
1937	3.867	1947	2.486	1957	1.973	1967	1.663		
1938	3.941	1948	2.307	1958	1.920	1968	1.596		
1939	3.998	1949	2.329	1959	1.905	1969	1.515		

	1973	1974	1975
January	1.302	1.190	1.065
February	1.293	1.175	1.058
March	1.281	1.162	1.054
April	1.272	1.156	1.049
May	1.265	1.143	1.044
June	1.256	1.133	1.035
July	1.253	1.124	1.025
August	1.231	1.109	1.021
September	1.227	1.096	1.017
October	1.217	1.087	1.101
November	1.209	1.078	1.004
December	1.201	1.070	1.000

Source: Office of the Secretary of the Treasury, Office of Tax Analysis, September 28, 1976

Capital Losses

With adequate adjustment for inflation, and for depreciation in the case of physical assets, capital losses under the model tax should measure real reductions in the current income of the taxpayer. There is, consequently, no reason to limit the deduction of such losses, as in current law. A forced postponement of the realization of such losses would be like requiring the taxpayer to make an interest-free loan to the government. Of course, some asymmetry in the treatment of gains relative to losses would remain, because taxpayers could benefit by holding gains to defer taxes but could always take tax-reducing losses immediately.

Taxation of Accruals in the Model Tax

Corporate Stock. As just described, the model tax would continue the present practice of recognizing income from increases in the value of capital assets only upon sale or exchange, but some income sources that presently are treated as capital gains would be put on an annual accrual basis.

If the individual and corporate income taxes were fully integrated into a single tax so that shareholders are currently taxed on retained earnings, a large portion of capital gains—the changes in value of common stock that reflect retention of earnings—would be subject to tax as accrued. The remainder of gains would be subject to tax only as realized. These gains would include changes in stock prices that reflect expectations about future earnings, and also changes in the value of other assets, such as bonds, commodities, and land.

Physical Assets. Depreciable assets, such as machinery and buildings, are also subject to price variations, but these variations would be anticipated, as nearly as possible, by the inflation adjustment and the depreciation allowance. If these allowances were perfectly accurate measures of the change in value of such assets, income would be measured correctly as it accrues, and sales prices would always match the remaining basis. Realized capital gain or loss on physical assets may, therefore, be regarded as evidence of failure to accurately measure past income from ownership of the asset. If under the model tax, depreciation is measured more accurately, the problem of tax deferral due to taxation of capital gains at realization will be reduced. However, as in the case of corporate stock, some unaccounted-for variation in asset prices undoubtedly will occur despite improvements in rules for adjustments to basis. Sales of depreciable assets will, therefore, continue to give rise to taxable gains and losses. Such gains and losses are the difference between sales price and basis, adjusted for depreciation allowances and inflation.

The taxation of capital gains on a realization basis would produce different results than current taxation of accrual of these gains. Even if capital gains were taxed as ordinary income (no exclusion, no alternative rate), the effective tax rate on gains would be lower than the nominal or statutory rate applied to the gains as if they accrued ratably over the period the asset was held. This consequence of deferral of tax may be significant, especially at high rates of return and for assets held for a long period. Table 2 shows the results for an assumed before-tax rate of return of 10 percent on alternative assets yielding an annually taxable income. Each item in the table is the percent by which the before-tax rate of return is reduced by the imposition of the tax at the time of realization.

Table 2

Effective Tax Rates on Capital Gains
Taxed as Realized at Ordinary Rates*

	Holding Period			
	1 year	5 years	15 years	30 years
Statutory rate of 50 percent	50%	45%	35%	23%
Statutory rate of 25 percent	25%	22%	15%	10%

*Assumes 10 percent annual return.

Accrual Taxation Alternative

Accrual taxation of capital gains poses three problems that, taken together, appear to be insurmountable. These are (1) the administrative burden of annual reporting; (2) the difficulty and cost of determining asset values annually; and (3) the potential hardship of obtaining the funds to pay taxes on accrued but unrealized gains. Under accrual taxation, the taxpayer would have to compute the gain or loss on each of his assets annually. For common stock and other publicly traded securities, there would be little cost or difficulty associated with obtaining year-end valuations. But for other assets, the costs and problems of evaluation would be formidable, and the enforcement problems would be substantial. It would be difficult and expensive to valuate assets by appraisal; valuation by concrete transactions, which taxing realizations would provide, has distinct advantages.

For taxpayers with little cash or low money incomes relative to the size of their accrued but unrealized capital gains, accrual taxation may pose cash flow problems. This circumstance is similar to that encountered with local property taxes assessed on homeowners. There is no cash income associated with the asset in the year that the tax liability is owed. However, in cases of potential hardship certain taxpayers could be allowed to pay a later tax on capital gains, with interest, at the time a gain is realized.

Realization-With-Interest Alternative

An alternative method that attempts to achieve the same economic effect as accrual taxation is taxation of capital gains at realization with an interest charge for deferral. But, in addition to the present complex rules defining realizations that would not be avoided in the model tax plan, rules would be required for the computation of interest on the deferred taxes. An appropriate rate of interest would have to be determined and some assumption made about the "typical" pattern of accruals. In order to eliminate economic inefficiency, the interest rate on the deferral should be the individual taxpayer's rate of return on his investments. However, because it is impossible to administer a program based on each investor's marginal rate of return, the government would have to charge a single interest rate. The single interest rate would itself tend to move alternatives away from neutrality. Moreover, for simplicity, it would have to be assumed that the gain occurred equally over the period or that the asset's value changed at a constant rate. This assumption would be particularly inappropriate in those cases where basis was changed frequently by inflation adjustments, depreciation allowances, capital improvements, etc. Because a simple time pattern of value change would reflect reality in very few cases, the deferral charge would introduce additional investment distortions. To the extent that gains occur early in the holding period, capital gains would be undertaxed; when gains occur late in the period, capital gains would be overtaxed.

The Income Averaging Problem

Under a progressive income tax system, the tax rate on a marginal addition to income differs depending on the taxpayer's other income. Generally, the higher the income level, the higher the tax rate. Similarly, under a progressive tax system, people with fluctuating incomes pay tax at a higher average rate over time on the same amount of total income than do those persons whose incomes are more nearly uniform over time.

Clearly, if a taxpayer's income (apart from any capital gains) is rising over time, the longer he delays realization, the higher his tax rate will be. Similarly, if he realizes gains only occasionally, his gains will tend to be larger, and the average tax rate on the gains will be increased. The bunching problem could be solved by spreading the gain, via income averaging, over the holding period of the asset. This flexibility would involve great complexity, but the result could be approximated reasonably well by fixed-period averaging similar to the general 5-year averaging system or the special 10-year averaging system for lump sum distributions, both of which are in present law.

The problem of postponement of tax to periods of higher marginal rates is a more difficult one. One possible solution would be to calculate an average marginal tax rate over a fixed number of years and to modify the amount of gain included in the tax base for the year of realization to reflect the ratio of the average marginal rate over the period to the marginal rate in the current year. Thus, if the current rate were higher, some of the gain could be excluded from income; if the current rate were lower, more than 100 percent of the gain would be included. As is the case with charges of interest for deferral, however, such systems would add significantly to the complexity of the tax law, and represent inexact adjustments besides.

Inflation Adjustment

The proper tax treatment of capital gains is further complicated by general price inflation. Capital gains that merely reflect increases in the general price level are illusory. For example, suppose an individual's capital assets increase in value, but at a rate precisely equal to the rise in the cost of living. His net worth will not have increased in real terms, and neither, therefore, will his standard of living. If no basis adjustment is made to account for inflation, the reported capital gain for an asset held over a period of time will largely reflect the level of prices in previous years. This contrasts with other income flows, such as salaries, that are always accounted for in current dollars.

Accounting for other transactions that are affected by inflation, such as borrowing and lending, is largely corrected for anticipated inflation by market adjustments. For example, a lender will insist on a higher interest rate to compensate for taxes against the depreciating value of the principal. Therefore, an adjustment of basis for inflation is desirable in the case of ownership of capital assets to avoid overtaxation of capital gains relative to other income sources, even if general indexing of income sources and/or taxes is not prescribed. Unfortunately, inflation adjustment would introduce additional complexity.

Clearly, there are competing objectives of simplicity, equity, and economic efficiency involved in the tax treatment of capital gains.

In this case, the model tax treatment would favor simplicity by foregoing accrual treatment that would require annual valuation of all assets, or interest charges for deferral. On the other hand, clear moves in the direction of accrual taxation are taken by introducing current taxation of corporate-retained earnings and more accurate measurement of depreciation. Adjustment of basis for general inflation also is judged to be worth the additional administration and compliance cost.

STATE AND LOCAL BOND INTEREST

The annual receipt or accrual of interest on State and local obligations unquestionably increases the taxpayer's opportunity to consume, add to wealth, or make gifts. It is, therefore, properly regarded as a source of income. However, such interest is not included in income under current law; this is not to say that owners of such bonds bear no consequence of the present income tax. Long-term tax-exempt bonds yield approximately 30 percent less than fully taxable bonds of equal risk—a consequence that may be regarded as an implicit tax. However, because problems of equity and inefficiency remain, this lower yield on tax-exempt bonds does not substitute for full taxation. *Under the model income tax, interest on State and local bonds would be fully taxable.*

Inefficiency of Interest Exclusion

The difference in interest costs that the State or local government would have to pay on taxable bonds and that which they actually pay on tax-exempt bonds is borne by the Federal Government in the form of reduced revenues. The subsidy is inefficient in that the total cost to the Federal Government exceeds the value of the subsidy to the State and local governments in the form of lower interest payments. Estimates of the fraction of the total Federal revenue loss that is not received by the State and local governments vary widely, but the best estimates seem to be in the 25- to 30-percent range.

Inequity of the Exclusion

The subsidy also may be regarded as inequitable. The value of the tax exemption depends on the investor's marginal tax rate. Thus, higher-income taxpayers are more willing than lower-income individuals to pay more for tax-exempt securities. The concentration of the tax savings among the relatively well-off reduces the progressivity of the Federal income tax as compared with the nominal rate structure. The exemption also results in differential rates of taxation among higher-income taxpayers who have incomes from different sources. Investors who would otherwise be subject to marginal rates above 30 percent may avoid these rates by purchasing tax-exempt bonds. Those with equal incomes from salaries or from active management of business must pay higher rates.

Alternatives to Tax-Exempt Bonds

The taxation of interest from State and local bonds would present no special administrative problems, except for transition rules, but alternative means of fiscal assistance to State and local governments may be desirable. Among the alternatives that have been suggested are replacement of the tax exclusion with a direct cash subsidy from the Federal Government (as under revenue sharing), or replacement with a direct interest subsidy on taxable bonds issued by State and local governments at their option. The mechanism for an interest subsidy may be either a direct Federal payment or a federally sponsored bank empowered to buy low-yield State and local bonds and issue its own fully taxable bonds.

OWNER-OCCUPIED HOUSING

Under present law, homeowners are allowed personal deductions for mortgage interest paid and for State and local property taxes assessed against their homes. Furthermore, there is no attempt to attribute to owner-occupiers the income implied by ownership of housing equity. (In the aggregate, this is estimated in the national income and product accounts at $11.1 billion per year, an amount that does not include untaxed increases in housing values.)

Imputed Rental Income

Any dwelling, whether owner-occupied or rented, is an asset that yields a flow of services over its economic lifetime. The value of this service flow for any time period represents a portion of the market rental value of the dwelling. For rental housing, there is a monthly contractual payment (rent) from tenant to landlord for the services of the dwelling. In a market equilibrium, these rental payments must be greater than the maintenance expenses, related taxes, and depreciation, if any. The difference between these continuing costs and the market rental may be referred to as the "net income" generated by the housing unit.

An owner-occupier may be thought of as a landlord who rents to himself. On his books of account will also appear maintenance expenses and taxes, and he will equally experience depreciation in the value of his housing asset. What do not appear are, on the sources side, receipts of rental payment and, on the uses side, net income from the dwelling. Viewed from the sources side, this amount may be regarded as the reward that the owner of the dwelling accepts in-kind, instead of the financial reward he could obtain by renting to someone other than himself. Since a potential owner-occupier faces an array of opportunities for the investment of his funds, including in housing for rental to himself or others, the value of the reward in-kind must be at least the equal of these financial alternatives. Indeed, this fact provides a possible method for approximating the flow of consumption he receives, constituting a portion of the value of his consumption services. Knowing the cost of the asset and its depreciation schedule, one could estimate the reward necessary to induce the owner-occupier to rent to himself.

In practice, to tax this form of imputed income, however desirable it might be from the standpoint of equity or of obtaining neutrality between owning and renting, would severely complicate tax compliance and administration. Because the owner-occupier does not explicitly make a rental payment to himself, the value of the current use of his house is not revealed. Even if market rental were estimated, perhaps as a fixed share of assessed value of the dwelling,[5] the taxpayer would face the difficulties of accounting for annual maintenance and depreciation to determine his net income.

The present tax system does not attempt to tax the imputed income from housing. This is, perhaps, because there would be extreme administrative difficulties in determining it and because there is a general lack of understanding of its nature. The incentive for home ownership that results from including net income from rental housing in the tax base while excluding it for owner-occupied housing also has strong political support, although the result is clearly a distortion from the pattern of consumer housing choices that would otherwise prevail.

Primarily for the sake of simplification, *the model plan continues to exclude from the tax base the portion of housing consumption attributable to owner-occupied dwellings. No imputation of the net income arising from these assets is proposed.*

Deductibility of Homeowners' Property Tax

Present law allows the homeowner to deduct State and local property taxes assessed against the value of his house as well as interest paid on his mortgage. The appropriateness of each of these deductions is considered next, beginning with the property tax.

The model tax would allow no deduction for the local property tax on owner-occupied homes or on other types of property that also have tax-free rental values, e.g., automobiles. This treatment is based on the proposition that deduction of the property tax results in further understatement of income in the tax base, in addition to the exclusion of net rental income. This cannot be justified, as can the exclusion of net income from the dwelling, on grounds of measurement difficulty. Allowing the deduction of property taxes by owner-occupiers results in unnecessary discrimination against tenants of rental housing. Elimination of the deduction would simplify tax administration and compliance and reduce the tax bias in favor of housing investment in general, and owner-occupancy in particular.

Local housing market adjustments normally will insure that changes in property taxes will be reflected in rental values. When the local property tax is increased throughout a market area, the current cost of supplying rental housing increases by the amount of the tax increase. Over time, housing supplies within the area will be reduced (and prices increased) until all current costs are again met and a normal return accrues to owners of equity and suppliers of mortgages. Accordingly, rents eventually must rise dollar-for-dollar with an increase in property tax. (Note that, in a market equilibrium, deductibility of the local tax against Federal income tax would not result in reduced Federal liability for *landlords* because the increase in gross receipts would match the increased deduction.) Tenants will experience an increase in rent and no change in their income tax liability.

Owner-occupiers provide the same service as landlords, and, therefore, must receive the same rental for a dwelling of equal quality. Hence, market rentals for their homes also would rise by the amount of any general property tax increase. If owner-occupiers were allowed to deduct the tax increase from taxable income while not reporting the increased imputed rent, they would enjoy a reduction in income tax that is not available either to tenants or to landlords.

To summarize the effect of the property tax increase: the landlord would have the same net income and no change in income tax; the tenant would have no change in income tax and higher rent; and the owner-occupier would have higher (imputed) rent as a "tenant," but the same net income and a *reduction* in his income tax as a "landlord." He would be favored relative to the renter first by receiving income from assets free of tax, and, in addition, his advantage over the tenant and landlord would *increase* with higher rates of local property tax. This advantage would not be present if the property tax deduction were denied to the owner-

occupier. He would be treated as the tenant/landlord that he is—
paying higher rent to himself to cover the property tax while his
net income and income tax were unchanged.

Deductibility of Mortgage Interest

The mortgage interest deduction for owner-occupiers is often
discussed in the same terms as the foregoing property tax argument. There are, however, quite significant differences, and,
because of these, the *model tax treatment would continue to allow
deductibility of home mortgage interest.*

The effect of this policy may be equated to allowing any taxpayer
to enjoy tax-free the value of consumption services directly produced by a house (or other similar asset), regardless of the method
he uses to finance the purchase of this asset. The tax-free income
allowed is thus the same whether he chooses to purchase the asset
out of funds previously accumulated or to obtain a mortgage loan
for the purpose.

This position is based on the reasoning that, given the pre-
liminary decision (based on measurement difficulty) not to attempt
to tax the net income received from his house by the person who
purchases it with previously accumulated or inherited funds, it
would be unfair to deny a similar privilege to those who must
borrow to finance the purchase.

There is a related reason in favor of allowing the mortgage interest deduction, having to do with the difficulty of tracing the
source of funds for purchase of an asset.

Prospective homeowners of little wealth are obliged to offer the
house as security to obtain debt financing. By contrast, an individual of greater wealth could simply borrow against some other
securities, use the proceeds to purchase housing equity, and take
the normal interest deduction. In other words, a mortgage is not
the only way to borrow to finance housing, and it is very difficult, if
not impossible, to correlate the proceeds of any other loan with the
acquisition of a house.

Nevertheless, a case may be made for disallowing the interest
deduction for borrowing identifiably for the purpose of financing
an owner-occupied home (or other consumer durable). There is no
doubt that most people finance home purchases with a mortgage
using the home as security. Mortgage interest payments are surely
highly correlated with net income produced by the associated
housing, and denying the deduction would increase the tax base by
an amount equal to a significant fraction of the aggregate net
income from owner-occupied dwellings. For those who cannot
otherwise finance home purchases, it would end the tax bias

against renting. These considerations deserve to be weighed against the view taken here that the efficiency and equity gains from denying the mortgage interest deduction are insufficient to counter-balance the equity losses and the increased administrative complexity of the necessary rules for tracing the sources of funds.

Consumer Durables

Precisely the same arguments that have been made concerning houses also apply to consumer durables, such as automobiles, boats, and recreational vehicles. These assets generate imputed incomes and may be subject to State and local personal property taxes. The model tax would treat these assets in the same way. That is, *property tax assessed against consumer durables would not be deductible, but all interest payments, including those related to purchase of durables, would be allowed as deductions.*

MEDICAL EXPENSES

The present tax law allows the deduction of uninsured medical expenses, in excess of a floor, and partial deduction for medical insurance premiums. The principal argument for deductibility is that medical expenses are not voluntary consumption. Rather, they are extraordinary outlays that should not be included in the consumption component of the income definition.

Opponents of deductibility can cite a fairly high degree of "consumer choice" in the extent, type, and quality of medical services that may be elected by persons of similar health. At the extreme, health care choices include cosmetic surgery, fitness programs at resorts and spas, frequent physical examinations, and other expenditures that are not clearly distinguishable from ordinary consumption. The remainder of medical expenditures is generally insurable, and insurance premiums may be regarded as regular, predictable consumption expenditures. Indeed, tax deductibility of medical expenses may be viewed itself as a type of medical insurance that is inadequate in amount for most taxpayers and has some quite unsatisfactory features.

Model Tax Treatment

The model tax would not allow deductions for medical expenses or medical insurance premiums. The benefits of medical insurance would not be included in income. Nondeductibility of medical expenses would simplify the tax law as well as recordkeeping for households. It also would eliminate the necessity of making the sometimes difficult administrative determination of eligibility of a medical expense for deduction.

An optional treatment is presented here that would provide a refundable tax credit for a share of large medical expenses. This optional approach is intended as an explicit medical insurance program, administered under the tax law. There is no presumption here, however, that administration of such a program by the tax authorities would be preferred to alternatives.

"Tax Insurance" Under Present Law

Under present law, eligible medical expenses in excess of 3 percent of adjusted gross income (AGI) are partially reimbursed by "tax insurance" equal to the deductible expenses multiplied by the taxpayer's marginal tax rate, e.g., 25 percent. The taxpayer pays only the coinsurance rate, in this example 75 percent, times the medical expenses. Therefore, itemizers are uninsured (by the tax system) for medical expenses up to an amount that varies in proportion to their income, and above that amount they pay a coinsurance rate that decreases as marginal tax rates increase. Low-income taxpayers are more likely to exceed the floor on deductibility (3 percent of AGI), but higher-income taxpayers receive a higher rate of insurance subsidy.

A family with $10,000 of salary receipts might be at the 19-percent marginal tax rate, and thus have a "tax insurance" policy that requires that family to pay 81 percent of medical expenses in excess of $300 per year. A family with $50,000 of salary at the 48-percent marginal rate has a "policy" that requires payment of only 52 percent of expenses above $1,500 per year. The same type of tax insurance is provided for medicines and drugs to the extent that they exceed 1 percent of AGI.

Present law also allows deduction of half of private insurance premiums (up to a deduction limit of $150) without regard to the floor, the balance being treated as uninsured medical expenses subject to the 3-percent floor. Insurance proceeds are not taxable so long as they do not exceed actual expenses. In the case of fully insured expenses, the result is the same as including all insurance proceeds in income, allowing deduction of all outlays without floor, and allowing deduction for a share of premiums as well. Hence, total medical costs—insurance premiums plus uninsured losses— are partially deductible without floor to the extent of insurance coverage and fully deductible above a floor for the uninsured portion. Those who cannot itemize have no "tax insurance," while itemizers pay a coinsurance rate—ranging from 30 percent to 86 percent—that varies inversely with income.

Optional Catastrophe Insurance Provision

Viewed as a mandatory government insurance program, the present tax treatment of medical expenses deserves reconsideration. One alternative is a policy that would provide a subsidy—either in the form of a refundable tax credit or direct appropriation—for very large medical expenses. Under such a scheme, the floor for the deduction would be raised, but the "coinsurance" rate would be increased for all taxpayers and made uniform, rather than dependent on the taxpayer's marginal rate. For example, if a tax credit were used, its amount might be equal to 80 percent of expenses in excess of a flat floor, say, $1,000 per year. Alternatively, the floor amount might be made a share of income.

While a catastrophe insurance provision would be a major change in the system of financing medical care, it need not have a large budgetary consequence when combined with repeal of the present deductions. For the level of medical expenses prevailing in 1975, elimination of the present deduction for premiums and expenses would finance complete reimbursement of all medical expenditures that exceed 10 percent of AGI. Full reimbursement would, however, have the undesirable effect of eliminating the market incentives to restrain medical costs. Some rate of coinsurance is desirable to help ration medical resources. Supplemental private insurance would undoubtedly be made available for insurable medical expenses not reimbursed by the tax credit. No deduction would be allowed for private medical insurance premiums, but proceeds would not be taxable.

STATE AND LOCAL TAXES

The way State and local governments should be treated in a comprehensive income measurement system presents difficult conceptual problems. These units might be treated simply as the collective agencies of their citizens. Ideally, in this view, the value of consumption services provided in-kind to the members of the group would be attributed to the individuals and counted on the uses side of their individual income accounts. The same amounts would appear on the sources side, as imputations for receipts in the form of services. Payments to the group would be deducted, as not directly measuring consumption, and payments received from the group would be added to the sources side of the individual income calculation.

The difficulty is in measuring the value of services provided by the collective unit. This problem is solved for such a voluntary collective as a social club by disallowing any deductions for payments made to it by members. In effect, these payments are regarded as measuring the consumption received by members. When it comes to a larger collective organization, such as a State government, this approach is much less satisfactory. The payments to the organization are no longer good proxies for the value of services received. For that reason there is a strong equity case for allowing a deduction of such payments in calculating individual income (including in individual income any grants received—"negative taxes").

Unfortunately, there is no practical method for imputing to individuals the value of services received, so that it is not possible to carry out the complete income measurement system. As in the case of services from owner-occupied homes, the model plan concedes that the value of most services provided collectively will be excluded from the tax base. And as with owner-occupied housing, there is a resulting bias introduced by the Federal tax system in favor of State and local collective expenditure over individual expenditures. The general principle, then, is that payments to the State or local government are excluded from the tax base other than in cases when there is a reasonable correspondence between payments and value of services received. There remains, however, the question of what constitutes "payment" for this purpose, and here particular difficulty is presented by indirect taxes such as sales taxes. Analysis of this issue, together with considerations of simplicity in administration, lead to the prescription of the model tax system that *a deduction is allowed only for State and local income taxes. Other taxes may be deducted only as costs of doing business.*

Income Tax Deductibility

Income taxes represent the clearest analogy with dues paid into a voluntary collective. These payments reduce the resources available to the payor for consumption or accumulation, and hence they are properly deductible.

Property Tax Deductibility

The issue of property tax deductibility for homeowners has been discussed above. Deduction of that tax should not be allowed so long as the associated implicit rental income from housing is excluded from taxable income. Other State and local taxes that are generally deductible under present law are general sales taxes, and motor fuel taxes.

Sales Tax Deductibility

General sales taxes, it may be argued, should not be deducted separately because they do not enter household receipts. Unlike the personal income tax, which is paid by households out of gross-of-tax wages, interest, dividends, and the like, the sales tax is collected and remitted to government by businesses that then pay employees and suppliers of capital out of after-sales-tax receipts. Therefore, the sum of all incomes reported by households must be net of the tax; the tax has already been "deducted" from income sources. To allow a deduction to individuals for the sales tax would be to allow the full amount of the tax to be deducted twice.

The argument above is modified somewhat to the extent that the rate of sales tax varies among States and localities that trade with each other. Jurisdictions with high sales tax rates may sustain locally higher prices if they can effectively charge the sales tax to their own residents who purchase goods outside the jurisdiction. In this case, compensating higher wages, rents, etc. (in money terms) must also prevail in the high-rate area to forestall outmigration of labor and capital. The additional tax will increase nominal income receipts in the region of high tax rates.

The question is an empirical one on the degree to which sales taxes do result in price level differences among jurisdictions. *In view of the difficulty of establishing this relationship and of measuring the individual expenditures on which sales taxes are paid, the deduction for sales taxes is not allowed in the model comprehensive income tax.* A disadvantage of this treatment is that to the extent sales taxes do cause price level differences, the choice of financing investment by State and local governments will be biased, toward income and away from sales taxes.

Alternative Treatments of Sales and Income Taxes

An alternative treatment of both sales and income taxes may be considered, whereby a deduction is allowed only for amounts in excess of a significant floor (possibly expressed as a fraction of the tax base). As at present, standard amounts of sales tax, related to income, could be included in the income tax form, with sales taxes on large outlays (e.g., for an automobile) allowed in addition. This approach would relieve most taxpayers of recordkeeping and be roughly equivalent to including at least some of consumption services that are provided by State and local governments in the tax base. (The floor could even be related to an estimate of the extent to which State and local taxes finance transfer payments, included in the base by recipients.)

Benefit Taxes

Certain State and local government services are financed by taxes and charges that are closely related to the taxpayer's own use of those services. Such taxes can be looked upon as measures of the value of consumption of those services and so should not be excluded from income. This argument holds especially for State and local taxes on motor fuels that are earmarked for the construction of highways and for other transportation services. The amount of gasoline consumed is a rough measure of the value of these services used, and, conversely, the consumer can choose the amount of highway services used, and taxes paid, by choosing the size of vehicle and the amount of his driving.

Other State and local user charges and special taxes, such as sewer assessments, fishing licenses, and pollution taxes, are not deductible under current law. This treatment is consistent with the arguments above. In addition, there are a number of local excise taxes that were enacted at least partly for the purpose of controlling consumption. Allowing deduction of such taxes, e.g., on gambling, alcohol, tobacco, firearms, etc., would be adverse to this purpose.

CONTRIBUTIONS TO CHARITIES

Contributions to qualified charitable organizations are presently deductible, subject to certain limits, as an indirect subsidy to philanthropy. Gifts are arguably also of a different nature than ordinary consumption for the donor, and therefore not part of income. Against this view, the voluntary nature of contributions may be cited as evidence that contributors derive satisfaction from giving just as they do from other uses of resources. Since contributions are not taxed to donees, either when received by philanthropic organizations or when distributed to ultimate beneficiaries, a component of income is clearly lost to the tax base as a result of the present policy. Taxation of the donor may be regarded as a substitute for taxation of the donee.

Accordingly, *the model tax would allow no deduction to the donor for gifts to charitable organizations and would not include benefits of such donations in income to recipients.*

The question of how to treat charitable contributions extends beyond issues of income measurement, however. Many persons would regard the benefits of a tax incentive to philanthropy as more valuable than the potential benefits of tax simplification and horizontal equity of the model tax treatment. Consequently, optional methods for providing an incentive to charity, in the form of donor deductibility or a tax credit, also are discussed.

Charity as Income to Beneficiaries

A charitable contribution is a transfer between a donor and beneficiaries with a philanthropic organization as an intermediary. The philanthropic organization usually converts cash contributions into goods and services, such as hospital care, education, or opera performances, that are subsidized or provided free to the beneficiaries. In many cases, e.g., cancer research, the benefits are very broadly diffused throughout society. The value of these services is a form of income-in-kind to the beneficiaries, but under present law there is no attempt to tax beneficiaries on that income.

The logic of the tax treatment of charitable contributions is much the same as that for gifts or bequests to individuals. A gift does not add to the standard of living of the donor, although it does for the beneficiary. If the taxpayer's standard of living is the appropriate criterion for taxability, proper treatment would be to allow deduction of the gift as at present, but with taxation to the recipient, subject only to the general exemption of very low-income taxpayers.

There is, however, no generally satisfactory way to measure or allocate the benefit-in-kind resulting from charitable donations. While total benefits might be measured by their cost, a large input to benefits-in-kind is voluntary effort that is very difficult to value.

Charities as Public Goods

Even if it were practical to tax benefits-in-kind, it still could be argued that the benefits should not be taxed because they flow to society generally as well as to the individual recipient. Many philanthropic activities provide services, e.g., basic research, education, etc., that benefit the public at large. Deductibility of contributions to such activities provides an incentive for this provision without direct government control.

On the other hand, some persons argue that this kind of hidden public finance should not be given to programs that are under private, and perhaps even individual, control. Moreover, it may be viewed as inequitable that some beneficiaries should receive untaxed benefits if others must pay the full cost for similar benefits (e.g., education, health care, etc.).

A Practical Alternative to Taxing Charitable Organizations

If it is considered logical but impractical to tax benefits to the beneficiary, an alternative approximation is to tax the donor by denial of deductibility. The charitable contribution is easily measurable and taxable in a practical sense. If the donor reduces his contributions by the amount of the additional tax he pays, the donor indirectly shifts the tax burden to beneficiaries. Denial of deductibility, therefore, may be viewed as a proxy for taxing beneficiaries. This describes the present treatment of gifts between individuals. The model tax repeats this treatment for gifts to organizations.

Alternative Tax Incentives for Philanthropy

The rationale for deductibility of gifts and exemption from tax of income of charitable institutions comes down to providing a tax incentive to encourage their activities. On the other hand, concern for tax equity only would suggest taxation of the full value of the charitable contribution on at least one side of the transfer. The latter conclusion may be reached whether one invokes a "standard-of-living" or an "ability-to-pay" criterion of equity.

Optional Tax Credit. The use of the tax system to provide an incentive for charitable activities may be accomplished by an alternative policy option—the replacement of the deduction with a tax credit. A flat credit (percentage of contribution) could be provided at a level that would just balance the revenue gain from denying deductibility. A credit of, for example, 25 percent would provide additional tax savings to those with marginal tax rates below 25 percent and impose more taxes on those with marginal rates in excess of 25 percent. In addition to this redistributive effect, this alternative tax incentive may result in certain activities, such as education, health care, and the arts, bearing the additional burden nominally imposed on the higher-income contributors. Other activities, such as religion and welfare, might be more likely to benefit from the tax savings given to lower-income contributors.

The choice between tax credits and deductions thus requires a judgment about the desired amount of stimulus among types of charities. The relative fairness of these devices may be judged according to one's concept of income. If gifts are regarded as reductions in the donor's income, and if rates of tax are chosen to produce a desirable degree of tax progressivity, then the deduction is to be preferred on equity grounds. Conversely, if charitable giving is a use of one's income that is to be encouraged by public subsidy, a subsidy per dollar of gift that does not vary with the taxable income of the donee may be more appropriate.

CASUALTY LOSSES

Model Tax Treatment

The issue of deductibility of casualty losses is analogous to that of the property tax deduction. Damage to property due to accidents or natural disasters reduces the present and potential income from ownership of that property. Consequently, casualty losses are properly deductible business expenses. However, as argued previously, owner-occupied houses and consumer durables produce incomes equal to a certain portion of the current rental value to the user, and that income is fully exempt from tax under present law and would be under the model tax. Deduction of casualty losses would represent an asymmetric treatment of these household assets—their income is exempt from tax, but interruption of the flow of income due to casualty would provide a tax reduction. *The model tax would allow no deduction for casualty losses except to business property. Casualty insurance premiums for household property would not be deductible and insurance benefits would not be included in income.*

Present Law Treatment

Under current law, insurance premiums are not deductible, but proceeds offset the deduction for actual losses. Hence, the effect for insured losses is the same as full deduction of losses, without floor, and inclusion of insurance proceeds in income.

The logic cited above for refusing the deduction of losses would suggest that insurance premiums for household assets also are a cost of maintaining tax-exempt income. Such costs, therefore, should not be deductible. Because insurance premiums are approximately equal to the expected value of insurance benefits, if no deduction is allowed for premiums, the aggregate of insurance benefits may be regarded as tax-prepaid. Consequently, these benefits should not be taxable as income when paid.

INTERNATIONAL CONSIDERATIONS

The Residence Principle

There are two basic prototype approaches to the taxation of international flows of income. The first is the *residence* principle, under which all income, wherever earned, would be defined and taxed according to the laws of the taxpayer's own country of residence. The second prototype is the source principle, which would require the taxpayer to pay tax according to the laws of the country or countries in which his income is earned, regardless of his residence. Adoption of one prototype or the other, as compared with the mixed system that now prevails, would have the desirable effect of insuring that no part of an individual's income would be taxed by more than one country, and would reduce the number of bilateral treaties necessary to assure against double taxation.

A number of considerations point to the residence principle as the more desirable principle to establish. First, the concept of income as consumption plus change in net worth implies that distinctions based on the geographical origins of receipts are inappropriate. Income, by this definition, is an attribute of individuals, not of places. Second, if owners of factor services are much less mobile internationally than the factor services they supply, variations among countries in taxes imposed by residence will have smaller allocation effects than tax variations among places of factor employment. Third, the income redistribution objective manifested by the use of progressive income taxes implies that a country should impose taxes on the entire income of residents. The usual concept of income distribution cannot be defined on the basis of income source.

For these reasons, the model plan recommends that the United States seek, as a long-run objective, a world wide system of residence principle taxation. This objective would be made much more feasible with the integration of individual and corporation income taxes. Clearly, the residence principle requires that taxable income be attributable to persons. If taxable income were attributed to corporations, they would be encouraged to move their residence to countries with low tax rates.

Even after establishment of the residence principle, some problems would remain. For example, individuals who live in countries that tax pensions upon realization might be induced to retire to those countries that require prepayment of taxes on pensions by including pension contributions in taxable income. Such international differences in tax structure would continue to require bilateral treaty agreements.

Establishing the Residence Principle

To encourage the establishment worldwide of the residence principle, the model tax would *reduce* in stages, and according to the outcome of international treaty negotiations, *the rates of U.S. withholding taxes on income paid to foreign residents and the foreign tax credit allowed to U.S. residents on foreign source income.* This process would depend upon corresponding reductions by foreign countries in the taxation of income of U.S. residents.

The first step in the process of establishing the residence principle is to define a unique tax residence for each individual. These definitions would be established initially by national statute, and ultimately settled by international tax treaty. The second step would be to devise a tax system that encouraged other countries to forego taxation of U.S. residents on income earned abroad. This fundamental change in tax jurisdiction will take time, and it is important that international flows of labor, capital, and technology not be hampered by double taxation during the transition period. Accordingly, transition to the model U.S. tax system would be designed as a slow but steady movement toward residence principle taxation.

Interim Rules

Foreign Shareholders. As a practical matter, it would not be feasible to exempt foreign shareholders from U.S. taxation until such time as the residence principle received broad political acceptance both in the United States and abroad. Initially, therefore, foreign shareholders might be subject to a withholding tax of perhaps 30 percent on their share of corporate income (whether or not distributed), with the rate of taxation subject to reduction by treaty. Other forms of income paid to foreign residents would continue to be subject to withholding tax at existing statutory or treaty rates. These rates also could be reduced by treaty.

Foreign Tax Credits. Eventually, a deduction—not a credit—should be allowed for foreign income taxes, because they are not significantly different from State and local income taxes, for which a deduction is also allowed. This approach would encourage foreign governments to provide U.S. firms operating abroad with benefits approximately equal to the amount of taxes. Otherwise, U.S. firms would gradually withdraw their investments. However, it will take time for foreign governments to accept the residence principle, just as the United States is not immediately willing to forego withholding taxes on U.S. source income paid to foreign residents. In the meantime, for reasons of international comity, and in order not to interrupt international flows of factor services, the United States would continue to allow a foreign tax credit to the extent of its own withholding tax on foreign income. In the case of corporate-source income, the initial credit limitation rate would be 30 percent (and the remainder of foreign taxes would be allowed as a deduction). In the case of other income, the credit limitation would be determined by the U.S. statutory or treaty withholding rate on the particular type of income.

Foreign Corporations. In keeping with the model income tax definition of income, the earnings of a foreign corporation controlled by U.S. interests would flow through to the domestic parent company and then to the shareholders of the domestic parent. The U.S. parent corporation would be deemed to receive the before-foreign-tax income of the subsidiary even if no dividends were paid. This would eliminate deferral here just as the integration plan eliminates shareholder deferral of tax as income in the form of corporate retained earnings. A foreign tax credit would be allowed for the foreign country's corporate income tax and withholding tax to the extent of the 30-percent limit. Excess foreign taxes would be deductible.

The earnings of foreign corporations that are not controlled by U.S. interests would be taxable in the hands of U.S. shareholders only when distributed as dividends, and, therefore, a deduction rather than a credit would be allowed for any underlying foreign corporate income tax. A foreign tax credit would be allowed to U.S. shareholders only to the extent of foreign withholding taxes, and limited by the U.S. withholding rate on dividends paid to foreign residents. (The remainder of foreign withholding taxes would be allowed as a deduction.)

Other Foreign Income. Other types of foreign income paid to U.S. residents would be similarly eligible for a foreign tax credit, again limited by the U.S. tax imposed on comparable types of income paid to foreigners. Thus, a U.S. resident earning salary income abroad would be allowed to claim a foreign tax credit up to the limit of U.S. withholding taxes that are imposed on the salary incomes of foreign residents in the U.S.

THE FILING UNIT

To this point, the concern of this chapter has been to develop a practical definition of income for purposes of a comprehensive income tax. That discussion has involved issues of timing, valuation, and scope, as well as considerations of administrability. The major issues that remain to be discussed have to do with assessment of the tax against income as defined.

Model Tax Treatment

Among the more difficult problems of translating an income definition into a tax system are (1) to determine what social or economic unit should be required (or allowed) to file a tax return and (2) how rates are to be applied to filing units having different characteristics. *The model tax would designate the family as the primary tax unit, with separate rate schedules, as under current law, for three types of families—unmarried individuals without dependents, unmarried individuals with dependents (heads of households), and married couples with or without dependents.* Other provisions for two-earner families and for dependent care are described below.

Problems of Taxation of the Filing Unit

To illustrate the issues involved in choosing among alternative tax treatments of families, consider the following potential criteria:
1. Families of equal size with equal incomes should pay equal taxes.
2. The total tax liability of two individuals should not change when they marry.

Both of these appear to be reasonable standards. Yet, there is no progressive tax system that will satisfy them simultaneously. This is readily illustrated by the following hypothetical case. Both partners of married couple A work, and each has earnings of $15,000. Married couple B has $20,000 of earnings from the labor of one partner and $10,000 from the other.

If individual filing were mandatory, with the same rate structure for all, couple A may pay less tax than couple B. This is a consequence of applying progressive rates separately to the earnings of each partner. Suppose marginal rates were 10 percent on the first $15,000 of income and 20 percent on any additional income. In this example, couple A would owe $1,500 on each partner's income, or a total of $3,000. Couple B would owe $2,500 on the larger income and $1,000 on the smaller, or a total of $3,500. This violates the first criterion.

Now consider a system of family filing in which all income within the family is aggregated and the tax is calculated without regard to the relative earnings of each partner. (Unmarried individuals would be subject to the same rates as a family.) In this case, the two couples would pay the same tax on their total income of $30,000. However, both couples would be financially worse off than if they were unmarried. Each couple would now pay a tax of $3,500 on the total of $30,000. As compared with separate filing, more income is taxed at the higher marginal rate. This violation of the second criterion is sometimes referred to as a "marriage tax."

The simplest device for dealing with this penalty on marriage is "income splitting," whereby the combined income of a married couple is taxed as though it were attributed half to one spouse, and half by the other. Each half is subject to the rate schedule applicable to an unmarried individual. To continue the above example, each couple with a total income of $30,000 would, with income splitting, pay a rate of 10 percent on each $15,000 share, or a total of $3,000 in tax. Notice that there may be a "marriage benefit" so long as each prospective spouse does not have the same income. Upon marriage, the combined tax for couple B would fall from $3,500 to $3,000.

Choice of the Filing Unit

Direct appeal to the concept of income does not settle these issues, because that concept presupposes the definition of an accounting unit. There are legal, administrative, and even sociological factors involved in the choice. The major arguments in favor of mandatory *individual* filing can be summarized as follows: (1) no marriage tax; (2) no discrimination against secondary workers; and (3) the administrative ease of identifying individuals without the requirement of a definition of families. By contrast, the arguments in favor of *family* filing are: (1) families with equal incomes should pay equal taxes; (2) families typically make joint decisions about the use of their resources and supply of their labor services; and (3) family filing makes it unnecessary to allocate property rights, as in the case of community property laws, and to trace intrafamily gifts.

The last point is critical. A concept of income as a use of resources implies that each individual's ability to pay includes consumption and net worth changes financed by transfers from other family members. Carried to extreme, this separate treatment of family members would suggest assessment of tax even to minor children. Chiefly because of this problem, *it is recommended that the family be made the primary tax unit.*

The definition of a family is, of necessity, somewhat arbitrary, as is the application of progressive rate schedules to families of different types. The following definition of a family is adopted here[6]: The family unit consists of husband and wife and their children. The children are included until the earliest date on which one of the following events occurs:

- They reach 18 years of age and they are not then attending school; or
- They receive their baccalaureate degree or;
- They attain age 26; or
- They marry.

Single persons are taxed separately. Persons not currently married and their children living with them are treated as family units.

The Problem of Secondary Workers

A system of joint family filing may cause an efficiency loss to the economy; namely, the discouragement of labor force participation by secondary workers in a family. If a partner not in the labor force is thinking of entering it, the tax rate that person faces is the marginal rate applying to the prospective total family income. This rate may be much higher than that for a single wage earner.

This consequence of family filing is sometimes referred to as the "wife tax."

Two-earner families and single-adult families with dependents also face expenses for dependent care, which may be regarded as altering such families' ability to pay taxes. Hence, taxability of families will vary according to the number of adults, the number of wage earners, and the number of children.

Compare the circumstances of three three-person families of equal income: family X has two adult wage earners; family Y has two adults, only one of whom is a wage earner; and family Z has only one adult, who is a wage earner. Family Y alone receives the full-time household and child care services of one adult member and may be regarded as better off on this account. Family X alone bears the wife tax associated with secondary wage earners. Family Z has the additional child care responsibility but also the smaller subsistence outlays associated with two children in place of an adult and one child. The model tax would recognize the difference of the type illustrated by these three families by two special adjustments to taxable income, and by separate rate schedules—one for families with one adult and another for those with two adults.

Tax Adjustments for Differences in Family Status

The first adjustment in the model tax is that *only 75 percent of the wage income of secondary earners would be included in family income.* This lower rate of inclusion would apply only to a limited amount of earnings of the secondary worker. In the model tax this limit would be $10,000. Earnings of the secondary worker means the income of all family wage earners, except that of the member with the largest wage income. This provision would reduce the "wife tax" on families with more than one wage earner.

The second adjustment would be *a child care deduction equal to half of actual child care costs* up to a limit of either $5,000 or the taxable earnings of the secondary worker, whichever is smaller. This deduction would be allowed only for a spouse who is a secondary worker, or for an unmarried head of household. The dependent care adjustment would provide some allowance for the reduced standard of living associated with the absence of full-time household services of a parent.

The model tax would provide separate rate schedules, as in present law, for single individuals, for families with a married couple, and for families with a single head of household. Rate schedules applicable to individuals would be set so that a two-adult family would pay slightly higher tax than two unmarried individuals whose equal taxable incomes sum to the same taxable income as the family. A single individual would, of course, owe more tax than a family with the same amount of taxable income. The schedule of rates for a family with a single head of household would be designed so that the tax liability would be the sum of (1) half the tax calculated from the single rate schedule and (2) half the tax from the rate schedule for couples.

The model tax also would have, as part of its rate schedule, a "zero rate bracket" that would exempt a fixed amount of income on each return from tax. The level of this exemption could be adjusted to reduce the potential marriage benefit that may result from different schedules of positive rates for married as compared to single filers. The desired relation in level and progressivity of tax among taxpayers of different family status would be achieved, therefore, by a combination of rates and rate brackets that is different for each type of family, and also by specifying a level of exemption per filing unit.

Provision of an exemption for each filing unit would have much the same effect as the standard deduction under present law. The exemption would provide a minimum level of income for each family or individual that would not be subject to tax. However, unlike the present law, the use of the exemption by a family would not disallow any other subtractions from receipts in the determination of taxable income. Under the model tax, deductions for employee business expenses, State and local income taxes, pension contributions, interest payments, etc. would not be reduced by, nor dependent upon, the exemption of a subsistence amount of income.

ADJUSTING FOR FAMILY SIZE

Most observers would agree that the tax treatment of families should vary by family size, as well as by marital status and the number of wage earners. *The model tax would adjust for family size by means of a specified exemption per family member*, as in present law.

Exemptions Versus Credits

The use of the personal exemption as an adjustment for family size has been much criticized. One line of criticism is that the dollar value of an exemption increases with the family's marginal tax rate, so that it is worth more for rich families than for poor families. This observation has led some people to suggest either a vanishing exemption, which diminishes as income increases, or institution of a tax credit for each family member in place of the exemption. The latter approach has been adopted, in a limited way, in the "personal exemption credit" provision of the 1975 Tax Reduction Act, which has been extended temporarily by the 1976 Tax Reform Act. A tax credit reduces tax liability by the same amount for each additional family member regardless of family income.

The argument for a vanishing exemption or family credit often reflects a misunderstanding of the relationship of these devices to the overall progressivity of the income tax. It is true that trading an exemption for a credit *without changing rates* will alter the pattern of progressivity, making the tax more progressive for large families, less for small families and single persons. But it is also true that, for any given level of exemption or credit, any degree of progression among families of equal size may be obtained by altering the rate schedule. Therefore, in the context of a basic reform of the tax system that involves revision of the rate structure, there is no reason that the substitution of tax credits for exemptions should result in a more progressive tax.

If the change in the standard of living that accompanies the addition of a family member is akin to a reduction in the family's income, then an exemption would be an appropriate family-size adjustment. If, on the other hand, one views the family-size adjustment as a type of subsistence subsidy for each member of a taxpayer's family, a credit may be more appropriate. The model tax reflects the former view.

The point to be emphasized here is that this choice is often argued in the wrong terms. If tax rates are adjustable, the issue of exemptions versus credits is essentially a question of the proper relative treatment of equal-income families of different sizes at various points of the income distribution. Should the tax reduction on account of additional family members be greater as family income increases? Or is this, per se, inequitable?

SAMPLE COMPREHENSIVE INCOME TAX FORM

In order to summarize the major provisions of the model Comprehensive Income Tax, and to provide a ready reference to its provisions, a listing of the items of information that would be required to compute the tax is provided below. In a few cases— unincorporated business income, capital gains and losses, and income from rents and royalties—supplemental schedules would be required to determine amounts to be entered. However, as compared with present law, recordkeeping requirements and tax calculation would be simplified greatly, despite the fact that several presently excluded items of income are added.

For most taxpayers, the only calculations that would be complicated would be the exclusion of a portion of wages of secondary workers and the child care allowance for working mothers and heads of households. The rest of the calculation would simply involve the addition of receipts, subtraction of deductions and exemptions, and reference to a table of rates. For single individuals and couples with one wage earner who have only employee compensation and limited amounts of interest and dividends, a still simpler form could be devised.

SAMPLE TAX FORM FOR THE
COMPREHENSIVE INCOME TAX

Filing Status

1. Check applicable status
   a. Single individual
   b. Married filing joint return
   c. Unmarried head of household
   d. Married filing separately

Family Size

2. Enter one on each applicable line
   a. Yourself
   b. Spouse
3. Number of dependent children
4. Total family size (add lines 2a, 2b, and 3)

Receipts

5. a. Wages, salaries, and tips of primary wage earner (attach forms W-2)*
   b. Wages, salaries, and tips of all other wage earners (attach forms W-2)*
   c. Multiply line 5b by .25; if greater than $2,500, enter $2,500
   d. Included wages of secondary workers, subtract line 5c from line 5b
   e. Wages subject to tax, add lines 5a and 5d
6. Receipts of pensions, annuities, disability compensation, unemployment compensation, workmen's compensation, and sick pay. (Includes social security benefits, except Medicare, and veterans disability and survivor benefits.)
7. Interest received (attach forms 1099)
8. Rents, royalties, estate and trust income, and allocated earnings from life insurance reserves (attach schedule E)
9. Unincorporated business income (attach schedule C)
10. Net gain or loss from the sale, exchange, or distribution of capital assets (attach schedule D)

---

*Wages reported by the employer would *exclude* employer and employee contributions to pension plans and disability insurance, and would also *exclude* both the employer's and employee's share of payroll taxes for social security retirement and disability (OASDI). Wages would *include* employer contributions to health and life insurance plans, the employee's allocated share of earnings on pension reserves, and the cash value of consumption goods and services provided to the employees below cost.

11. Allocated share of corporate earnings (attach forms W-x)
12. Public assistance benefits, Food Stamp subsidy, fellowships, scholarships, and stipends (attach forms W-y)
13. Alimony received
14. Total receipts (add lines 5e and 6-13)

Deductions

15. Employee business expense (includes qualified travel, union and professional association dues, tools, materials, and education expenses)
16. Nonbusiness interest expense (attach statement)
17. State and local income tax
18. Alimony paid
19. Child care expenses
    a. If line 1c is checked and line 3 is not zero, or if line 1b is checked and both lines 3 and 5b are not zero, enter total child care expenses
    b. Multiply line 19a by .5
    c. Enter smaller of line 19b or $5,000
    d. Child care deduction. If unmarried head of household, enter smaller of line 19c or line 5a
    e. If married filing joint return, enter smaller of line 19c or line 5d
20. Total deductions (add lines 15-18, and 19d or 19e)

Tax Calculation

21. Income subject to tax. Subtract line 20 from line 14 (if less than zero, enter zero)
22. Basic exemption. Enter $1,600
23. Family size allowance. Multiply line 4 by $1,000
24. Total exemption. Add lines 22 and 23
25. Taxable income. Subtract line 24 from line 21 (if less than zero, enter zero)
26. Tax liability (from appropriate table)
27. a. Total Federal income tax withheld
    b. Estimated tax payments
    c. Total tax prepayments (add lines 27a and 27b)
28. If line 26 is greater than line 27c, enter Balance Due
29. If line 27c is greater than line 26, enter Refund Due

CHAPTER **4**

A Model Tax Based
On Consumption

INTRODUCTION

This chapter presents a proposal for a consumption base tax as an alternative to a comprehensive income tax. Called the Cash Flow Tax because of the simple accounting system used, this system is designed to replace the current taxes on the income of households, individuals, trusts, and corporations.

The major difference between the Cash Flow Tax and the Comprehensive Income Tax outlined in chapter 3 is that the change in an individual's net worth is effectively excluded from the base of the Cash Flow Tax. In many other respects, the two taxes are alike. Consumption is included in both tax bases. The measure of consumption in the cash flow proposal is broadly similar to that in the Comprehensive Income Tax proposal; it differs mainly in that it includes the flow of consumption from consumer durables and owner-occupied housing and certain other forms of in-kind consumption. The treatment of the family unit for tax purposes is the same in both the Comprehensive Income and Cash Flow proposals.

The concern of this chapter is to define the base of the Cash Flow tax system. The issue of the progressivity of the tax system is a separate problem that would have to be resolved for either the Cash Flow Tax or the Comprehensive Income Tax. This issue is considered for both taxes in chapter 5.

Cash Flow Accounting

The central feature of the model tax system is the use of cash flow accounting for financial transactions to obtain a measure of annual consumption for any individual or household. The principle involved is very simple. A household could use monetary receipts

101

in a year for three purposes: personal consumption, saving, and gifts. By including *all* monetary receipts in the tax base, including the entire proceeds of sales of assets and gifts received, and allowing deductions for purchases of assets and gifts given, the annual consumption of a household could be measured without directly monitoring the purchases of goods and services.

The use of cash flow accounting of financial asset transactions to compute the tax base is illustrated, for an average wage earner, in the following example. Suppose a worker earns $10,000 per year in wages, of which he uses $9,000 for personal consumption and $1,000 for saving. Under the Cash Flow Tax outlined in this proposal, the worker could deduct $1,000 from his $10,000 of wages, if he had deposited the $1,000 in a qualified account.

Use of Qualified Accounts. Qualified accounts would be established by banks and other financial institutions, which would keep records of deposits and withdrawals. The worker's $1,000 deposit in the account could be used to purchase any type of financial asset—savings bank deposits, corporate shares, bonds, mutual funds, or any other claim to current or future income. The future balance in the qualified account would depend, of course, on the profitability of his investments. No tax would be assessed against interest, dividends, or capital gains as they are earned, *but the taxpayer would be required to include in his tax base the full value of any withdrawals from his qualified account that were not reinvested in similar accounts*. The use of qualified accounts to handle financial transactions would ease the taxpayer's recordkeeping burden and would enable tax authorities to trace the annual flow of funds available for consumption uses.

The qualified accounts described here are very similar to qualified retirement accounts under current law. These accounts include Keogh plans and Individual Retirement Accounts (IRA's), which provide the taxpayer a current deduction for contributions to funds for retirement and, then, include withdrawals from the fund in the tax base after retirement. There are two major differences between the qualified accounts proposed here and qualified retirement accounts provided for in the current tax code. First, withdrawal of funds from the qualified account would be allowed without penalty at any time during a taxpayer's lifetime. Second, there would be no statutory limit to the amount a taxpayer could contribute to a qualified account.

Thus, in the example above, if the worker deposited $1,000 in a savings account, his tax would be computed on an annual cash flow base of $9,000. If, in the following year, he consumed his entire salary of $10,000 and in addition withdrew $500 from his savings account to purchase a color television set, his cash flow tax base in that year would be $10,500. His tax base is geared to the use of his receipts for consumption, currently or in the future.

Alternative Treatment of Investments. An alternative way of handling investments that would enable an individual to alter the timing but not the expected present value of his cash flow tax base would be to include the *purchases* of assets in the tax base, but to exempt *all returns* from assets from tax. To continue the example above, the worker could deposit $1,000 of his $10,000 of annual wages in a savings bank, but without using a qualified account. If he did so, the entire $10,000 of wage receipts would be included in his tax base in the initial year, but any future interest earned on the savings deposit and any withdrawal of the principal would be excluded from the tax base. As will be discussed more fully below, the expected present value of the worker's lifetime tax base would be the same for either method of accounting, if he consumes the proceeds of his account during his lifetime.

Investments handled in this alternative way would be treated very simply for tax purposes. The amount invested would be included in the tax base—the same as consumption—but all subsequent returns on the investment would be untaxed. In effect, the tax that would otherwise be due on consumption from the proceeds of the investment would be prepaid at the time the investment is made. Allowing taxpayers the choice of this alternative way of handling investment accounts has some advantages, but could create problems, which are discussed below.

The possibility is discussed of dealing with these problems by introducing restrictions on the types of investments that may or must be made through qualified accounts. Although few restrictions are recommended in the model plan, it should be stressed that to increase their number or stringency would be consistent with the basic concept of the Cash Flow Tax and would not alter its most important features.

The remainder of this chapter presents the details of the model Cash Flow Tax base and discusses its most important characteristics. The next section points out the tax issues that have common solutions in the model Comprehensive Income Tax and the model Cash Flow Tax. Then, a section is devoted to the major differences between the two tax bases, including a full description of the Cash Flow Tax treatment of investment assets and consumer durables. Another section discusses the economic consequences of adopting the Cash Flow Tax, and the final section presents a sample tax calculation form.

ELEMENTS IN COMMON WITH THE
COMPREHENSIVE INCOME TAX

Several of the issues discussed in the preceding chapter would be resolved similarly for the Cash Flow Tax. These questions include the measurement of consumption—to be taxed alike in both models—and the related issue of the appropriate treatment of families of varying size and circumstances.

Family Size and Family Status

Under this proposal, the family would be taxed as a unit for reasons analogous to those argued in chapter 3. In order to assess tax to each family member as an individual, it would be necessary to allocate consumption among family members. This would destroy much of the administrative simplicity of the Cash Flow Tax, which rests upon deducting from receipts certain cash outlays that are usually made on behalf of the family as a unit. Receipts are also usually combined at the family level. The argument that standard of living varies by family size holds for a consumption measure of living standard as well as for an income standard. The adjustment device in the model Cash Flow Tax plan discussed in this chapter—one exemption per family member—is the same as that proposed for the Comprehensive Income Tax. However, differences in the size of the tax base under the two taxes might require that the exemption levels be different for model taxes intended to raise the same revenue. As in the case of the Comprehensive Income Tax, other approaches to the adjustment for family size would be fully consistent with the Cash Flow Tax base.

Adjustments that account for differences among families in the number of wage earners and the availability of a full-time adult in the household apply to labor-related earnings and expenses only. They would be just as appropriate, therefore, under a consumption tax as under an income tax. However, the structure of rates required to achieve the desired pattern of progressivity might be different.

Deductions for Charitable Contributions,
Medical Expenses, and Taxes

Contributions to Charities. As in the case of the Comprehensive Income Tax, deductions for charitable contributions would not be allowed under the model Cash Flow Tax. Conceptually, under a "standard-of-living" consumption tax, itemized gifts should be deductible by the donor and included in the receipts of the donee. Following the discussion in chapter 3, including receipts from charities in the tax base of the recipient is rejected as impractical.

Charity is not usually given in cash or in goods that are easy to value, and sometimes the benefit is to society generally, so that beneficiaries cannot be separately identified. Nor should the charitable institutions be taxed. They do not consume; they merely act as intermediaries to distribute the benefits to the ultimate recipients. The foregoing suggests that the best way to tax consumption resulting from charitable activities would be to count charitable contributions as consumption by the donor and not to allow a tax deduction.

In opposition to this proposal, it may be argued that tax-free consumption of goods and services provided by charities should be maintained because these goods and services provide a public service function. Proponents of this view would argue for either a deduction or some form of tax credit for charitable contributions. As noted in chapter 3, however, the decision whether or not to allow the deduction of charitable contributions is not essential to the basic integrity of the overall proposal.

One element of the Comprehensive Income Tax discussion of charities that does not apply to the Cash Flow Tax is the undistributed portion of endowment earnings of charitable organizations which should not be taxed even if taxation of organizations on the basis of contributions is viewed as feasible and recommended as a general policy.

Medical Expenses. The issues involving medical expenses and medical insurance are exactly the same for the Cash Flow Tax as for the income tax. Consequently, the same policy options are prescribed for both model taxes.

State and Local Income Taxes. The model Cash Flow Tax treatment of state and local taxes also would be the same as that under the model accretion tax: income taxes would be fully deductible because they are not regarded as part of consumption. Other taxes would not be deductible, except as business expenses.

Property Taxes. No property tax deduction would be allowed to homeowners under either of the model taxes. The rationale for denying deduction of the property tax for owner-occupied homes is, however, somewhat different in the case of the cash flow tax. The Cash Flow Tax would measure the owner's consumption of housing services as the purchase price (or capital value) of the dwelling. In a market equilibrium, this price is the present value of the prospective stream of imputed rents less current costs. These costs include property taxes. Therefore, a higher local property tax, if uncompensated by services to the property, would result in a lower market price of the dwelling. In this way, the property tax is excluded from the base of the Cash Flow Tax without an explicit deduction.

Health, Disability, and Unemployment Insurance

Those types of insurance that are purchased for a 1-year term and pay benefits directly to the insured—health, disability, and unemployment insurance—are no different in concept or model tax treatment under the Cash Flow Tax than under the accretion tax. They are included in the definition of consumption. The differences in treatment among them—taxation of benefits in the case of disability and unemployment, and of premiums for health insurance—are explained in the preceding chapter. The model tax treatment is the same for each of these items whether the insurance is public or private, employer-paid or employee-paid. However, life, casualty, and old-age insurance do present differences in concept under the consumption tax and will be discussed below.

Casualty Losses

Casualty losses would not be deductible under the model Comprehensive Income Tax or under the Cash Flow Tax. Again, however, the rationale for not allowing the deduction under the Cash Flow Tax is slightly different. Under the Cash Flow Tax, changes in net worth would not be included in the tax base, and, therefore, reductions in net worth, in general, should not be deducted. Further, as explained below, all taxation for the consumption of consumer durables would be prepaid at the time of purchase, and subsequent sales of consumer durables, at whatever price, would not be included in the tax base. Following the same reasoning, the premiums for casualty insurance would *not* be deductible under the Cash Flow Tax proposal, and the proceeds would be excluded from the tax base.

DIFFERENCES BETWEEN THE CASH FLOW TAX AND THE COMPREHENSIVE INCOME TAX

The major difference between the Cash Flow Tax outlined here and the Comprehensive Income Tax presented in chapter 3 follows directly from the definition of the two bases. Under the cash flow system, changes in net worth would not be included in the tax base, but the Comprehensive Income Tax would attempt to include all changes in net worth to the extent administratively feasible. Thus, the Cash Flow Tax and the income tax differ in their treatment of purchases of assets and returns from asset ownership. Specifically, the two taxes differ most in the handling of corporate profits, income from unincorporated business, capital gains, interest received on savings and interest paid on loans, rental income, income accrued in retirement plans and life insurance, and casualty losses.

The first part of this section discusses in some detail the treatment of investment assets and consumer durables under the Cash Flow Tax proposal. In the second part, a comparison is made between specific provisions of the model Comprehensive Income Tax and the handling of corresponding items under the model Cash Flow Tax.

The Treatment of Assets Under a Cash Flow Tax

The Cash Flow Tax would greatly simplify tax accounting and tax administration regarding real and financial assets. Accounts to determine capital gains, depreciation, and inventories—among the most complex necessitated by the current tax code—would no longer be required. For many individuals, no accounting would be necessary for asset purchases nor for receipts associated with asset ownership. For other taxpayers, simple annual cash flow data would provide all the necessary information for computing tax liability. The taxpayer would merely record the net annual deposits or withdrawals from qualified accounts. Accounting for the Cash Flow Tax would rest solely on marketplace transactions for the current year, thus minimizing the need for long-term record-keeping.

Family-Owned Businesses. The simplicity of Cash Flow Tax accounting is best illustrated by the model tax treatment of a family-owned business. All cash in-flows would be counted as receipts. Cash outlays that represent business expenses—including all purchases of equipment, structures, and inventories—would be deducted from receipts; that is, instantaneous depreciation for tax purposes would be allowed on all investments regardless of the durability of the asset purchased. The difference between receipts and cash outlays would be included in the individual's tax base. If cash outlays exceed business receipts in any year, the difference would reduce receipts from other sources.

For example, suppose a family derived all its receipts from a family-owned grocery store. To compute its tax base, the family would add up all cash receipts from sales and subtract from this amount all business outlays, including payments to employees and cash outlays for electricity, rent payments for the store, purchases of machinery, and purchases of inventories. These would be the only calculations the family would make to determine its tax base under the Cash Flow Tax. No data on capital gains or depreciation would be required to determine taxable receipts.

Financial Assets. Financial assets, including stocks, bonds, and savings deposits, owned by taxpayers via qualified accounts would be recorded for tax purposes in the same way as annual purchases and sales associated with a family-owned business. All deposits would be deducted from other receipts in computing the tax base. All withdrawals, whether arising from dividends, interest, or asset sales, would be included in the tax base. No distinction would have to be made between the gain from sale of an asset and the return of capital invested.

For example, suppose an individual deposits $100 in a qualified savings bank account, where it earns 10 percent annual interest. In the year he makes the $100 deposit, he would be allowed to deduct $100 from current receipts in computing his tax base. If, in the following year, he withdraws the principal plus earned interest— now equal to $110—the amount withdrawn would be added to receipts from other sources in computing the tax base. If, instead, the savings deposit were left in the bank to accumulate interest, there would be no current tax consequences. Any future withdrawal would add to taxable receipts in the year it is made.

Deductions for the purchase of financial assets would be allowed only if the purchase were made through a qualified account. This device would offer a simple way to insure compliance with the Cash Flow Tax. Individuals would be permitted to keep qualified accounts with savings banks, corporations, stockbrokers, and many other types of financial institutions. The net amount of deposits in, and withdrawals from, qualified accounts during the year would be reported by the institution to both the taxpayer and tax authorities. The present dividend-reporting requirements for corporations may be viewed as a model for the way financial institutions would report net withdrawals and deposits from qualified accounts for the Cash Flow Tax.

The tax base of an individual would include the sum of net withdrawals from all qualified accounts. If deposits exceeded withdrawals, the excess would be subtracted from other receipts in computing the tax base. The sale of one asset out of a qualified account and subsequent purchase in the same year of another asset of equal dollar value would have no net tax consequences if the new asset were also purchased in a qualified account.

Consumer Durables. It is technically feasible, but practically unattractive, to apply the cash flow concepts just described to the purchase of consumer durables. Unlike financial assets, consumer durables such as automobiles, houses, and major home appliances, all yield flows of services to the owners that are not measured by annual monetary payments. Thus, to allow a deduction for consumer durable purchases and then to include only future *monetary* receipts in the tax base would amount to excluding from the tax base the value of consumption services yielded by durable goods. Because it is difficult to determine the annual value of the use of consumer durables the same concepts used for financial assets cannot be easily applied.

For example, suppose an individual purchased an automobile for $4,000 and sold it for $2,000 3 years later. If a deduction were allowed for the purchase and, then, the sale value included in receipts, the individual's total tax liability would be lowered by owning the automobile. However, the individual would have expended $2,000 plus some foregone interest for the consumption services of the automobile over the 3-year period. The depreciation and foregone interest measure the cost of the consumption services and should be included in the tax base. If the automobile were taxed the same way as an asset in a qualified account, this consumption value would escape the tax.

To assure that the entire consumption value is included in the tax base, the appropriate treatment of consumer durables is to allow no deduction on purchase and to exclude sales receipts from the tax base. In other words, purchase of a consumer durable would be treated the same way as current consumption of goods and services. The reason for this approach is that the price paid for a consumer durable should reflect the present value of future services the buyer expects to receive. Including the value of durable goods in the tax base at the time of purchase produces, in effect, a prepayment of the tax on the value of future consumption services.

According to this treatment, the $4,000 for the purchase of the automobile would not be deducted from the tax base. Similarly, the $2,000 from sales of the automobile 3 years later would not be included in the tax base. Thus, if an individual sold a used car and bought another used car for the same price, or used the proceeds for current consumption, there would be no tax consequences. If he sold a used car for $2,000 and invested the proceeds in a qualified asset, he would deduct $2,000 from his tax base in the year of the transaction.

In summary, the purchase of a durable good would be treated as present consumption even though the good yields consumption services over time. The reason for this approach is that the price of the good reflects the expected present value of its future stream of services. Measuring annual service flows directly would require the measurement of annual depreciation and annual imputed rent on the value of the asset. This would introduce unwanted and unnecessary complexity into the Cash Flow Tax system.

Checking Accounts. Deductions should also be denied for purchases of certain types of financial assets that yield their primary benefits in the form of services received, rather than monetary returns. For example, non-interest-bearing demand deposits provide services for depositors in place of interest. Deductions, therefore, should *not* be allowed for deposits in checking accounts, and withdrawals from checking accounts should *not* be included in the tax base. That is, checking accounts should not be qualified accounts.

Equivalence of Qualified Account Treatment and Tax Prepayment Approach

The equivalence noted above between the purchase price of a consumer durable good and the present value of its expected future services suggests an analogous equivalence between the price of a business or financial asset and the present value of its expected future stream of returns. This equivalence can best be illustrated by a simple example. Suppose an individual deposits $100 in a savings account at 10 percent interest in year 1. In year 2, he withdraws the $100 deposit plus $10 earned interest and uses it to buy consumption goods.

Qualified Accounts Treatment. If the savings account is a qualified account, the individual would reduce his tax base by $100 in year 1 and raise it by $110 when he withdraws his funds from the account in year 2. At an interest rate of 10 percent, the discounted present value in year 1 of his second-year tax base would be $110/1.10, or $100.

Tax Prepayment Approach. Now, suppose instead that the savings account is not a qualified account. In this case, the individual is not allowed a deduction for the deposit and is not taxed on interest earned or on funds withdrawn in year 2. The discounted present value of his tax base would be the same in this case as under the cash flow rules initially presented. The tax base in year 1 would be $100 higher, and the discounted present value of the tax base in year 2 would be $100 lower, than if a qualified account were used. In other words, allowing a deduction for purchases of assets and taxing withdrawals—the qualified accounts treatment—is equivalent to allowing no deduction for the asset purchase and exempting all interest earnings from tax—the "tax prepayment" approach.

The consequences to the government of the two ways of taxing the purchase of assets would also be the same *in present value terms.* If the individual bought the asset through a qualified account, the Government would collect revenue on a tax base of $110 in year 2. If the interest were exempt from tax, and no deduction for the asset purchase allowed, the government would collect revenue on a tax base of $100 in year 1. This revenue would grow to $110 by year 2 at 10 percent interest. Ignoring possible variations in average tax rates, the government would be left with the same revenue at the end of year 2 in both cases.

The example above suggests that all assets may be treated according to the tax prepayment method required for consumer durables. Asset purchases would *not* be deducted from the tax base, and all earnings from assets and sales of assets would *not* be included in the tax base. Thus, for assets not purchased through qualified accounts, it would not be necessary to keep any records for tax purposes. The expected present value of the tax base would be the same for both methods of tax treatment of assets, although the timing of payments would be different. Both methods of tax treatment of assets are consistent with a cash flow approach to taxation.

It is worth repeating that allowing an alternative treatment of financial assets outside of qualified accounts, tax prepayment, is not essential to the integrity of the proposal, but it would provide convenience and some other advantages. In the cash flow proposal presented in this study, purchases of financial assets except for investments in a family business or closely held corporation, would be allowed to have tax-free returns if the investment were not deducted. Alternative rules are possible: (1) to require all asset purchases, except for consumer durables, to be made through qualified accounts; or (2) to continue to tax returns from assets purchased outside of qualified accounts (i.e., dividends, interest, rental income, capital gains) as they would be taxed under either a comprehensive income base (described in chapter 3) or under the current tax law. The current taxation of returns would strongly encourage, but not require, taxpayers to purchase income-earning assets through qualified accounts. Otherwise, the present value of tax liability would ordinarily be higher and recordkeeping and tax accounting more costly.

Treatment of Borrowing and Lending

The equivalence between the amount invested in an asset and the expected present value of returns also permits two alternative ways of treating loan transactions. Normally, under cash flow accounting, receipts from a loan would be handled through qualified accounts. An individual would be required to report the loan proceeds in his tax base in the initial year. (Of course, if he used the loan proceeds to purchase investment assets through a qualified account in the same tax year, there would be no net tax consequence.) Subsequent interest and principal payments would then be deductible from the tax base in the following years. If the individual sold assets that had been purchased through qualified accounts in an amount just sufficient to pay the loan interest and principal, the net tax consequence would, again, be zero. On the other hand, if the loan were taken outside a qualified account, proceeds of the loan would *not* be included in the tax base, and repayments of interest and principal would *not* be deductible. Note, again, that the present value of the tax liability would be the same in either case. The discounted value of future interest and principal payments on a loan would be equal to the current proceeds of the loan.

Advantages of Taxpayer Option Treatment of Asset Purchases and Borrowing

There are significant advantages to a flexible approach under the Cash Flow Tax that allows a taxpayer to chose, subject to certain limits, whether or not to use qualified accounts to make financial transactions.

Averaging of Consumption. One advantage is the potential for evening out over time large outlays that are made irregularly, such as the purchase of a house or an automobile, or payment for college. According to the rules suggested above, cash outlays for consumer durables would not be deductible, so that borrowing via a qualified account would produce taxable receipts for which there would be no immediate offset. In buying a home, an individual probably would wish to borrow outside a qualified account. Otherwise he would pay tax on the entire mortgage in the year of the purchase. If the loan were not obtained through a qualified account, the proceeds of the loan would not be included in the tax base, but future principal and interest payments would not be deductible. Thus, tax liabilities from consumption of the good financed by such a loan would be spread out over the period of repayment, as the taxpayer used receipts from other sources, such as current wages, to pay the loan interest and principal.

The existence of alternative ways of treating financial assets and loans for tax purposes would give individuals considerable flexibility in the timing of their tax liabilities. This feature of the Cash Flow Tax is desirable because it would minimize the need for special averaging provisions. Averaging is desirable because increasing marginal rates would be applied to increases in the tax base for any single year.

With increasing marginal rates, an individual with a tax base of $10,000 in year 1 and $30,000 in year 2 will pay higher taxes than an individual with a tax base of $20,000 in both years. Whether the tax base is comprehensive income or consumption, it is hard to see why the first individual should be considered to be in a better position to pay taxes than the other.

An example of the optional use of qualified accounts for the purpose of averaging consumption is the following: Suppose an individual purchased a $40,000 house, on which the bank made available a $30,000 mortgage. If the individual chose not to include the loan proceeds from the $30,000 mortgage in his tax base, he could not deduct mortgage payments in future years. In effect, the individual could pay the principal and interest on the mortgage every year out of current receipts from other sources. The receipts used for the annual mortgage payments would be included in the tax base. Thus, the tax base on the mortgage could be made to approximate the schedule of mortgage payments on the house.

This leaves the problem of the down payment. The $10,000 used for the down payment, if withdrawn from a qualified account, would be included in its entirety in the tax base in the year the house was purchased. The individual, if he had foreseen buying a house, could have avoided this problem by saving outside the qualified account. The money devoted to acquiring these financial assets would have been included in the tax base every year but, the tax having been prepaid, the lump sum withdrawal would not be subject to tax. These savings could then be transferred to the purchase of equity in housing. The prepayment of taxes would continue to apply to the stream of consumption services from housing, as it did to the yield from financial assets.

In most other cases, individuals would probably want to save in *qualified* accounts for averaging purposes. Most people save during their most productive years, when income is highest. The savings are used to finance consumption after retirement. By saving in qualified accounts, an individual could reduce his tax liability in the years when his income is high relative to consumption, and raise it in the future when income is low. On the other hand, saving outside of qualified accounts might be an individual's best strategy when he anticipates large consumption expenditures such as a down payment for a house or college expenses. To the extent that the taxpayer remains in the same tax bracket for substantial variations in his tax base, the choice among types of accounts for reasons of averaging would be unnecessary.

Privacy. A second advantage of allowing optional treatment of asset purchases is that taxpayers would not be compelled to make all financial investments through a third-party broker. The existence of assets not monitored by third parties, or by the government, would allow a person to maintain the privacy of his accounts without changing the present value of his tax base.

Equality of Treatment Among Asset Types. A third advantage of allowing optional treatment for financial assets is that it would give investors in such assets the same opportunities available to investors in consumer durables. For both types of investments the initial and subsequent amounts would not be deductible and all returns, including sale of the asset, would not be subject to tax.

Lifetime Perspective of the Cash Flow Tax

At this point, it is worth emphasizing again the lifetime perspective of the Cash Flow Tax system. The flexibility of asset treatment and the use of individual discretion over *any 1 year's* tax liability would allow both postponement and advancement of tax liabilities. By allowing individuals to avoid taxes totally in some years by judicious rearrangement of asset purchases, these provisions might appear to provide a tax loophole. However, this loophole is apparent only—any reduction in tax base must be matched by an increase in future tax base equal in present value. There could be no advantage to deferral if interest earnings were positive. Furthermore, because of progressive tax rates, *it would be to the advantage of taxpayers to try to average their tax base over time.* Thus, taxpayers would have an incentive to pay some tax every year, even though the means to postpone the tax is available.

An Example. To see how an individual could use the system to avoid taxes in a given year, and why it would not be to his advantage, consider this example. Suppose a worker earned $20,000 per year and accumulated wealth equal to $20,000 by saving outside a qualified account. In another year, he deposits the entire $20,000 in a qualified account, deducting the deposit from his wages. He would then report taxable receipts of zero in that year and, thereby, succeed in "sheltering" his consumption. (Less than $20,000 would need to be switched to a qualified account if there are personal exemptions.) However, this way of managing his financial portfolio probably would increase, rather than decrease, the present value of his tax payments *over his lifetime.*

This point can be illustrated by showing that taking part of the $20,000 deduction in either a previous or future year would yield tax savings. For example, suppose he deposited only $19,000 in a qualified account in the year in question, deducting the additional $1,000 by depositing it in a qualified account on the first day of the following year. With increasing marginal tax rates, the increased tax liability from increasing the tax base from zero to $1,000 in the current year will be much smaller than the reduction in tax liability from the $1,000 reduction in tax base in the following year, when taxable consumption is much higher.

Alternatively, the individual might have taken a $1,000 deduction by depositing money in a qualified account in the last day of the previous year, leaving only $19,000 in assets outside qualified accounts in the year in question. Again, the increased tax liability from a $1,000 increase in tax base in the year in question would be smaller than the reduced tax liability from a $1,000 reduction in tax base through taking the deduction in the previous year, when taxable consumption is much greater than zero.

Thus, with increasing marginal rates, the taxpayer who uses the asset flexibility features of the model Cash Flow Tax to acquire a year of tax-free consumption pays for that privilege. The present value of his tax liability would be increased in either prior or future years by an amount greater than the present value of tax saving in the "tax-free" year.

Uncertain Outcomes: A Problem with the Tax-Prepayment Approach

Tax Liability Can Be Independent of Outcome for Risky Investments. An apparent disadvantage of allowing a wide variety of financial assets to be purchased *outside* qualified accounts is that some large gains would go untaxed. When an asset has been purchased through a qualified account, the government could be viewed as participating in the investment, by allowing a tax deduction, and also participating in the return on the investment, by taxing the gross proceeds. For assets purchased outside of qualified accounts, however, the investment would not be deducted and the entire proceeds of the investment could be liquidated for consumption purposes tax-free.

Note, however, that if taxes were proportional, the after-tax *rate of return* would be the same in both cases. With qualified accounts, the Government would be a partner in the investment, sharing in the cost and appropriating a fraction of the return. When the tax is prepaid, however, the Government "share" in the returns would be zero. For assets bought outside of qualified accounts, large winners would not pay a higher tax and losers would not receive a loss offset. Although both types of tax treatment would allow investors equal opportunity to earn after-tax dollars, the tax treatment of assets purchased outside of qualified accounts would not distinguish between winners and losers of investment gambles. Thus, a lucky investor who acquired an asset on a tax-prepaid basis (thereby sharing none of the costs with the government) would incur no additional tax liability on the extra future consumption out of any positive payoff. Conversely, unlucky investors will have prepaid a tax on expected returns and will then obtain no deduction for the losses they incur.

It is easily overlooked that, except when the risky asset is unique (e.g., a particular work of art), the difference between tax-prepaid and qualified account treatment is largely cosmetic. A 50 percent tax bracket investor can, for example, obtain exactly the same results by buying $1,000 worth of a given stock on a tax-prepaid basis, or $2,000 worth on a qualified account basis. Either approach means an initial outlay of $1,000, in view of the tax saving of $1,000 on the qualified-account purchase. If the stock triples in value, the investor can similarly realize the same $3,000 under either approach: the $6,000 total value of the qualified-investment acquisition carries with it a $3,000 tax liability.

Graduated rates lead to a modification of this outcome, since large gains may be subject to a higher rate of tax than that applied to the original deductions under the qualified account approach. Conversely, losses will be offset at a lower rate; the government-partner shares more in the gains than in the losses. It does not follow, however, that taxpayers would therefore always choose to make investments on a tax-prepaid basis. The sharing of risk with the government may be of value to them. By the same token, the extra revenue the government would reap on average from qualified account investments (because of graduated rates) can be viewed as a form of insurance premium, paid to taxpayers in general for the risk-sharing enjoyed by the investor.

A second potential problem with tax-prepayment of returns from assets would arise if tax rates were subsequently increased sharply—for example, to finance a war. In that case, individuals who had prepaid tax on assets at the lower rates would escape taxation at the higher rates even if they were using the proceeds of profitable investments to finance current consumption. Of course, in making the tax-prepaid investments, those individuals ran the risk that tax rates might have been lowered, in which case they would have reduced their tax liability had they bought assets through a qualified account.

Conversely, individuals who undertake saving on a qualified account basis may experience unexpectedly heavy burdens if tax rates are increased, unexpectedly light burdens if rates decline. Some may consider it desirable in view of these problems to impose a greater uniformity of results by restricting, or even eliminating, the provision for purchase of income-earning assets outside of qualified accounts. One possible treatment, addressing uncertain returns but not uncertain tax rates, would be to force all "speculative" investments, i.e., land, stocks, etc., to be purchased through qualified accounts but to allow the tax-prepayment option for fixed interest securities and savings deposits.

Consumer Durables. A similar problem would exist for consumer durables. Because consumer durables could not be purchased using qualified accounts, unanticipated increases in the value of consumer durables would be untaxed and there would be no tax offset for unanticipated losses. For example, if the value of an individual's house doubled in a year, his tax liability would not be affected. The option of requiring qualified-account treatment is not available here, as it is in the case of financial assets, because of the difficulty of measuring the value of the consumption services these assets provide.

No Optional Treatment for Nonfinancial Business Assets

As explained above, investments in individual businesses would be eligible *only* for tax treatment on a current cash flow basis. All outlays for the business would be eligible for deduction, while all net receipts would be subject to tax. The reason for not allowing the alternative "tax-prepayment" treatment is that it is sometimes difficult to distinguish between the profits and wages of individual businessmen. If profit alone were exempted from tax, the businessman would have an incentive to avoid tax on the value of his labor services by paying himself a low wage and calling the difference return from investment. This problem would exist for individual proprietorships and possibly for small partnerships and closely held corporations. For such enterprises, all net receipts should be taxable and outlays for capital goods should be eligible for immediate deduction.

Table 1 below summarizes the proposed rules for tax treatment of financial assets, durable goods, loans, and closely held business enterprises. Note that the only restrictions are that all investments in a closely held business must be treated as if they were purchased in qualified accounts and consumer durable goods could *not* be purchased through qualified accounts. Financial assets could be purchased, and loans obtained, either through qualified accounts or outside of the system.

Table 1

Summary: Tax Treatment of Certain Assets Under Cash Flow Tax

	Qualified Accounts	Accounts outside of system
1. Financial assets	purchases deductible; all withdrawals of earnings and principal taxed	purchases not deductible; interest and return of capital not taxed
2. Durable goods	not available	purchases not deductible; sales not included in tax base
3. Loans	receipts in tax base; repayments including interest, deductible	receipts not in tax base; repayments not deductible
4. Closely held business	all outlays deductible, including capital outlays; all receipts taxed	not available

DIFFERENCES BETWEEN CASH FLOW AND COMPREHENSIVE INCOME TAXES: SPECIFIC PROVISIONS

Pension Plans and Social Security

Under the Cash Flow Tax, all contributions to pension plans may be viewed as contributions to qualified accounts, whether by the employee or by the employer. By this logic, contributions would not be included in the tax base, while retirement benefits would be included in full. Similarly, all contributions for Social Security would be excluded from the tax base, while all Social Security retirement benefits would be taxable. There would be no need, under the Cash Flow Tax, to compute the income on pension funds attributable to individual employees because the accumulation would not be subject to tax.

Life Insurance

Both term life insurance and whole life insurance would be treated differently under the Cash Flow Tax than under the Comprehensive Income Tax.

With term life insurance, there is no investment income and, thus, no expected change in net worth. Under the Comprehensive

Income Tax proposal, premiums for term life insurance, whether paid by the employer or the employee, would be included in the insured's tax base, while proceeds from term life insurance policies would be tax-exempt. The treatment of gifts under the Cash Flow Tax emphasizes the standard-of-living notion of consumption. (Note, though, as discussed in chapter 2, the Comprehensive Income Tax treatment is also of the "standard-of-living" type.) Term life insurance may be viewed as a wealth transfer from the policyholder to the beneficiary. Purchase of a term life insurance policy lowers the lifetime consumption of the policyholder and raises the expected lifetime consumption of the beneficiary. Thus, a cash flow tax that taxes consumption of individuals should not tax premiums paid by the policyholder but should include proceeds from a term life insurance policy in the tax base of the beneficiary. In practice, this would mean that employer contributions to term life insurance would not be imputed to the tax base of the policyholder, while term life insurance premiums paid directly by the policyholder would be deductible.

Whole life insurance poses a different issue, although it would receive the same treatment as term insurance under the Cash Flow Tax. A whole life insurance policy does provide investment income to a policyholder in the form of an option to continue to buy insurance at the premium level appropriate for the initial year. Under the Cash Flow Tax, unlike the comprehensive income tax, the increase in the value of the option would not need to be computed for tax purposes because it would represent a change in net worth and not in consumption. However, if the individual cashed in the option value, the receipts from this transaction would be included in the Cash Flow Tax base.

Under the model Cash Flow Tax, all premiums paid by policyholders for whole life insurance would be tax deductible, while premiums paid by employers for policyholders would not be imputed to policyholders' tax bases. All receipts from life insurance policies, whether in the form of cash surrender value to policyholder or proceeds to beneficiaries, would be included in the tax base of the recipient.

State and Local Bond Interest

Under the model Cash Flow Tax, State and local bond interest for securities not purchased through a qualified account would remain tax-exempt, as under the present law. However, as with the Comprehensive Income Tax proposal, State and local bonds would lose their special status relative to other assets. Under the Comprehensive Income Tax, these bonds would lose their special status because their interest would become taxable. Under the Cash Flow Tax, the bonds would lose their special status because returns from all other assets would also become tax-exempt.

If State and local bonds were purchased through a qualified account, all contributions to the account would be deductible from the cash flow tax and all withdrawals from the account would be subject to tax. Thus, the purchase price of a State or local bond would be deductible, while withdrawals of interest payments and principal from the bond to pay for consumption would be subject to tax.

Interest Paid

Under the Comprehensive Income Tax, all interest paid would be tax deductible because such outlays represent neither consumption nor additions to net worth. This would include interest payments for mortgages on owner-occupied homes. Under the Cash Flow Tax, however, if a loan were taken through a qualified account, the initial proceeds of the loan would be taxable, while subsequent interest and principal repayments would be tax deductible.

Neither interest payments nor repayment of principal would be deductible on a loan not made on a qualified account basis. In that case the proceeds of the borrowing would not be subject to tax. In present-value terms, the net effect of a loan on the tax base would be zero under *either* the qualified account or the tax-prepayment approach.

Corporate Income

Corporations would not be taxed as entities under either the Cash Flow Tax or the Comprehensive Income Tax. However, under the Cash Flow Tax, there would be no need to impute undistributed income to individuals because taxes would be assessed only on funds available for personal consumption. Consequently, a single Cash Flow Tax applied at the household level could be accomplished without the rules for integrating corporate and household accounts that are conspicuous features of the model income tax.

The treatment of returns from corporate activity under the Cash Flow Tax would be exactly the same as the treatment of returns from other kinds of investments. There would be no separate tax at the corporation level. Individuals would be permitted to purchase corporate stock through qualified accounts held with brokers. The initial purchase price would be deductible from the tax base at the time of purchase, and subsequent withdrawals from the account as dividends received, return of capital, or proceeds from the sale of stock would be added alike to the tax base. For stock purchased outside of a qualified account, no deduction would be allowed for purchases, and neither dividends nor proceeds of future sales would be added to the tax base. Capital gains and capital losses would, therefore, have no tax consequences.

Capital Gains and Losses

Under the Cash Flow Tax, there would be no need to keep records of the basis of asset purchases to compute capital gains. As explained above, when assets are purchased outside of qualified accounts, capital gains would be exempt from tax and capital losses would not be deductible. If assets are purchased within qualified accounts so that a deduction may be taken for the initial purchase price, no distinction would be made between the part of the sale that represented capital gain and the part of the sale that represented return of basis. In the latter case, the full amount of the sales proceeds, if not reinvested, becomes part of the tax base. The size of the capital gain would affect the amount of withdrawals for future consumption. Hence, when qualified accounts are used, the size of capital gains would have tax consequences even though no explicit calculation of gains (or losses) is necessary.

Because the Cash Flow Tax does not tax accumulation as it occurs, the issues of deferral, inflation adjustment, and the appropriate rate of tax on capital gains need not be considered, as they were in the discussion of the accretion income tax. The concept of deferral of tax would be relevant for the Cash Flow Tax only if one could postpone without interest the tax liability associated with current consumption. Similarly, the value of assets or changes in the value of assets, whether related to general inflation or not, would not be relevant for the Cash Flow Tax until they are withdrawn to finance consumption.

Business Income Accounting

Income accounting for any individual's business under the Cash Flow Tax would be strictly on a cash accounting basis. The individual would have to compute in any year net receipts from operating the business. To perform this computation, he would add to the sale of goods and services during the accounting year any receipts from borrowing and would subtract the purchases of goods and services from other firms, wages paid to employees, interest paid to suppliers of debt finance, and all purchases of plant and equipment. Net receipts calculated by this method would be included in the individual's tax base, if positive, and would be deducted, if negative.

Note that the major difference between the Cash Flow Tax and the Comprehensive Income Tax with respect to business accounting is the treatment of assets. Under the Cash Flow Tax, purchases of assets would entitle the businessman to an immediate deduction for the amount of purchase. Under the Comprehensive Income Tax, deductions each year would be limited to a capital consumption allowance (depreciation), which estimates the loss in value during the year of those assets.

Also, business loans would be treated differently under the Cash Flow Tax. All receipts of loans to a business would be included in the base, while interest and amortization payments would be deductible. Under the Comprehensive Income Tax, loan receipts and amortization payments would have no tax consequences; only the interest payments would be deductible. When the proceeds of the loan are used immediately to purchase materials or services for the business, the deduction allowed under the Cash Flow Tax just matches the addition of loan proceeds to the base.

For partnerships, the rules are simpler. A partnership would be required to report the annual cash contribution of each owner to the business and the annual distribution to each owner. The difference between distributions from partnerships and net contributions to partnerships would enter the individual owner's tax base. If the owner sold his shares, it would enter the tax base as a negative contribution.

SPECIAL PROBLEMS: PROGRESSIVITY, WEALTH DISTRIBUTION, AND WEALTH TAXES

The Cash Flow Tax outlined in this proposal would tax consumption but not individual accumulation of assets. People are likely to conclude that such a tax would be regressive and that it would encourage excessive concentration of wealth and economic power. This section examines both these concerns, showing that concern about regressivity is a misconception and suggesting that the Cash Flow Tax could be complemented in any desired degree by a transfer tax to influence wealth distribution. The complexities in the tax treatment of transfers at death caused by the existence of two kinds of financial assets are discussed below and some potential solutions are proposed.

Progressivity of the Tax

Exemption of Capital Earnings. The assertion that a consumption base tax is regressive stems from the fact that wealth is concentrated among relatively few households as compared to labor earnings. Because the Cash Flow Tax is equivalent in present-value terms to exemption of earnings from capital, it would necessarily tax labor earnings more heavily to raise the same revenue. Thus, it might appear that the Cash Flow Tax is a way of shifting the tax burden to wage earners and relieving the wealthy taxpayer.

Such criticism of the Cash Flow Tax may be superficially plausible but it is misleading on several grounds. First, much of what is generally labeled capital income is really a reward for postponing immediate consumption of past wages. Laborers as a group do not necessarily lose when the tax rate applied to wages immediately consumed is raised to enable forgiveness of taxes on the returns for saving out of wages. Second, the only other source of funds for investment aside from wages is transfers received (including inheritances), and these would be subject to tax at the same rate schedule applied to labor earnings under the Cash Flow Tax. (This point is elaborated below.) Finally, the progressivity of any individual tax is to a large degree determined by the rate structure. The choice between an income and a consumption base is independent of the degree of vertical progressivity of the rate structure.

Transfers of Wealth. The mechanism by which gifts and inheritances would be included in the tax base is simple. In order to be eligible for deduction by the donor, all gifts would have to be included in the tax base of the recipient. Gifts would be recorded only if they were transfers between taxable entities. Thus, a gift of a father to his 9-year-old son would not be included in the family's taxable receipts (unless it were removed from a qualified account). When the son left the family unit, say when he turned 26, he would become a separate taxpayer. At that point, all accumulated wealth from past gifts and inheritances would be included in his initial tax base and deducted from the family's base. If the initial base were large, the individual would have an incentive to purchase a qualified account to avoid a steep progressive tax, but would have to pay tax on subsequent withdrawals for consumption out of that account. Thus, an individual would *not* have the opportunity to realize tax-free consumption from a past inheritance.

Similarly, if the family's deduction for transfers to the son were large, the family would have an incentive to withdraw assets from a qualified account and treat such assets thereafter as held outside a qualified account. The family need suffer no adverse tax consequence, thereby.

The taxation of gifts and accessions to the donee, and the deduction of itemized gifts by the donor are a logical, integral part of the Cash Flow Tax system necessary to assure that the tax base is related to the lifetime consumption of every individual.

To see how inheritances would be included in the tax base of the Cash Flow Tax, consider the following example. Suppose a man died on January 2, 1977 at the age of 70, leaving $300,000 in qualified accounts to his 35-year-old son. The tax base of the decedent in 1977 included a $300,000 withdrawal from the qualified account in receipts and a $300,000 deduction for the bequest of funds, for a net tax base of zero. The tax base of the son included the receipt of $300,000. With progressive rates, it is likely that the son would wish to deposit a large part of the $300,000 in a qualified account, paying tax only as the money was withdrawn for consumption.

A difficulty would arise if the $300,000 of the decedent, or a fraction thereof, were held outside a qualified account. While the tax treatment of the recipient's inheritance would be the same ($300,000 of receipts), the estate of the decedent has a large deduction, possibly with no current tax base to offset. The estate might then be entitled to a tax refund before the estate were divided up. This treatment would be appropriate because the decedent had, in effect, prepaid tax for consumption of the proceeds of the investment that was never consumed in his lifetime. However, an amount, or rate, of refund must be specified. One possibility would be to allow a refund to the estate equal to the value of investment assets outside of qualified accounts multiplied by the rate applicable to the lowest tax bracket. An alternative solution would be to give no refund at all. The inability to consume expected proceeds of a tax-prepaid investment because of death may be viewed as one of the risks an individual knowingly undertakes when he invests in a tax-prepaid asset. This treatment would provide an incentive for investments to be made through qualified accounts.

If initial financial endowments and receipts of transfers are included in the tax base, there would be no difference in tax treatment between an individual who invests an inheritance and one who invests his savings out of wages. Neither would have any additional tax until he consumes the amount invested or the earnings. In effect, earnings from investment could be viewed as a reward for deferring consumption from wage income or inheritance. If the rate structure were appropriately progressive, so that the high-wage earners with large accessions would be paying a significantly higher tax than low-wage earners with small accessions, there would seem to be no particular reason to discriminate in tax liability between persons with different patterns of lifetime consumption. Viewed in that manner, the Cash Flow Tax would not favor the wealthy but would favor, relative to the Comprehensive Income Tax, those individuals who, *at any given income level*, chose to postpone consumption.

Lucky Gambles. Another potential objection is to the opportunity the proposed system would afford individuals to acquire wealth by a lucky investment gamble, and to have paid only a small tax on the amount wagered. Some regard this possibility as inequitable. As noted above, this possibility could be largely avoided, at a price in complexity and compliance costs, by taxing the future returns on some or all investments that are not made through qualified accounts, or by restricting the types of investment that could be made outside of qualified accounts.

Accumulation of Wealth. A second concern about the Cash Flow Tax is that it would place no restraint on the accumulation of wealth. Although all consumption out of accumulated wealth would be taxed, the Cash Flow Tax, compared with an income tax, would make it easier for individuals to accumulate wealth. The effect of this on the distribution of wealth in the United States cannot be forecast precisely. Presumably, individuals at all levels would tend to hold more wealth, so that the *dispersion* of wealth might either increase or decrease. At the same time, there might be an increase in the size of the largest wealth holdings.

The Cash Flow Tax—with wealth transfers deductible to the donor and included in the tax base of the recipient—would be a tax on the standard of living of individuals (with some exemption, or credit, for a small consumption amount). Like the model Comprehensive Income Tax, it could be converted to the concept of "ability-to-pay" discussed in chapter 2. According to that concept, wealth transfers would be regarded as consumption by the donor and included in the tax base of both donor and recipient. To accomplish this conversion, the deduction of gifts and bequests would be eliminated.

A simpler approach, and one that is more consistent with present policies, would be to retain the estate and gift tax as the principal instrument for altering the distribution of wealth. Such a tax, which is levied according to the situation of the donor, would be a logical complement to the model Cash Flow Tax. The existence of a separate estate and gift tax would not damage either the basic simplicity inherent in the treatment of assets under the cash flow tax or the neutrality in tax treatment of those individuals with the same endowment who have different time patterns of labor earnings or consumption. Under this option, all features of the Cash Flow Tax would remain exactly as explained above, except for the wealth transfer tax. Tax rates on gifts and bequests could be designed to achieve any desired degree of equalization in initial wealth of individuals.

SAMPLE TAX FORM FOR
THE CASH FLOW TAX

Filing Status

1. Check applicable status
   a. Single individual
   b. Married filing joint return
   c. Unmarried head of household
   d. Married filing separately

Family Size

2. Enter one on each applicable line
   a. Yourself
   b. Spouse
3. Number of dependent children
4. Total family size (add lines 2a, 2b, and 3)

Receipts

5. a. Wages, salaries, and tips of primary wage earner (attach forms W-2)*
   b. Wages, salaries, and tips of all other wage earners (attach forms W-2)*
   c. Multiply line 5b by .25; if greater than $2,500, enter $2,500
   d. Included wages of secondary workers, subtract line 5c from line 5b
   e. Wages subject to tax, add lines 5a and 5d
6. Receipts of pensions, annuities, disability compensation, unemployment compensation, workmen's compensation, and sick pay. (Includes social security benefits, except Medicare, and veterans disability and survivor benefits.)
7. Net receipts from unincorporated business (from Schedule C) (if positive)
8. Royalties and distributions from trusts (Schedule D)
9. Net distributions from partnerships and closely held corporations (from Schedule E) (if positive)
10. Net withdrawals from qualified accounts (attach forms Q)

---

*Wages reported by the employer would *exclude* employer and employee contributions to pension plans, life insurance plans, and disability insurance, and would also *exclude* both the employer's and employee's share of payroll taxes for social security retirement and disability (OASDI). Wages would *include* employer contributions to health insurance plans and the cash value of consumption goods and services provided to the employee below cost.

11. Public assistance benefits, Food Stamp subsidy, fellow-ships, scholarships, and stipends (attach forms W-y)
12. Gifts and inheritances received.
13. Alimony received
14. Total receipts (add lines 5e and 6-13)

Deductions

15. Employee business expense (includes qualified travel, union and professional association dues, tools, materials, and education expenses)
16. Net outlay for unincorporated business (from Schedule C) (if positive)
17. Contributions to trusts; gifts and bequests to identified recipients (from Schedule F)
18. Net contributions to partnerships and closely held corporations (from Schedule E) (if positive)
19. Net deposits to qualified accounts (attach forms Q)
20. State and local income tax
21. Alimony paid
22. Child care expenses
    a. If line 1c is checked and line 3 is not zero, or if line 1b is checked and both lines 3 and 5b are not zero, enter total child care expenses
    b. Multiply line 22a by .5
    c. Enter smaller of line 22b or $5,000
    d. Child care deduction. If unmarried head of household, enter smaller of line 22c or line 5a
    e. If married filing joint return, enter smaller of line 22c or line 5d
23. Total deductions (add lines 15-21, and 22d or 22e)

Tax Calculation

24. Cash flow subject to tax. Subtract line 23 from line 14 (if less than zero, enter zero)
25. Basic exemption. Enter $1,500
26. Family size allowance. Multiply line 4 by $800
27. Total exemption. Add lines 25 and 26
28. Taxable cash flow. Subtract line 27 from line 24 (if less than zero, enter zero)
29. Tax liability (from appropriate table)

30. a. Total Federal income tax withheld
    b. Estimated tax payments
    c. Total tax prepayments (add lines 30a and 30b)
31. If line 29 is greater than line 30c, enter Balance Due
32. If line 29 is less than line 30c, enter Refund Due

Form Q — Supplied by administrators of qualified accounts

1. Total deposits
2. Total withdrawals
3. Net withdrawal (line 2 minus line 1), if positive
4. Net deposit (line 1 minus line 2), if positive

CHAPTER **5**

Quantitative Analysis

This chapter presents quantitative analyses of the two model plans and compares them to present law. The first section discusses briefly the nature of the data base used to develop and simulate the effects of the model plans. The chapter then discusses the estimated magnitudes of the various income concepts used in the report and the following section uses these data to derive exemption and rate structures for the Comprehensive Income Tax consistent with achieving present revenue yield. This is followed by estimates of the magnitude of the Cash Flow Tax base. Finally, the chapter develops specific provisions of the Cash Flow Tax—exemptions and rates—and compares the two model plans and current law.

THE DATA BASE

The first step in the quantitative analysis of the reform plans was to construct a data base representative of the relevant characteristics of the U.S. population. A file of records was created and stored in a computer, with each record containing information for a tax return filing unit, such as the amount of wages earned by the member or members of that unit, dividends received, etc. In all, some 112,000 records are contained in the file.

Each of these records stands for a group of taxpayers with similar characteristics. Thus, a given record may be taken to represent 100 or 1,000 filing units in the U.S. population as a whole. To simulate the effect of some change on the whole population, the effect on each record in the file is calculated and multiplied by the number of units represented by that record.

The records in the file were constructed by combining information from two separate sources: a sample of 50,000 tax returns provided by the Statistics Division of the Internal Revenue Service, and a sample of 50,000 households (representing about 70,000 tax filing units) from the Current Population Survey of the Census Bureau. The two data sets were needed because the reform plans base tax liabilities on information not now provided on tax returns. Furthermore, a realistic picture of the U.S. economy requires obtaining characteristics of "nonfilers," individuals and families who are not obliged to file income tax returns because they do not have sufficient taxable income.

To represent the incomes generated by the U.S. economy, these two data sets were merged by matching records of taxpayers from the sample of tax returns with records of participants in the Current Population Survey. Since confidentiality strictures on the release of identifier information from each of these sources prevented the literal pairing of data on any given taxpayer, the matching was accomplished by matching records of similar characteristics (age, race, total income, etc.). The resulting file of records is not quite the same as if the information in each record had been obtained for the same individual or family. For technical reasons, it has been possible to achieve a more faithful representation of the U.S. population by using some records more than once. Therefore, the number of records in the final data file reflects an artificial expansion of the number of records in the two original files.

Both samples use 1973 data. Because more recent data would be more relevant, the 1973 population and its attributes were adjusted by extrapolation to represent the 1976 population.

The resulting simulations of the U.S. population should be interpreted with some sense of the nature of the data set. The original data were subject to the usual sampling and processing errors. The processes of merging the two data sources and extrapolating the resulting file to a later year represent further sources of error. Furthermore, many items needed were not recorded in either of the original surveys, and had to be estimated and imputed to each record. For these reasons, the file should not be regarded as a perfect description of the U.S. population.

Nonetheless, the data have been assembled with great care. In some cases, adjustments were made to insure that the data file produces aggregate figures (say, on total wages paid in the economy) in line with those derived from independent statistical sources. In other cases, such aggregates were used to "validate" the file; that is, to check its reasonableness. By and large, the data pass the test of these checks, and the file may be used with some confidence. At the same time, it would be a mistake to equate the data file with the real world, for example, by being concerned about small differences in a simulated tax burden.

ESTIMATION OF THE INCOME CONCEPTS

The first few tables present various definitions of income that were used in the computer simulations.

Table 1 describes adjusted gross income, or AGI, the broadest before-tax concept used for the present income tax. Like all of the income concepts, its source is primarily current money wages and salaries. The remainder, labeled "other AGI" in the table, comes from net self-employment and partnership income, capital income, such as interest and dividends, capital gains, and miscellaneous other elements of income. The table shows that "other AGI" is a larger share of adjusted gross income in the highest income classes.

The data in table 1 cannot be compared directly with AGI as reported on tax returns because information is included for non-filers as well as filers. Thus, table 1 shows adjusted gross income that would be reported if all families and individuals were required to file tax returns under current law, and displays the distribution of all such filing units by income class.

Table 1

Present Law
Adjusted Gross Income
(1976 levels)

Economic income class	Number of filing units[1]	Current money wage income	Other adjusted gross income	Total adjusted gross income
($000)	(..millions..)	(.................$ billions................)		
Less than 0	0.2	0.9	−1.8	−0.9
0-5	38.0	29.5	12.2	41.7
5-10	19.5	81.3	20.6	101.9
10-15	13.9	117.4	16.1	133.5
15-20	12.1	151.9	16.3	168.1
20-30	15.0	261.0	25.8	286.8
30-50	7.1	157.1	34.4	191.5
50-100	2.3	56.0	30.9	86.9
100 or more	0.5	20.0	25.7	45.7
Total	108.6	875.1	180.1	1,055.2

Source: Office of the Secretary of the Treasury, Office of Tax Analysis

[1]Includes all filing units whether or not they actually file returns or pay tax under present law. The estimated number of filing units that do not currently file tax returns is 21.5 million; their adjusted gross income is $4.1 billion.

The income classes in table 1 are defined in terms of "economic income," the broadest before-tax income concept used in this report. As discussed more fully below, this income concept is even broader than the tax base described in the Comprehensive Income Tax proposal of chapter 3. Economic income is used as the classifier in the early tables of this chapter. In later tables, other classifiers are used for reasons explained below.

Adjusted gross income is not the base of the present individual income tax. Starting from AGI, taxpayers are allowed several kinds of deductions to arrive at income subject to tax. Table 2 displays the major elements of the present individual income tax base. Again, as in table 1, the information shown includes data for nonfilers as well as filers, although nonfilers do not add anything to the aggregate taxable income under present law because their exemptions and deductions reduce their taxable incomes to zero.

In each category of table 2, the amounts shown include only income that enters into the calculation of AGI. Thus, for example, portfolio income includes only one-half of realized net long-term capital gains. As appropriate, expenses were netted against the associated income. Thus, wage receipts are net of the recognized expenses of earning it. Similarly, "portfolio income," consisting of interest, dividends, rent, estate and trust income, and realized capital gains, is net of interest expense. "Miscellaneous income minus deductions" is an amalgam of income not otherwise classified, net of all deductions not directly allocable to particular income sources. Its negative value results from the fact that the itemized deductions allowed under present law and not separately deducted from other components of income are much larger than the miscellaneous income items included here, such as State income tax refunds, alimony received, prizes, and the like.

The present tax base is shown in the column labeled "tax base." Exemptions and standard deductions (but not itemized deductions) are thus treated here as part of the rate structure. As table 2 shows, the tax base under present law is somewhat larger than AGI less itemized deductions because negative net income is never allowed to reduce the tax base for an individual return to below zero. Similarly, the value of the standard deduction and exemptions cannot reduce income subject to tax to below zero.

Table 2 indicates that present law income subject to tax is only about 63 percent of adjusted gross income. Exemptions, the standard deduction, and itemized deductions account for this difference.

Table 2

Components of the Present Law Individual Income Tax Base

(1976 levels)

Economic income class ($000)	Net money wage income	Pension income	Self-employment income	Portfolio income	Deductions for state and local taxes	Miscellaneous income minus deductions	Total[1]	Tax base[2]	Standard deductions	Exemptions[3]	Present law income subject to tax
	(· $ billions ·)
Less than 0	0.8	0.2	-4.2	1.5	-0.1	0.2	-1.6	0.5	0.0	-0.1	0.4
0-5	29.2	5.5	0.1	4.9	-0.5	0.8	40.0	40.6	-26.3	-7.7	6.6
5-10	80.4	4.7	4.3	10.3	-1.9	-1.6	96.2	96.7	-28.7	-24.3	43.7
10-15	115.6	2.6	5.6	5.5	-4.1	-3.9	121.3	121.5	-19.2	-26.5	75.8
15-20	149.8	1.9	6.9	2.5	-7.3	-5.9	147.9	148.1	-14.6	-27.8	105.7
20-30	257.5	2.1	11.2	3.6	-15.2	-10.3	248.9	249.3	-16.9	-37.2	195.2
30-50	154.8	1.7	16.4	11.1	-12.1	-8.5	163.4	163.7	-5.4	-18.0	140.3
50-100	55.1	0.8	15.2	12.6	-6.1	-4.7	72.9	73.1	-1.5	-5.8	65.8
100 or more	19.7	0.3	9.8	14.2	-3.3	-3.7	37.0	37.3	-0.1	-1.4	35.8
Total	863.0	19.8	65.3	66.3	-50.6	-37.6	926.0	930.7	-112.7	-148.7	669.2

Source: Office of the Secretary of the Treasury, Office of Tax Analysis

Note: The amounts shown in each category include only the income that actually enters into adjusted gross income under present law.

[1] The amounts shown in this column are the sum of the amounts in the preceding column.

[2] The amounts shown in this column differ from the amounts in the "total" column because of the exclusion of negative amounts in the total column for individual filing units.

[3] The amounts shown in this column exclude the value of exemptions that would reduce income subject to tax to below zero.

The major components of economic income are tabulated separately in table 3. Many of these components require some explanation. "Deferred compensation" consists of employer contributions to pension and insurance plans, including social security. "Household property income" consists of rents, interest income net of interest expense, estate and trust income, dividends, capital income of the self-employed, and imputed returns from homeownership, life insurance policy reserves, and pension plans. "Noncorporate capital gains accruals" represents the growth in the real value of assets held by individuals except for corporate stock. The latter accruals are assumed to be included in corporate retained earnings, as indicated in the next column. In constructing the simulation of the U.S. taxpayer population, corporate retained earnings were allocated to shareholders in proportion to their dividend income.

The entries in the columns "corporation income tax" and "implicit taxes" are derived from concepts that may not be generally familiar. Since the corporation income tax is before-tax income that would be received by individuals were it not taken by taxation first, this tax is included in before-tax economic income. The burden of the corporation income tax was assumed to fall evenly on all individual owners of capital. The logic underlying this position is that, in a market system, capital is allocated to equalize rates of return. Because of the corporation income tax, the capital stock in the corporate sector is smaller than it would be otherwise, and the before-tax rate of return higher. By the same reasoning, the capital stock in the noncorporate sector is higher and rates of return lower than they would be otherwise. Through this tax-induced movement of capital from the corporate to the noncorporate sector, the burden of the corporate tax, that is, its effect on reducing after-tax returns, is spread across all capital income.

Cases can be constructed in which labor income as well as capital income bears the real burden of the corporation income tax, but for the simulations presented in this chapter, this tax has been allocated in proportion to all capital income, with the result shown in table 3. Capital income in this table is composed of household property income, noncorporate capital gains accruals, corporate retained earnings, corporation income tax, and implicit taxes.

The "implicit taxes" shown in table 3, although small in amount, illustrate an important phenomenon affecting the progressivity of the tax structure. Implicit taxes are best explained by an example. Present law does not tax the interest on municipal bonds; therefore, a holder of such bonds receives less interest than he might receive if he invested his funds in fully taxable securities. The difference between what he receives and what he could receive is his implicit

Table 3
Economic Income
(1976 levels)

Economic income class ($000)	Net money wage income	Deferred compensation	Self-employment labor income	Household property income	Non-corporate capital gains accruals	Corporate retained earnings	Corporation income tax	Implicit taxes	Net transfers	State and local income tax deductions	Economic income
					$ billions						
Less than 0	0.8	0.0	0.1	-3.9	0.1	0.1	-0.6	0.4	0.3	-0.1	-2.8
0-5	29.2	2.6	1.0	4.3	0.6	0.3	0.9	-0.5	41.4	-0.1	79.9
5-10	80.4	8.8	4.7	11.5	1.4	1.1	2.5	-1.2	34.3	-0.3	143.2
10-15	115.6	14.4	5.9	11.6	1.8	1.0	2.6	-1.0	20.8	-1.0	171.9
15-20	149.8	18.7	9.0	14.3	2.9	1.1	3.4	-0.7	15.1	-2.1	211.5
20-30	257.5	33.7	14.8	30.4	5.2	2.3	7.1	-0.8	17.8	-4.9	362.9
30-50	154.8	20.9	17.7	44.8	6.2	3.4	10.5	0.3	9.6	-4.7	263.5
50-100	55.1	6.8	13.9	51.9	5.8	4.0	12.3	2.6	3.0	-3.0	152.4
100 or more	19.7	1.6	9.4	28.5	3.6	6.2	7.5	0.8	10.2	-2.0	85.4
Total	863.0	107.6	76.5	193.3	27.7	19.6	46.0	0.0	152.4	-18.1	1,467.9

Source: Office of the Secretary of the Treasury, Office of Tax Analysis

tax. It is *implicit* because no revenue is paid to the U.S. Treasury. It is nonetheless a *tax* because the bondholder's after-tax income is reduced in the same way as if he paid a tax. Of course, the implicit tax may be lower than the actual tax payable on fully taxable bonds, and this is why tax-exempt securities are attractive to high-bracket taxpayers.

Other persons receive benefits from the tax exemption of municipal bonds. The attractiveness of municipal bonds draws capital out of the private sector, thereby increasing slightly the before-tax return to investors in other forms of capital. The *increase* in their return is an implicit subsidy or negative implicit tax. If total income is kept constant in the economy, and efficiency losses ignored, the positive and negative implicit taxes must balance exactly in the aggregate, although not for any particular taxpayer or any income class.

There is an implicit tax corresponding to many tax benefits to capital income in the current tax structure. The simulations included implicit taxes for real estate, agriculture, mining, capital gains arising from corporate retained earnings, and tax-exempt bonds. In each case, the tax preference accorded to the activity in question attracts capital that would otherwise be applied elsewhere, and thus reduces the before-tax returns. Since the advantages of these tax benefits—even taking into account the reduced before-tax returns—are worth more to those in high tax brackets, positive implicit taxes are paid by higher income taxpayers. Therefore, implicit taxes make the present tax structure as measured by effective tax burdens somewhat more progressive than it may at first appear.

Nonetheless, some positive implicit taxes are borne by filing units in the below-zero income class. This income class consists of households sustaining real economic losses. To the extent that these losses occurred in tax-preferred activities, they are even greater than they would have been in the absence of the tax preference, and, accordingly, implicit taxes are generated for this income class.

"Net transfers" include income support in cash and in kind and the excess of accruing claims to future social security benefits over current employer and employee contributions.

Finally, economic income is net of some State and local taxes. Since property taxes are netted in calculating capital income in the previous columns and sales taxes as discussed in chapter 3 are treated as consumption outlays, only State and local income taxes are subtracted here.

Economic and Comprehensive Income

Economic income is an accrual concept. However, as chapter 3 makes clear, a pure accrual income concept is not practical as a tax base. Table 4 shows the difference between economic income and "comprehensive income," which was the starting point for developing the tax base used in the Comprehensive Income Tax proposal.

Four categories of adjustments are involved in moving from economic income to comprehensive income. The first adjustment is for pensions. Economic income includes the accruing value of future pension benefits for both private pensions and social security. Comprehensive income, however, is on a realization basis in that actual social security and pension benefits, rather than their accruing value, are included. The difference is shown in column 2.

The second adjustment is for homeowner preferences and agricultural income. Comprehensive income does not include the imputed rental income from owner-occupied housing. Furthermore, all agricultural activity cannot reasonably be placed on the accrual accounting standard applied in calculating economic income. The third adjustment accounts for the fact that capital gains on noncorporate assets are included in comprehensive income when realized rather than accrued. Finally, in-kind transfers, such as Medicaid, are not included in comprehensive income. As table 4 makes evident, the partial shift from an accrual to a realization concept of income results in a substantial shrinkage in the value of the income measure that serves as the starting point for the model Comprehensive Income Tax.

As discussed in chapter 3, it was principally the difficulties in measuring income on an accretion basis that underlay the decision to use comprehensive rather than economic income as the tax base. This decision also influenced the way in which taxpayers were classified and tax burdens calculated in the simulations. While economic and comprehensive income are generally highly correlated, there are some classes of taxpayers for whom income as accrued and income as realized are quite different. This is especially the case for the taxpayers receiving pension income, who are drawing down their past accruals of pension plan assets. Such taxpayers would find themselves in relatively low economic income classes but would be in higher comprehensive income classes as a result of realizing the benefits of past contributions to pension plans.

Table 5 presents a cross-tabulation by economic income and comprehensive income of the number of filing units receiving

Table 4

Economic and Comprehensive Income
(1976 levels)

Economic income class ($000)	Economic income	Pensions	Nontaxed homeowner preferences and agricultural income	Non-corporate capital gains	In-kind transfers	Comprehensive income
			$ billions			
Less than 0	-2.8	-0.2	0.1	0.1	0.1	-2.8
0-5	79.9	-18.4	1.0	0.4	6.4	90.4
5-10	143.2	4.6	2.1	0.9	4.0	131.6
10-15	171.9	21.5	4.4	1.1	1.5	143.4
15-20	211.5	26.2	8.3	1.7	0.8	174.5
20-30	362.9	43.7	15.9	3.1	0.8	299.4
30-50	263.5	24.5	10.7	3.7	0.4	224.1
50-100	152.4	7.0	3.6	3.5	0.1	138.3
100 or more	85.4	11.3	1.0	2.2	0.0	71.0
Total	1,467.9	120.1	47.2	16.6	14.1	1,269.9

Source: Office of the Secretary of the Treasury, Office of Tax Analysis

pensions in excess of $500. While this table indicates that pensioners in higher economic income classes are in higher comprehensive income classes as well, it also reveals that, in general, their comprehensive income tends to be larger than their economic income. If taxes were assessed on the basis of comprehensive income and filing units were arrayed by economic income class, the tax structure would appear less progressive. This is because pensioners, who are generally in lower income classes, have comprehensive income that exceeds economic income. During their earning years, both economic and comprehensive income are relatively high but economic exceeds comprehensive income.

Both of these effects tend to tilt the structure of effective tax rates as measured using economic income in the direction of lower effective rates on higher economic income and higher effective rates on lower economic income. What appears to be a phenomenon of the aggregate distribution of the tax burden is actually a matter of the timing of taxes at different points in the life cycle of the same taxpayer. A consequence of these lifetime effects, which are discussed in more detail later in this chapter, is that comprehensive income is a more meaningful classifier for analyzing a tax system using a realization basis. Hence, in the tables that follow, comprehensive rather than economic income is used to identify the income classes of the taxpayers. Even more desirable would be a comparison of lifetime tax burdens with lifetime income.

Present Law Tax

Table 6 displays the progressivity of the present income tax system, the total amount of revenue that it raises, and the effective tax rates by comprehensive income class. The individual income tax is only part of the present tax structure. The proposals in this report also would replace the corporation income tax and, by including virtually all income in the tax base, would reduce implicit taxes to near zero. Present tax burdens, however, include all three forms of tax. As shown in table 6, effective tax rates so derived rise with comprehensive income.

Table 5
Cross-Tabulation of the Number of Filing Units with Substantial Pension Income by Economic Income and by Comprehensive Income[1]
(1976 levels)

Economic income ($000)	Comprehensive income ($000) (·· thousands ··)									
	Up to 0	0-5	5-10	10-15	15-20	20-30	30-50	50-100	100 or more	Total
Less than 0	49	22	7	4	0	0	0	0	0	81
0-5	4	9,705	3,221	526	88	33	3	0	0	13,581
5-10	4	453	2,839	1,539	318	70	6	0	0	5,230
10-15	1	61	170	1,080	472	172	22	1	0	1,978
15-20	0	27	17	152	640	382	55	0	0	1,273
20-30	1	22	4	13	185	914	208	12	0	1,360
30-50	0	10	2	1	4	118	681	77	0	894
50-100	0	6	0	0	0	0	26	276	22	331
100 or more	0	4	2	0	0	0	0	6	55	68
Total	60	10,311	6,262	3,316	1,707	1,689	1,001	372	77	24,796

Source: Office of the Secretary of the Treasury, Office of Tax Analysis
[1]Pension income of $500 or more.

Table 6

Present Law Tax and Effective Tax Rates
(1976 levels)

Comprehensive income class	Individual income tax	Corporation income tax	Implicit taxes	Total present law income tax	Effective tax rate[1]
($000)	(.................... $ billions ....)				(percent)
Less than 0	0.2	-0.6	0.4	0.0	-0.6
0-5	1.0	0.7	-0.3	1.4	1.7
5-10	9.5	2.5	-1.1	10.9	6.4
10-15	17.8	3.6	-0.9	20.5	9.9
15-20	22.9	4.3	-0.7	26.5	12.7
20-30	32.6	7.3	-0.8	39.1	15.4
30-50	22.8	10.1	0.5	33.4	19.8
50-100	16.5	11.3	2.5	30.3	25.2
100 or more	13.3	6.7	0.5	20.6	32.4
Total	136.6	46.0	0.0	182.6	14.4

Source: Office of the Secretary of the Treasury, Office of Tax Analysis
[1]Tax as a percentage of comprehensive income.

A Proportional Comprehensive Income Tax

It would be possible to replace the present individual and corporate income tax with a proportional or flat-rate tax on individuals, choosing the rate in such a way as to raise the same total revenue. A reasonable exemption could be allowed for a taxpayer and dependent, or the exemption could be eliminated altogether in favor of a lower rate. Two versions of a proportional tax on comprehensive income, raising the same revenue as the present income tax, are shown in table 7. One has no exemption and a tax rate of 14.35 percent of the comprehensive income base, and the other has an exemption of $1,500 per taxpayer and dependent and a flat rate of 19.35 percent of comprehensive income in excess of exemptions. Table 7 shows comprehensive income by income class, present law tax burdens, and the results of the two proportional rate plans. As compared to present law, both plans would result in a tax decrease for the higher income taxpayers and an increase for those with lower incomes. The plan that allows an exemption would come somewhat closer to the present distribution of tax burdens, but some form of graduated rates is required to achieve a close approximation.

Table 7

Distribution of the Tax Burden
Under Present Law and Illustrative
Flat Rate Income Taxes
(1976 levels)

Compre-hensive income class	Comprehensive income	Amount of income tax under		
		Present law	Flat rate of 14.35 percent	Flat rate of 19.35 percent with exemption[1]
($000)	(		$ billions	)
Less than 0	-3.6	0.0	0.0	0.0
0-5	81.0	1.4	11.6	5.7
5-10	171.2	10.9	24.6	19.6
10-15	205.7	20.5	29.5	26.6
15-20	209.1	26.5	30.0	29.5
20-30	253.7	39.1	36.4	39.1
30-50	169.0	33.4	24.2	28.6
50-100	120.2	30.3	17.2	21.6
100 or more	63.5	20.6	9.1	11.9
Total	1,269.9	182.6	182.6	182.6

Source: Office of the Secretary of the Treasury, Office of Tax Analysis
[1]Exemption of $1,500 per taxpayer and dependent.

THE MODEL COMPREHENSIVE INCOME TAX RATE STRUCTURE

Table 8 shows the steps from comprehensive income to the income subject to tax under the model Comprehensive Income Tax plan and compares that amount to present law taxable income.

Adjustments. The first adjustment is for child care and secondary workers and applies to joint and head-of-household returns. Only 75 percent of the first $10,000 of earnings of workers other than the primary wage earner is included in income subject to tax. A deduction of one-half of child care expenses, up to a maximum deduction of $5,000, is allowed against wage earnings of unmarried heads of households and against the included wages of secondary workers on joint returns.

Exemptions. The combination of exemptions and structure of rates is designed to yield about the same total revenue, with about the same distribution by income class, as the present tax. The model Comprehensive Income Tax would allow exemptions of $1,000 per taxpayer and dependent, plus $1,600 per return (half for married persons filing separately). The value of these exemptions is shown in table 8. A deduction for these amounts yields "comprehensive income subject to tax," the amount to which the rate schedule is applied in the model tax.

Table 8 also indicates the change in taxable income from current law as a result of using the model Comprehensive Income Tax. The increase in income subject to tax is large, approximately one-third of present taxable income. Such a substantial broadening of the tax base can permit a marked reduction in tax rates throughout the entire income range.

Rates. The rate structure for joint returns would be as follows:

Income Bracket	Marginal Tax Rate
$0 - $4,600	8 percent
$4,600 - $40,000	25 percent
Over $40,000	38 percent

For single returns, the rate structure would be as follows:

Income Bracket	Marginal Tax Rate
$0 - $2,800	8 percent
$2,800 - $40,000	22.5 percent
Over $40,000	38 percent

"Heads of households," as under present law, would pay the average of the amounts they would pay using the single and joint schedules.

The tax revenues that would be raised by this plan, and their distribution by income class, are shown in table 9, along with the corresponding information for the present tax. The agreement is quite close and the aggregate tax change for each income class is small. Table 10 shows tax liabilities by filing status under both the present law and the comprehensive income tax proposal. Again, the changes are small. The proposed tax plan would favor larger families slightly compared to present law. Filing units with one or more aged members would pay somewhat higher taxes because they would lose the extra age exemption and because social security cash grants are included in the tax base.

Although tax liabilities by income class and filing status do not change greatly on the average, the proposed comprehensive income tax would alter significantly the tax liabilities of many individual taxpaying units. Those whose income is not fully taxed under current law would pay more tax under this comprehensive plan, while others would benefit from the generally lower rates. Also, many would be relieved of the burden of double taxation on corporate income.

Table 8

Tax Base for Comprehensive Income Tax Proposal

(1976 levels)

Comprehensive income class ($000)	Comprehensive income	Child care and secondary worker provisions	Exemptions[1]	Comprehensive income subject to tax[2]	Present law taxable income	Change in taxable income
	(· $ billions ·)
Less than 0	-3.6	0.0	0.0	0.0	0.8	-0.8
0-5	81.0	-0.1	-68.0	12.9	10.1	2.8
5-10	171.2	-1.5	-83.5	86.1	69.2	16.9
10-15	205.7	-4.4	-71.7	129.6	111.3	18.3
15-20	209.1	-6.6	-57.1	145.4	129.9	15.5
20-30	253.7	-8.2	-51.4	194.1	164.6	29.5
30-50	169.0	-3.1	-21.4	144.5	97.0	47.5
50-100	120.2	-1.0	-8.5	110.7	54.7	56.0
100 or more	63.5	-0.3	-2.0	61.2	31.7	29.5
Total	1,269.9	-25.3	-363.6	884.5	669.2	215.2

Source: Office of the Secretary of the Treasury, Office of Tax Analysis

[1]The amounts shown do not include the value of exemptions that, if allowed, would reduce comprehensive income subject to tax to below zero.

[2]Since comprehensive income subject to tax cannot be less than zero, it is greater than the sum of the first three columns by the amount of the negative income in the first comprehensive income class.

Table 9

Amount of Tax and Effective Tax Rates Under the Present Law Income Tax and Model Comprehensive Income Tax
(1976 levels)

Comprehensive income class	Present law		Comprehensive Income Tax	
	Tax	Effective tax rate[1]	Tax	Effective tax rate[1]
($000)	($ billions)	(percent)	($ billions)	(percent)
Less than 0	0.0	-0.6	0.0	0.0
0-5	1.4	1.7	1.0	1.3
5-10	10.9	6.4	10.4	6.1
10-15	20.5	9.9	20.5	10.0
15-20	26.5	12.7	27.0	12.9
20-30	39.1	15.4	40.1	15.8
30-50	33.4	19.8	32.6	19.3
50-100	30.3	25.2	31.2	26.0
100 or more	20.6	32.4	20.8	32.7
Total	182.6	14.4	183.7	14.5

Source: Office of the Secretary of the Treasury, Office of Tax Analysis
[1]Tax as a percentage of comprehensive income.

Table 10

Amount of Tax According to Filing Status Under the Present Law Income Tax and Model Comprehensive Income Tax
(1976 levels)

Filing status	Present law income tax	Comprehensive Income Tax
	(........... $ billions ....)	
Single..	32.3	32.3
Married filing separately.....................	2.5	3.0
Head of household	6.4	6.9
Joint and certain surviving spouses	141.4	141.5
No dependents............................	54.3	57.3
One dependent............................	28.2	27.8
Two dependents	29.0	27.9
Three dependents.........................	17.5	16.8
Four dependents..........................	7.8	7.4
Five or more dependents	4.6	4.3
All returns	182.6	183.7
Returns with one or more aged	21.6	25.8

Source: Office of the Secretary of the Treasury, Office of Tax Analysis

Table 11 shows the number of filing units in various categories that would have their tax liabilities either increased or decreased by more than 5 percent of present law tax or by more than $20. The average amount of decrease for those returns with decreases is almost $380, while the average amount of increase among the gainers is nearly $650. The average gains and losses are similarly large for virtually all the categories shown on the table.

This finding of large average amounts of gains and losses should be interpreted with great care. It is inevitable that any such tax change will involve substantial redistribution within income classes even if the total tax collected within each class remains the same. Furthermore, to some degree, the simulated comparisons are spurious because it is not proposed to adopt the model plan overnight. Indeed, the existence of a large number of gainers and losers is in itself evidence that careful transition rules are needed to facilitate the movement toward a reformed tax structure.

It should also be noted that the nature of the data base biases the result in the direction of a finding of extensive redistribution. This is so because the individual records in the file of taxpayers in the simulation were constructed by matching information about different individuals in the taxpayer and Current Population Survey samples. As a result, current and new tax liabilities for a given record in the data base may, in fact, be based on information concerning different people.

Aside from such statistical details and the question of transition rules, comparisons of gainers and losers may be misleading on other grounds. The redistributions of income indicated may reflect not only changes in tax burdens among different taxpayers, but, perhaps more importantly, changes between the taxpayer at one point in his life and the same taxpayer at another point. For example, employee contributions to social security are excluded from taxable income, but social security benefits are included. As a result, the simulations show a decrease in tax for present wage earners and an increase in tax for pensioners.

Indeed, table 11 shows that almost half of those with tax increases are receiving $500 or more in pension income. This gives a misleading impression of the distributional consequences of the change, because present wage earners are future retirees. A more satisfactory comparison would be one that reflected the overall lifetime tax burden of different individuals under various plans. It has not been possible to perform simulations of such lifetime effects. Thus, the simulations that are shown tend to be biased toward a finding of greater redistribution than actually would be implied by the model plan.

Table 11

Filing Units with Gains and Losses Under the Comprehensive Income Tax as Compared to the Present Law Income Tax[1]
(1976 levels)

	Tax decrease			Tax increase		
	Number of filing units	Amount of tax change	Average decrease for filing units with decrease	Number of filing units	Amount of tax change	Average increase for filing units with increase
	(millions)	($ billions)	(dollars)	(millions)	($ billions)	(dollars)
All filing units with gains and losses	60.9	23.0	378	37.2	24.1	648
Filing units with $500 or more of pension income	5.0	2.2	431	17.7	13.5	764
Filing units with less than $500 of pension income	55.9	20.9	373	19.5	10.6	543
Single filers	27.7	4.1	148	3.6	1.2	331
Age less than 22	13.7	0.6	46	1.0	0.1	107
Age 22 to 61	13.0	3.2	245	2.4	1.0	427
Age 62 or over	1.0	0.3	293	0.2	0.1	254
Joint filers	24.2	15.8	654	12.9	8.4	653
Earning status:						
One earner	10.2	6.7	657	8.6	5.2	608
Two or more earners	14.0	9.1	652	4.3	3.2	742
Dependency status:						
No dependents	6.9	5.1	745	4.4	2.9	643
Two dependents	5.8	3.5	607	2.8	1.7	624
Four dependents	1.7	1.1	649	0.7	0.5	747
Filing units with means-tested cash grant income	2.7	0.2	59	3.9	1.1	270

Source: Office of the Secretary of the Treasury, Office of Tax Analysis

[1] Filing units whose tax liabilities would change by more than 5 percent of present law tax or by more than $20.

THE CASH FLOW TAX RATE STRUCTURE

Table 12 shows, for each comprehensive income class, the derivation of gross consumption from comprehensive income. "Imputed consumption from owner-occupied housing" consists of the net rental value of owner-occupied dwellings, and is included in gross consumption even though a cash outlay may not be made for the rental services. "Corporate retained earnings" are deducted because they represent saving on behalf of households. Similar saving occurs in the form of earnings on life insurance policies, contributions to and earnings of private pension plans, and employee contributions to social security. "Direct saving" represents household net purchases of real and financial assets. In table 12, gross consumption is derived by subtracting the sum of all forms of saving from the sum of comprehensive income plus imputed consumption.

The term "gross consumption" is used because consumption is here considered to be gross of income taxes paid under current law; in other words, gross consumption represents before-tax consumption. Gross consumption is the starting point of the Cash Flow Tax in the same way that comprehensive income is the starting point of the Comprehensive Income Tax.

As was explained earlier in connection with the Comprehensive Income Tax, taxpayers must be classified properly before the distribution of tax burdens can be analyzed. All tables dealing with the cash flow tax will use gross consumption for classification purposes.

Adjustments and Exemptions. Table 13 shows the derivation of the Cash Flow Tax base. The provisions for child care and secondary workers are the same for the cash flow tax as for the comprehensive income tax. Exemptions under the cash flow tax are $1,500 per return and $800 per taxpayer and dependent. Adjusting gross consumption for child care and secondary worker provisions, and for exemptions, yields the amount of cash flow subject to tax. A comparison of the amounts subject to tax in the two model plans, as shown in tables 8 and 13, indicates that the amount of cash flow subject to tax is about 7 percent less than the amount of comprehensive income subject to tax. Nonetheless, the amount of cash flow subject to tax is 23 percent more than present taxable income, as shown in table 8. Thus, even though saving is deducted, the model Cash Flow Tax accomplishes a substantial broadening of the tax base.

Table 12
Comprehensive Income and Gross Consumption
(1976 levels)

Comprehensive income class ($000)	Comprehensive income	Imputed consumption from owner-occupied housing	Savings — Corporate retained earnings	Savings — Saving in life insurance, pension plans, and social security	Savings — Direct saving	Gross consumption
	(· $ billions ·)
Less than 0	-3.6	0.1	0.1	0.0	-5.9	2.3
0-5	81.0	1.3	0.3	0.4	3.0	78.6
5-10	171.2	3.6	0.9	2.1	8.1	163.7
10-15	205.7	7.0	1.1	3.3	14.0	194.4
15-20	209.1	8.3	1.3	4.0	18.3	193.8
20-30	253.7	9.7	2.4	5.6	26.7	228.7
30-50	169.0	4.9	3.5	3.2	18.9	148.3
50-100	120.2	2.1	4.0	1.3	16.8	100.2
100 or more	63.5	0.7	6.0	0.5	6.8	51.0
Total	1,269.9	37.8	19.6	20.5	106.7	1,160.9

Source: Office of the Secretary of the Treasury, Office of Tax Analysis

Note: Gross consumption equals comprehensive income plus imputed consumption from owner-occupied housing minus all of the following forms of savings: corporate retained earnings, saving in life insurance plans, social security contributions, and direct saving.

Rates. The rate structure for joint returns under the cash flow tax would be as follows:

Cash Flow Bracket	Marginal Tax Rate
$0 - $5,200	10 percent
$5,200 - $30,000	28 percent
Over $30,000	40 percent

For single returns, the rate structure would be as follows:

Cash Flow Bracket	Marginal Tax Rate
$0 - $3,200	10 percent
$3,200 - $30,000	26 percent
Over $30,000	40 percent

Heads of households, as under present law, would pay the average of the amounts under the single and joint schedules.

Table 14 shows the distribution of tax liabilities and effective rates of tax under the model Cash Flow Tax and present law. The Cash Flow Tax nearly reproduces the progressivity of the present tax structure. It is clear that taxing consumption is perfectly consistent with a progressive structure of tax liabilities.

Table 13

Cash Flow Tax Base
(1976 levels)

Gross consumption class	Number of filing units[1]	Gross consumption	Child Care and second-ary worker provisions	Exemp-tions[2]	Cash flow subject to tax
($000)	(millions)	(.................. $ billions ....)			
Less than 0	0.0	0.0	0.0	0.0	0.0
0-5	40.7	84.2	-0.1	-66.2	17.9
5-10	24.3	178.9	-1.8	-76.6	100.5
10-15	17.9	221.4	-5.7	-67.1	148.6
15-20	11.8	202.9	-7.3	-47.8	147.8
20-30	8.7	208.5	-6.8	-36.0	165.6
30-50	3.7	136.3	-2.6	-14.9	118.8
50-100	1.3	88.2	-0.8	-5.5	81.9
100 or more	0.3	40.6	-0.2	-1.1	39.2
Total	108.6	1,160.9	-25.3	-315.2	820.4

Source: Office of the Secretary of the Treasury, Office of Tax Analysis

[1]Includes all filing units whether or not they actually file returns or pay tax under current law.

[2]The amounts shown do not include the value of exemptions that, if allowed, would reduce cash flow subject to tax to below zero.

Although the Cash Flow Tax preserves the average progressivity of current law, a shift to it would redistribute tax burdens. Table 15 tabulates filing units whose tax change would be more than 5 percent of present law tax or more than $20. This table yields essentially the same results as those presented in table 11 for the Comprehensive Income Tax. The caveats in interpreting the results of table 11 apply with equal force to table 15.

COMPARISONS OF TAX LIABILITIES UNDER THE DIFFERENT PLANS

Up to this point, this chapter has presented simulations of the effects of the model tax plans on all taxpayers. This section examines the tax liabilities of taxpayers in particular situations. These materials illustrate the differences among the present law income tax and the two model plans. Since the data are hypo-thetical, they do not represent the situations for any particular taxpayer.

Table 14

Amount of Tax and Effective Tax Rates Under the Present Law Income Tax and under Model Cash Flow Tax
(1976 levels)

Gross consump-tion class	Present law tax		Cash Flow Tax	
	Tax	Effective tax rate[1]	Tax	Effective tax rate[1]
($000)	($ billions)	(percent)	($ billions)	(percent)
Less than 0	0.0	0.0	0.0	0.0
0-5	1.8	2.2	1.8	2.1
5-10	13.2	7.4	13.7	7.7
10-15	26.2	11.8	26.3	11.9
15-20	30.0	14.8	30.6	15.1
20-30	37.5	18.0	38.2	18.3
30-50	32.2	23.6	31.4	23.1
50-100	27.1	30.7	26.8	30.3
100 or more	14.6	36.0	14.5	35.7
Total	182.6	15.7	183.3	15.8

Source: Office of the Secretary of the Treasury, Office of Tax Analysis
[1]Tax as a percentage of gross consumption.

Table 15

Filing Units with Gains and Losses Under the Cash Flow Tax Compared with Present Law Income Tax[1]
(1976 levels)

	Tax Decrease			Tax Increase		
	Number of filing units	Amount of tax change	Average decrease for filing units with decrease	Number of filing units	Amount of tax change	Average increase for filing units with increase
	(millions)	($ billions)	(dollars)	(millions)	($ billions)	(dollars)
All filing units with gains and losses	53.6	31.0	577	44.7	31.7	708
Filing units with $500 or more of pension income	5.1	3.5	700	17.9	13.7	765
Filing units with less than $500 of pension income	48.6	27.4	564	26.8	18.0	671
Single filers	24.5	4.9	199	6.6	2.0	309
Age less than 22	12.6	0.5	43	2.0	0.3	130
Age 22 to 61	11.0	3.9	360	4.3	1.7	392
Age 62 or over	0.9	0.4	410	0.3	0.1	313
Joint filers	20.6	21.4	1,037	16.6	14.6	880
Earning status:						
One earner	8.9	9.6	1,075	10.0	8.8	876
Two or more earners	11.7	11.8	1,007	6.6	5.9	885
Dependency status:						
No dependents.........	6.8	8.0	1,174	4.6	4.1	889
Two dependents	4.6	4.3	933	4.0	3.5	884
Four dependents........	1.3	1.3	1,060	1.1	1.0	924
Filing units with means-tested cash grant income	2.4	0.2	73	4.4	1.5	352

Source: Office of the Secretary of the Treasury, Office of Tax Analysis
[1]Filing units whose tax liabilities would change by more than 5 percent of present law tax or by more than $20.

The Marriage Penalty

A subject of continuing controversy and interest is the division of the tax burden between married and unmarried individuals. Table 16 shows, for current law, the additional tax paid by a married couple filing a joint return over what would be paid if both persons could file single returns. The left-hand column shows the couple's total income. The subsequent columns present different shares of the total income earned by the lesser-earning spouse. For example, in the first column, one spouse earns all of the income. This column shows that a married couple would pay a lower tax than would a single individual with the same income because of the favorable rate structure of the joint return schedule. In the last column, earnings are derived equally from the wages of both spouses. In this case, the married couple would pay a higher tax than would two unmarried individuals, with a marriage penalty of $4,815 on a joint income of $100,000.

Table 17 shows the same data for the model Comprehensive Income Tax plan. The area of marriage penalty has increased somewhat as compared to current law. However, the rate structure and exclusion of a portion of the earnings of the secondary worker would result in some changes relative to current law. This may be seen most clearly in the last column. Although the marriage penalty paid by a couple earning $100,000 would increase, for all other families in which equal earners marry, the marriage penalty would be reduced compared to current law. As the first column shows, the differences between married couples and unmarried individuals are, in general, reduced in the Comprehensive Income Tax plan compared to current law. This is because the broader tax base permits a less steep progression of marginal tax rates. Table 18 shows the marriage penalties under the model Cash Flow Tax.

Lifetime Comparisons

As suggested above, a desirable point of view from which to assess the relative tax burdens among individuals is that of the complete lifetime. The tables presented thus far do not reflect this lifetime perspective. If either of the model tax plans had been in effect as long as the present tax, the income and tax situations of taxpayers would be different from those shown in the simulated results.

This is particularly true of saving, which is subject to considerably different treatment under the model plans. For persons accumulating for their retirement years in savings accounts, the present law would collect tax on the income from which the saving

Table 16

Marriage Penalties in 1976 Law[1]

Total family income	Dollar amount of marriage penalty when share of income earned by lesser-earning spouse is:[2]					
	None	10 Percent	20 Percent	30 Percent	40 Percent	50 Percent
(dollars)	(........................... No Marriage Penalty ....)					
0	0	0	0	0	0	0
3,000	-42	0	0	0	0	0
5,000	-233	-149	-69	12	87	130
7,000	-266	-137	-18	101	201	212
10,000	-383	-163	43	191	216	221
15,000	-527	-187	97	162	237	263
20,000	-762	-240	56	189	258	243
25,000	-1,085	-324	29	235	319	365
30,000	-1,406	-442	13	320	497	565
40,000	-2,013	-657	149	661	1,034	1,188
50,000	-2,697	-799	334	1,188	1,743	1,910
100,000	-6,810	-2,532	605	2,819	4,275	4,815
			(..................... Marriage Penalty ....)			

Source: Office of the Secretary of the Treasury, Office of Tax Analysis

[1]The marriage penalty is the excess of the tax a couple pays with a joint return over what it would pay if both persons could file single returns.

[2]In all tax calculations, deductible expenses are assumed to be 16 percent of income, and the maximum tax is not used.

Table 17

Marriage Penalties in the Model Comprehensive Income Tax[1]

Total family income	Dollar amount of marriage penalty when share of income earned by lesser-earning spouse is:					
	None	10 Percent	20 Percent	30 Percent	40 Percent	50 Percent
(dollars)						
0	0	0	0	0	0	0
3,000	-32	-8	0	0	0	0
5,000	-80	-50	-20	10	40	62
7,000	-312	-169	-25	46	72	58
10,000	-441	-278	-116	15	97	122
15,000	-316	-72	140	263	300	206
20,000	-191	134	347	425	300	175
25,000	-66	340	555	456	300	300
30,000	59	515	675	488	425	425
40,000	309	847	800	675	675	675
50,000	244	1,477	1,432	1,432	1,432	1,432
100,000	244	1,835	3,385	4,935	6,485	6,888

(Upper region: No Marriage Penalty ..... Lower region: Marriage Penalty .....)

Source: Office of the Secretary of the Treasury, Office of Tax Analysis

[1]The marriage penalty is the excess of the tax a couple pays with a joint return over what it would pay if both persons could file single returns.

Table 18

Marriage Penalties in the Model Cash Flow Tax[1]

Total family income (dollars)	Dollar amount of marriage penalty when share of income earned by lesser-earning spouse is:					
	None	10 Percent	20 Percent	30 Percent	40 Percent	50 Percent
0	0	0	0	0	0	0
3,000	-70	-40	-10	0	0	0
5,000	-80	-42	-5	32	70	88
7,000	-320	-156	9	77	80	63
10,000	-494	-304	-114	6	96	106
15,000	-394	-109	106	241	296	191
20,000	-294	86	296	396	256	116
25,000	-194	261	486	391	216	216
30,000	-94	406	596	386	316	316
40,000	-144	886	1,244	1,044	1,044	1,044
50,000	-144	1,086	1,366	2,066	2,444	2,444
100,000	-144	1,366	2,766	4,166	4,488	4,488

(No Marriage Penalty . . . .)

(. . . . Marriage Penalty . . . .)

Source: Office of the Secretary of the Treasury, Office of Tax Analysis

[1]The marriage penalty is the excess of the tax a couple pays with a joint return over what it would pay if both persons could file single returns.

is made and again on the interest earned on the savings. Withdrawal of funds, however, would have no tax consequence. Under the Cash Flow Tax, savings would not be subject to tax; rather, taxes would be assessed when the proceeds are withdrawn for consumption. The Comprehensive Income Tax would be levied both on income saved as well as on interest earned, but the broader base would permit lower rates than under present law.

Since one objective of saving is the reallocation of lifetime consumption, these three tax systems would be expected to alter the timing of income, consumption, and tax liabilities. Table 19 summarizes these effects. It shows summary statistics for a family whose saving strategy is to maintain a constant level of consumption throughout working and retirement years. This table provides a very direct and convenient way of comparing the different systems, since tax burdens may be determined directly from the level of consumption. The higher is the level of consumption attainable, the lower is the tax burden. In this example, the present law tax burden is somewhat higher (consumption is lower) than that implied by the model Comprehensive Income Tax, which in turn is higher than that under the Cash Flow Tax.

Table 19
Lifetime Comparison of Present Law Income Tax and Model Tax Plans
(Married couple; one earner, wages $16,000 per year for 40 years; consumes at maximum possible steady rate over entire lifetime)

	Present law tax	Comprehensive Income Tax	Cash Flow Tax
Consumption:			
All ages	$ 11,456	$ 11,524	$ 11,713
Savings account balance:			
Age 40	60,114	53,759	58,764
Age 60	151,185	137,651	164,900
Taxes:			
Working years:			
Age 21	2,102	2,318	2,100
Age 40	2,272	2,696	2,100
Age 60	2,582	3,312	2,100
Retirement years:			
Age 61	845	42	2,100
Age 75	505	0	2,100

Source: Office of the Secretary of the Treasury, Office of Tax Analysis

Note: This example assumes a 3-percent real rate of return (before taxes) on savings and that the corporation income tax under present law is borne by the return from all savings at the rate of 19.1 percent.

CHAPTER **6**

Transition Considerations

INTRODUCTION

Major changes in the tax code which would accompany a switch to either the Comprehensive Income Tax or Cash Flow Tax may lead to substantial and sudden changes in current wealth and future after-tax income flows for some individuals. Transition rules need to be designed to minimize unfair losses, or undeserved windfalls, to individuals whose investment decisions were influenced by the provisions of the existing code.

This chapter discusses the major issues in transition and suggests possible solutions to problems arising from transition to both the Comprehensive Income Tax and the Cash Flow Tax. It outlines the major wealth changes that can be expected under a switch to either of the two model taxes, and discusses the relevant equity criteria to be applied in the design of transition rules. Instruments for ameliorating transition problems, including phasing-in provisions of the new law and grandfathering, or exempting, existing assets from the new rules are discussed. The effects of applying these transition instruments to different types of changes in the tax law are outlined. Transition rules to be applied to specific changes in the tax law included in the model Comprehensive Income Tax in chapter 3 are considered. Special problems of transition to a consumption-based tax are discussed also, and a plan is suggested for transition to the Cash Flow Tax proposal described in chapter 4.

WEALTH CHANGES AND THEIR EQUITY ASPECTS

Two separate problems requiring special transition rules can be identified: carryover and price changes. Carryover problems would occur to the extent that changes in the tax code affect the taxation of income earned in the past but not yet subject to tax or, conversely, income taxed in the past that may be subject to a second tax. Price changes would occur in those instances where changes in the tax code altered the expected flow of after-tax income from existing investments in the future.

Carryover Problems

Under the present tax system, income is not always taxed at the time it accrues. For example, increases in net worth in the form of capital gains are not taxed before realization. A change in the tax rate on realized capital gains, therefore, would alter the tax liability on gains accrued but not realized before the effective date of the tax reform. Application of the new rules to past capital gains would either raise or lower the applicable tax on that portion of past income, depending on the rates and on whether the increase in tax from including all capital gains in the income base exceeded the reduction in tax caused by any allowance of a basis adjustment for inflation.

The problem of changes in the timing of tax liability might be especially severe if the current tax system were changed to a consumption base. Under a consumption base, purchases of assets would be deductible from tax and sales of assets not reinvested would be fully taxable. Under the current tax system, both the income used to purchase assets and the capital gain are subject to tax, the latter, however, at a reduced rate. Recovery of the original investment is not taxed. An immediate change to a consumption base would penalize individuals who saved in the past and who are currently selling assets for consumption purposes. Having already paid a tax on the income used to purchase the asset under the old rules, they would also be required to pay an additional tax on the *entire* proceeds from the sale of the asset. On the other hand, if owners of assets were allowed to treat those assets as tax-prepaid, they would receive a gain to the extent they planned to use them for future consumption. Future income on past accumulated wealth would then be free from future taxes, and the government would have to make up the difference by raising the tax rate on the remaining consumption regarded as non-pretaxed. A change-over in the treatment of gifts and bequests, to deduction by donors and inclusion by donees, would typically increase the burden of tax on past accumulations devoted to this purpose.

Other carryover problems include excess deductions or credits unused in previous years and similar special technical features of the tax law. In general, carryover can be viewed as being conceptually different from changes in the price of assets. In the case of capital gains tax, for example, the change in an individual's tax liability for gains that have arisen because asset values increased, does not affect the tax liability of another individual purchasing an asset from him; in general, the asset price depends only on *future* net-of-tax earnings. However, the new tax law *and* the transition rules, by altering future net-of-tax earnings, would change the price of assets.

In most cases, carryover problems could be handled by special rules that define the amount of income attributable to increases in asset values not realized before the effective date of implementation of the new law. Changes in the definition of an individual's past income would alter asset prices only if they provided an incentive for pre-effective date sales of existing assets. For example, if, under the new system, past capital gains were taxed at a higher rate than under the old system, an incentive might be created for sales of assets prior to the effective date.

Price Changes

Adoption of a broadly based tax system would change prices of some assets by changing the taxation of future earnings. Under the Comprehensive Income Tax, for example, the following changes in the tax code would alter tax rates on income from existing assets: integration of the corporate and personal income taxes; taxation of all realized capital gains at the full rate; adjustment of asset basis for inflation (or deflation); inclusion of interest on State and local government bonds in the tax base; elimination of accelerated depreciation provisions that lower the effective rate of tax on income arising in special sectors, including minerals extraction, real estate, and some agricultural activities; and elimination of the deductibility of property taxes by homeowners. Adoption of these and other changes in the tax code would alter both the average rate of taxation on income from all assets and the relative rates imposed among types of financial claims, legal entities, and investments in different industries.

The effects of changes in taxation on asset values would be different for changes in the average *level* of taxation of the associated returns and changes in the *relative* rates of taxation on different assets. A change in the average rate of taxation on all income from investment, while it would affect the future net return from wealth or accumulated past earnings, would not be likely in itself to change individual asset prices significantly. For any single asset, an increase in the average rate of taxation of returns would reduce net after-tax earnings roughly in proportion to the reduction in net after-tax earnings on alternative uses of funds, including lending at interest. Thus, the market value of the asset, which can be roughly thought of as the ratio of returns net of taxes to the interest rate after tax, would not tend to change. On the other hand, an increase in the *relative* rate of taxation on any single asset generally would lead to a fall in the price of that asset, because net after-tax earnings would fall relative to the interest rate. The opposite holds for a decrease in the *relative* rate of taxation.

The behavior of the price of any single asset in response to a change in the relative rate of taxation of its return depends on the characteristics of the asset and the nature of the financial claim to it. For example, suppose the asset is a share in an apartment project. In the long run, the price of the asset will depend on the cost of building apartments; if unit construction costs are independent of volume, they will not be altered by changes in the tax rate on real estate profits.

Now, suppose the effective rate of taxation on profits from real estate is increased. The increase in tax will drive down the after-tax rents received by owners. Because the value of the asset to buyers depends on the stream of annual after-tax profits, the price a purchaser is willing to pay also will fall. With the price of the structure now lower than the cost of production, apartment construction will decline, making rental housing more scarce and driving up the before-tax rentals charged to tenants. In final equilibrium, the before-tax rentals will have risen sufficiently to restore after-tax profits to a level at which buyers are again willing to offer a price for the asset equal to its cost of production. However, for the interim before supply changes restore equilibrium, after-tax returns would be lowered by the price change.

Thus, the immediate effect of the change in the rate of taxation would be to lower the price of equity claims to real estate. The wealth loss to owners of those shares at the time of the tax change would depend both on the time required for adjustment to final equilibrium and the extent to which future increases in the gross rentals (from the decline in housing supply) were anticipated in the marketplace. The faster the adjustment to equilibrium and the larger the percent of gross rentals change that is anticipated, the smaller the fall in asset price will be for any given increase in the tax on the returns.

If the asset is a claim to a fixed stream of future payments (e.g., a bond), a change in the rate of taxation would alter its price by lowering the present value of the future return flow. For example, if interest from municipal bonds became subject to tax, the net after-tax earnings of holders of municipal bonds would fall, lowering the value of those claims. New purchasers of municipal bonds would demand an after-tax rate of return on their investment comparable to the after-tax return on other assets of similar risk and liquidity. The proportional decline in value for a given tax change would be greater for bonds with a longer time to maturity.

The effect of corporate integration on the price of assets is less certain. If the corporate income tax is viewed as a tax on the earnings of corporate equity shareholders, integration would increase the rate of taxation on income from investment of high-bracket shareholders and lower the rate of taxation on such income of low-bracket shareholders.[1] In addition, many assets owned by corporations also can be used in the noncorporate sector. To the extent that relative tax rates on income arising in the two sectors were altered by integration, those assets could easily move from one sector to the other, changing relative before-tax earnings and output prices in the two sectors, but keeping relative after-tax earnings and asset prices the same.

In conclusion, raising the relative rate of taxation on capital income in industries and for types of claims currently receiving relatively favorable tax treatment would likely cause some changes in asset prices. Immediate asset price changes generally would be greater for long-term fixed claims, such as State and local bonds, than for equity investments; greater for assets specific to a given industry (e.g., apartment buildings) than for assets that can be shifted among industries; and greater for assets the supply of which can only be altered slowly (e.g., buildings and some mineral investments) than for those the supply of which can be changed quickly.

The net effect of integration on asset values may not be large. On the other hand, changes in the special tax treatment currently afforded in certain industries, for example in real estate and mineral resources, and changes in the treatment of State and local bond interest, would likely cause significant changes in values of those assets.

The Equity Issues

Considerations of equity associated with changes in tax laws are different from equity considerations associated with the overall design of a tax system. Changes in the tax code would create potential inequities to the extent that individuals who made commitments in response to provisions of the existing law suffer unanticipated losses (or receive unanticipated gains) as a result of the change. These gains (and losses) can be of two types: (1) wealth changes to individuals resulting from changes in tax liabilities on income accrued in the past but not yet recognized for tax purposes, and (2) changes in the price of assets or the value of employment contracts brought about by changes in future after-tax earnings. These two types of problems, carryover and price change, pose somewhat different equity issues.

Carryover poses the problem of how to tax equitably income attributable to an earlier period, when a different set of tax laws was in effect. For example, consider one aspect of the proposed change in the tax treatment of corporations under the Comprehensive Income Tax. At present, capital gains are subject to lower tax rates than dividends, especially when realization is deferred for a long period of time. Individuals owning shares of corporations paying high dividend rates relative to total earnings pay more tax than individuals owning shares of corporations with low dividends relative to total earnings. As both types of investment are available to everyone, individuals purchasing shares in high-dividend corporations presumably are receiving something (possibly less risk or more liquidity) in exchange for the higher tax liability they have to assume. To subject shareholders of low-dividend corporations to the same rate of taxation they would have paid if income had accumulated in the form of capital gains before the effective date had been distributed would be unfair.

Carryover poses another equity problem: some taxpayers may be assessed at unusually high or low rates on past income because of changes in the timing of accrual of tax liability. The above example can be used to illustrate this point too. Under current law, the special tax treatment of capital gains in part compensates shareholders for the extra tax on their income at the corporate level. Under the integration proposal presented in chapter 3, the separate corporate income tax would be eliminated, but shareholders would be required to pay a full tax on their attributed share of the corporation's income, whether or not distributed.

Now, suppose integration is introduced and a shareholder has to pay the full tax on the appreciation of his shares that occurred before the effective date.[2] The taxpayer would, in effect, be taxed too heavily on that income, because it was subject to taxation at the corporate level before being taxed at the full individual income tax rate. Before integration, he would, in effect, have paid the corporate tax plus the reduced capital gains rate on the gains attributable to that income; after integration, he would be liable for the tax on ordinary income at the full rate. Thus, in the absence of transition rules, he would be subject to a higher tax on income in the form of capital gains accrued before, but not recognized until after, the effective date of the new law than on income earned in a similar way under a consistent application of either present law or the comprehensive income tax.

The most desirable solution to the problem of equity posed by carryover is to design a set of transition rules that insure that, to the maximum extent consistent with other objectives, tax liabilities on income accrued before the effective date are computed according to the old law and tax liabilities on income accrued after the effective date are computed according to the new law.

Changes in future after-tax income brought about by tax reform raise a different set of equity issues. A complete change in the tax system, if unexpected, would cause losses in asset value to investors in previously tax-favored sectors. Imposition of such losses may be viewed as unfair, especially since past government policy explicitly encouraged investment in those assets.

For example, as between individuals in a given tax bracket one of whom held State and local bonds producing a lower interest rate because such interest was tax-exempt and the other of whom held taxable Treasury bonds producing higher interest but the same after-tax return, it seems reasonable to compensate the holder of the State and local bonds for the loss suffered upon removal of the tax exemption so that he ends up in the same position as the holder of Treasury bonds. Note that this concept of distributive justice does not imply that a third taxpayer, who earns higher after-tax income from tax-free bonds than from Treasury bonds because he is in a higher tax bracket than the other two, should retain the privilege of earning tax-free interest. Equity does not require that the tax system maintain loopholes; it does require some limitation on wealth losses imposed on individuals because they took advantage of legal tax incentives.

The counterargument to the view that justice requires compensation for such wealth changes is that all changes in public policy alter the relative incomes of individuals and, frequently, asset values. For example, a government decision to reduce the defense budget will lower relative asset prices in defense companies and their principal supplying firms and also lower relative wages of individuals with skills specialized to defense activities (e.g., many engineers and physicists). Although some special adjustment assistance programs exist,[3] it is not common practice to compensate individuals for changes in the value of physical and human assets caused by changes in government policies. In addition, it can be argued that, because investors in tax-favored industries know the tax subsidy may end, the risk of a public policy change is reflected in asset prices and rates of return. If, for example, it is believed that the continuing debate over ending remaining special tax treatment of oil industry assets poses a real threat, it can be argued that investors in oil are already receiving a risk premium in the form of higher than normal net after-tax returns, and further compensation for losses upon end of the subsidy is unwarranted.

The discussion above suggests that a case can be made both for and against compensation of individuals for losses in asset values caused by radical changes in tax policy. Because the asset value changes resulting from the tax change alone are virtually impossible to measure precisely, designing a method to determine the appropriate amount of compensation would be difficult on both theoretical and practical grounds. However, it would be desirable to design transition rules so that unanticipated losses and gains resulting from adoption of a comprehensive tax base would be moderated. Two possible design features, grandfathering existing assets and phasing in the new rules slowly, are discussed next.

INSTRUMENTS FOR AMELIORATING TRANSITION PROBLEMS

Objectives

The main criteria that transition rules should satisfy are: (1) simplicity, (2) minimizing incentive problems, and (3) minimizing undesirable wealth effects.

Simplicity. The transition rules in themselves should not introduce any major new complexity in the tax law. To the extent possible, transition rules should not require that corporations or individuals supply additional data on financial transactions or asset values.

Minimizing Incentive Problems. The transition rules should be designed to minimize the probability of action in response to special features of the change from one set of tax rules to another. In particular, there should not be special inducements either to buy or to sell particular kinds of assets just before or after the effective date of the new law.

Minimizing Undesirable Wealth Effects. Transition rules should moderate wealth losses to individuals holding assets that lose their tax advantages under basic tax reform as well as gains to those whose assets are *relatively* favored. At the same time, special transition rules to protect assetholders from loss should not give them the opportunity to earn windfall gains.

Alternatives

Two alternative methods of reducing capital value changes are discussed here: grandfathering existing assets and phasing in the new law.

Grandfathering. The grandfather clause was originally used by some southern States as a method for disenfranchising black voters following the Civil War. It exempted from the high literacy and property qualifications only those voters or their lineal descendants who had voted before 1867. More recently, grandfather clauses have been used to exempt present holders of positions from new laws applicable to those positions, e.g., setting a mandatory age of retirement. In the context of tax reform, a grandfather clause could be used either to exempt existing assets from the new law as long as they are held by the current owner or to exempt existing assets from the new law regardless of who holds them. A grandfather clause also could be applied to capital gains accrued but not yet realized at the time the new law went into effect.

Consider, for example, the effect of eliminating the special depreciation rules that result in a low rate of taxation on income from real estate investments. A grandfather clause that exempts existing buildings only so long as they are held by the current owner(s) would mean that current owners could depreciate their buildings to zero according to the old rules, but that new owners could not do so. Grandfathering the buildings independently of their owners would allow subsequent purchasers to depreciate according to the old rules.[4] This would have the effect of raising the value of the buildings. Elimination of tax incentives in real estate would discourage new construction, reducing the supply of housing and raising gross rentals before tax. Thus, grandfathering, by making existing property more valuable, would give a windfall gain to investors in real estate tax shelters. On the other hand, grandfathering the buildings only for current owners would not prevent a wealth loss to real estate investors, because the value to new buyers would decline. The loss would be mitigated by the anticipated increase in after-tax profits to current investors (because of the decline in housing supply).

The effect of grandfathering on asset prices for fixed-interest securities is less certain. For example, if existing municipal bonds were grandfathered, annual interest received net of tax would be unchanged. However, the value of the tax saving from owning municipal bonds would change for two reasons. First, there would be no new tax-exempt municipal bond issues under the new rules; with fewer available tax-exempt bonds, the price of tax-exempt securities will rise, as will the marginal tax bracket at which such securities offer a net advantage. Second, the other changes in the tax system which would enable marginal tax rates in the highest brackets to fall, would reduce the gain from tax exemptions, driving down the demand for, and the price of tax-exempt securities. As demand and supply will both fall, it is not clear in what direction the price of the grandfathered securities would change, though the price change would be smaller than if the new rules were adopted immediately for all tax-exempt securities.

One problem of grandfathering is that it can provide an unanticipated gain to current owners of assets subject to favorable tax treatment. These owners would receive a gain because the new tax law would reduce the supply of previously favored assets, thus raising before-tax profits.

Grandfathering probably should be limited to cases where gross returns are not likely to be altered significantly by the change in taxation. For example, changes in the tax treatment of pensions would not be likely to affect before-tax labor compensation significantly, assuming the supply of labor to the economy is relatively fixed. While grandfathering tax treatment of pensions in current employment contracts would not be likely to raise significantly the value of those contracts relative to their value under the old law, an immediate shift to the new law would reduce the value of previously negotiated pension rights.

Phasing In. An alternative method of avoiding drastic changes in asset values is to introduce the new rules gradually. For example, taxation of interest on currently tax-exempt State and local bonds could be introduced slowly by including an additional 10 percent of interest in the tax base every year for 10 years. Phasing in the new rules would not alter the direction of asset value changes, but it would reduce their magnitude by delaying tax liability changes.

Assuming that the market incentives under the new law are preferable to the incentives under the current law, phasing in poses distinct disadvantages. Phasing in would delay application of the new rules, thus reducing the present value of the economic changes that would be encouraged, and which are an important objective of the new rules. Phasing in also may introduce substantial complexity. The length of the phase-in period would depend on the desired balance of the gains in efficiency and simplicity from changing the tax system against the distributive inequities resulting from imposition of asset value changes on some investors.

Combination of Phasing In and Grandfathering. A possible variant on the two approaches outlined above is to adopt the new rules immediately for new assets while phasing in the new rules for existing assets. In many cases, grandfathering existing assets when new assets would be taxed more heavily under the new tax law would raise the market price of the old assets. By phasing in the new rules for the old assets, it would be possible to moderate the increase in present value of future tax liabilities, while at the same time reduced supply of new assets would raise before-tax returns on both new and existing assets. The two effects may roughly cancel out, leaving asset prices almost the same throughout the early transition period. For example, a gradual introduction of new, and more appropriate, depreciation schedules for existing residential real estate,[5] with a concurrent adoption of the new rules for new buildings, would have the same incentive effects on new building as immediate adoption of the new law. Before-tax rentals on existing real estate would rise gradually, as supply growth is reduced, while tax liabilities on existing real estate also would rise. It is likely that, for an appropriate phase-in period, the asset value change to existing owners would be small. However, tax shelters on new construction would be totally eliminated immediately.

PROPOSED SOLUTIONS TO SELECTED PROBLEMS IN THE TRANSITION TO THE COMPREHENSIVE INCOME TAX

Adoption of the Comprehensive Income Tax would have significant impact on the taxation of capital gains, corporate income, business and investment income, and personal income. The following discussion examines the problems that these changes present for transition. In most cases, possible solutions to these problems are suggested.

Capital Gains

Under the Comprehensive Income Tax, no distinction will be made between capital gains and ordinary income, and losses will be fully deductible against income from other sources. The transition mechanism proposed is to allow capital gains (or losses) that have accrued as of the general effective date of the proposal to continue to qualify for capital gains treatment upon a sale or other taxable disposition for 10 years following such date. This "capital gain account" inherent in each asset could be determined in either of two ways:

1. By actual valuation on the general effective date of enactment of the proposal (or on an elective alternative valuation date to avoid temporary distortions in market value), or

2. By regarding the gain (or loss) recognized on a sale or exchange of the asset as having accrued ratably over the period the seller held the asset. The portion of the gain (or loss) thus regarded as having accrued prior to the effective date would be taxed at capital gain rates (or be subject to the limitation on capital losses) provided that the asset continued to meet the current requirements for such treatment. Recognition of capital gain (or loss) on the asset after the effective date would extinguish the capital gain (or loss) potential of the asset. Thus, gains on sale or exchange of an asset purchased after the effective date would not receive any special tax treatment.

Both of these systems have been employed in the Tax Reform Act of 1976 in connection with the so-called carryover basis provisions at death—the former for securities traded on established markets, and the latter for all other assets.

A number of technical rules relating to transfers and subsequent adjustments to basis would have to be provided. In general, the account should carry over to the transferee in certain tax-free transfers that reflect a change in the transferor's form of ownership of, or interest in, the asset, such as contributions to a controlled corporation (under section 351) or partnership (section 721) or a complete liquidation of certain controlled subsidiaries (section 332). In the case of a transfer of an asset to a controlled corporation or partnership, it may be appropriate to allow the shareholder or partner to elect to transfer the capital gain account of the asset to his stock or partnership interest, and have the asset lose its capital gain character in the hands of the corporation or partnership. Also, in the case of a sale or exchange where the seller is allowed nonrecognition of gain on the transaction because he acquires an asset similar to the asset disposed of, the capital gain account should attach to the newly acquired asset. For example, if a taxpayer is to be allowed nonrecognition treatment on the sale of a personal residence where another residence is acquired within a specified time, the capital gain account would attach to the new residence.

Rules also would be needed to take into account an increase or decrease in the basis of the property after the effective date. An increase in the basis of the property generally should not decrease the capital gain account, since the increase in basis generally will be accompanied by an increase in the fair market value of the asset (for example, where a shareholder contributes cash to a corporation); the increased fair market value due to the increase in basis would, when recognized, represent a return of the investment increasing the basis. On the other hand, a decrease in basis resulting from a deduction against ordinary income should reduce the capital gain account (i.e., code sections 1245, 1250, and other recapture provisions currently in the code that prevent the conversion of ordinary income into capital gain because of excess depreciation deductions or other means should continue to apply). In general, if the taxpayer's basis in an asset is required to be allocated among several assets (such as is required with respect to a nontaxable stock dividend) the capital gain account should be allocated in a similar manner.

Special rules also would be needed for section 1231 property, since net gains from the sale of such assets qualify for capital gains treatment.[6] A workable rule would be to apply section 1231 to assets that qualify as section 1231 assets in the hands of the taxpayer on the general effective date, and continue to so qualify as of the date of sale or other taxable disposition. Such property would have a "section 1231 account" similar to the capital gain account attaching to each asset. Similar rules relating to transfers, basis adjustments, etc., also would apply.

Since an asset may be held for an indefinite period, a cutoff date for capital gains treatment is needed; otherwise, the complexity of the capital gains provisions in the code would continue for at least a generation. (Under the proposal, donors and decedents would be required to recognize gain or loss on the assets transferred, subject to certain exceptions and, thus, the capital gain account would not carry over to a donee or heir.) Accordingly, at the end of a specified period (say, 10 years), the capital gains deduction and the alternative tax treatment would expire. Admittedly, some of the equity problems resulting from immediate repeal of the capital gains provisions would remain even if complete repeal were delayed 10 years. The 10-year phase-out period, however, would allow gradual market adjustments and help protect the interests of investors who purchased assets in reliance on the current capital gains provisions.

An alternative to the capital gain account (and section 1231 account) procedure would be to phase out the deduction for capital gains (and the alternative tax) ratably over a specified number of years. For example, the 50-percent deduction for capital gains could be reduced five percentage points a year, so that at the end of 10 years the deduction would be eliminated. The simplicity of this alternative is the best argument for its adoption, since no valuation as of a particular date would be required.

Corporate Integration

Under the Comprehensive Income Tax, corporations would not be subject to tax. Instead, shareholders would be taxable on their *prorata* share of corporate income, or would be allowed to deduct their *prorata* share of corporate loss. (See the discussion in chapter 3.)

The most significant transitional problems involve the question of timing and the treatment of income, deductions, credits, and accumulated earnings and profits that are earned or accrued before the effective date of the change-over to integration but that would be taken into account for tax purposes after such date. Other transition problems related to the foreign area are discussed in chapter 3.

Pre-effective Date Retained Earnings. Perhaps the most difficult transition problem posed by corporate integration is the treatment of corporate earnings and profits that are undistributed as of the effective date of integration. Such earnings would have been taxed to the shareholders as dividends if distributed before the effective date. Under corporate integration, distributions made by a corporation to its shareholders would be tax-free to the extent of the shareholder's basis; distributions in excess of the shareholder's basis in his stock would be taxable. However, corporate earnings and profits accumulated before the effective date but distributed afterward should not be accorded tax-free treatment; to do so would discriminate against corporations that distributed (rather than accumulated) their earnings and profits in preintegration taxable years.

The problem of accumulated earnings can be addressed by continuing to apply current law to corporate distributions that are made within 10 years after the effective date of integration and that (1) are made to persons who held the shares on such effective date with respect to which the distribution is made, and (2) are made out of earnings and profits accumulated before such date. Thus, a distribution to such shareholders out of earnings and profits accumulated by the corporation before the first taxable year to which corporate integration applies would be a dividend, taxable as ordinary income, unless the distribution would qualify for different treatment under current law. For example, a distribution received pursuant to a redemption of stock that is not essentially equivalent to a dividend under current law would continue to be treated as a distribution in part or full payment in exchange for the stock. On the other hand, an attempt to bail out the pre-effective date earnings and profits by means of a partial redemption of stock that would be treated as a dividend distribution under current law would continue to be so treated. The provisions of current law relating to electing small business (subchapter S) corporations would be helpful as a model in drafting this particular transition proposal. For purposes of determining how much of a distribution that is treated as a sale or exchange under current law would qualify for special capital gains treatment, the transition rules outlined above for changes in taxation of capital gains would apply.

In general, distributions with respect to stock acquired in a taxable transaction after the effective date would be subject to the new rules, and would reduce basis and not constitute income (unless such distributions exceeded the shareholder's basis). However, in those cases where the transferee acquired the stock after the effective date without recognition of gain by the transferor, current law would continue to apply to distributions from pre-effective date accumulated earnings and profits.

Distributions after the effective date would be deemed to be made first from the shareholder's distributable share of the corporation's post-effective date income and then from pre-effective date earnings and profits (similar to the subchapter S rules). Distributions in excess of these amounts would be applied against and reduce the shareholder's basis in his stock. Amounts in excess of the shareholder's basis generally would be considered income.

In order to avoid indefinite retention of such a dual system of taxation, the special treatment of pre-effective date earnings and profits would cease after a specified number of years following the effective date of integration. Distributions received after such date, regardless of source, first would be applied against basis and would be income to the shareholder to the extent they exceed basis. As previously indicated, pre-integration accumulated earnings and profits remaining after this date will not escape taxation completely at the shareholder level, since such earnings will be reflected in the gain recognized on a subsequent taxable transfer of the stock (such as a sale or a transfer by gift or at death), or may be taxed as a distribution in excess of basis. Before fixing the cutoff date for this provision, an effort should be made to determine quantitatively the extent of the benefit to the shareholders of the deferral of such taxation.

An alternative proposal was considered in an attempt to preserve the ordinary income character of distributions from pre-effective date earnings. This proposal would treat a shareholder as receiving a "deemed dividend" (spread ratably over a 10-year or longer period) in an amount equal to the lesser of the excess of the fair market value of the share of stock as of the effective date over its adjusted basis, or the share's *prorata* portion of undistributed earnings and profits as of such date. This proposal was rejected because of its complexity and because of the likelihood of substantial liquidity problems for certain shareholders.

Carryovers and Carrybacks. The carryover or carryback of items of income, deduction, and credit between taxable years to which the corporate income tax applies, and taxable years to which it does not, must be considered for purposes of the transition rules. To the extent practicable, an attempt should be made to treat such items in a manner that reflects the impact of the corporate income tax as in effect when such items were earned or incurred. In following this approach, however, no attempt should be made to depart from the general rules requiring that an item of income or loss be recognized before it is taken into account in computing gross income. Accordingly, unrecognized appreciation or decline in value of corporate assets (or stock of the corporation) attributable to the pre-effective date period should not be "triggered" or recognized solely because of the shift to full integration.

In general, certain deductions and credits may carry back to a preceding taxable year or carry over to a subsequent taxable year because of a limitation on the amount of such deduction or credit that the taxpayer may claim for the taxable year in which the deduction is incurred or the credit earned. Thus, for example, a net operating loss carryback or carryover arises because the taxpayer's deductions exceed his gross income. Capital loss deductions are limited to capital gains, deductions for charitable contributions are limited to a certain percentage of income, and the investment tax credit is limited to a percentage of the tax due. Also, the recapture as ordinary income, after the effective date, of deductions allowed and other amounts of income upon which tax has previously been deferred in pre-effective date years, has the effect of shifting that income to post-effective date years.

If income sheltered by a deduction (or income that would have been sheltered had the deduction been utilized in an earlier year) had been distributed as a taxable dividend, the net after-tax effect on the shareholder of the deferral or acceleration of a deduction would depend on his marginal tax bracket. In general, if the shareholder is in a lower bracket, he may realize more total after-tax income if the deduction is utilized in a pre-effective date year in which the corporate tax applies and in which the tax savings at the corporate level are distributed as a dividend. If the taxpayer is in a higher bracket, he may realize more total after-tax income if the deduction is utilized in computing his distributable share of taxable income after integration. To best approximate the net result that would occur if such items could be used in the year incurred or earned, unused deductions and credits incurred or earned in pre-effective date years should be given an unlimited carryback to earlier years of the corporation. In many cases this would benefit the taxpayer because he would receive a tax refund from such carryback earlier than he would under current law. Such benefits could be avoided to a large extent by charging the taxpayer an appropriate amount of interest for advancement of the refund.

Deductions that could not be absorbed in pre-effective date years would be allowed to be carried in full to post-effective date years, subject to the limits established on the number of succeeding taxable years to which the item may be carried. In general, however, deductions carried over from a pre-effective date year should not flow through to the shareholders, either directly or indirectly, for use in offsetting the shareholder's income from other sources, but should be available only as deductions at the corporate level in order to determine the shareholder's *prorata* share of corporate income. This would avoid retroactive integration with respect to such deductions, since the deduction would not flow through when incurred; it also would avoid possible abuses by means of trafficking in loss corporations. Ordinary income upon which tax was deferred in pre-effective years should continue to be subject to recapture as ordinary income.

Generally, the carryover to a post-integration year of a tax credit earned in a pre-effective date taxable year would result in a windfall for the shareholder. If the credit had been used to offset corporate income tax in the year in which it was earned, the amount representing the tax at the corporate level offset by the credit would have been taxable to the shareholder, either when distributed as a dividend or when realized by means of sale of the stock. Accordingly, a rule should be devised by which the tax benefit of a credit carryover approximates the benefit that would result if the amount of the credit first offset a hypothetical corporate tax and then was distributed to the shareholder as a taxable dividend (or, perhaps, realized as capital gain).

In general, no losses incurred or available credits earned in post-effective date years would carry back to pre-effective date years, since such items would flow through to the shareholders after the effective date of integration.

Under present law, certain taxpayers, such as regulated investment companies, real estate investment trusts, and personal holding companies, receive a dividends-paid deduction for a taxable year even though the distribution is actually made in a subsequent year. Such distributions in post-effective date years should be allowed to relate back to the extent provided by current law for the purpose of determining the corporate tax liability for the appropriate pre-effective date year. The distribution would be considered to be out of pre-effective date earnings and profits (whether or not it exceeds the amount in such account) and taxable to the shareholders as a dividend from that source.

Rules will have to be provided to insure that, if an investment tax credit earned by a corporation in a pre-effective date taxable year is subject to recapture because of an early disposition of the property, the credit also is recaptured, either from the corporation or the shareholders. This could be accomplished at the corporate level by imposing an excise tax on the transfer or other recapture event in an amount equal to the appropriate income tax recapture.

Flow-Through of Corporate Capital Gains. During the phase-out period for capital gains, the net capital gain or net capital loss for taxable years after the effective date of corporate integration should be computed at the corporate level with respect to sales or exchanges of capital assets or section 1231 property by the corporation. The character of such net capital gain or net capital loss should flow through to the shareholders.

Flow-Through of Tax-Exempt Interest. If the character of capital gains is to flow through to shareholders, consistency would require that the character of any remaining tax-exempt interest received or accrued by a corporation after the effective date of corporate integration from any State or municipal bonds that are grandfathered also should flow through as tax-exempt interest to the shareholders. The tax-free character of the interest to shareholders would be preserved by increasing the shareholder's basis by the amount of the interest attributable to him, but not including such interest in taxable income. Distribution would be treated as under the new law—as a reduction of basis, but not included in income. Thus, such interest, if distributed, would leave both taxable income and basis unchanged.

Generally, under present law, State and municipal bond interest is received tax-free by the corporation, but is taxable as a dividend when distributed to shareholders. The 1976 Tax Reform Act, however, provides that, in certain cases, the character of tax-exempt interest distributed by a regulated investment company flow through as tax-exempt interest to its shareholders.[7] If it is determined that the tax-exempt character of State and municipal bond interest received by all corporations should not flow through to shareholders, an exception should be made for regulated investment companies that have relied on the flow-through provisions of the 1976 Tax Reform Act.

Unique Corporate Taxpayers. The provisions of the tax code relating to taxation of insurance companies and other unique corporate taxpayers will have to be examined to determine what adjustments, if any, are required to take into account the effect of corporate integration on the special rules applying to such taxpayers. The determination of appropriate transition rules will depend on the nature of any changes made to the basic provisions.

Business and Investment Income, Individual and Corporate

In general, the repeal of code provisions that provide an incentive for certain business-related expenditures or investments in specific assets should be developed to minimize the losses to persons who made such expenditures or investments prior to the effective date of the new law. The principal technique to effectuate this policy would be to grandfather actions taken under current law. For example, any repeal of a tax credit (such as the investment tax credit) and any requirement that an expenditure that is currently deductible (such as soil and water conservation expenditures) must be capitalized should be prospective only.[8] Subject to the rules prescribed above for corporations, unused tax credits earned in pre-effective date years should be available as a carryover to taxable years after the effective date to the extent allowed under current law. The repeal of special provisions allowing accelerated amortization or depreciation of certain assets generally should apply only with respect to expenditures made or assets placed in service after a specific cutoff date. The revised general depreciation and depletion rules should apply to property placed in service or expenditures made after an effective date. Thus, for example, buildings would continue to be depreciable in the manner prescribed by current law only in the hands of their current owners. A taxpayer who acquires a building and places it in service after the effective date would be subject to the new rules. Although this could result in losses in asset value for the current owners, grandfathering the asset itself could, particularly in the case of buildings, delay the effect of the new rules for an unacceptable period.

The deduction for local property taxes on personal residences should be phased out by allowing deduction of a declining percentage of such taxes.

The exclusion from gross income of interest on State and municipal bonds and certain earnings on life insurance policies should continue to apply to such interest and earnings on bonds and insurance policies that are outstanding as of the effective date.

When adoption of the Comprehensive Income Tax results in ending those provisions of current law that allow the nonrecognition of gain (or loss) on sales or exchanges of particular assets, such changes should be effective immediately, with no grandfather clause. It is unlikely that the original decision to invest in such assets depended on an opportunity to make a subsequent tax-free change in investment. An exception may be appropriate, however, with respect to a repeal of the provision that excludes from gross income the value of a building constructed by a lessee that becomes the property of the lessor upon a termination of the lease. A grandfather clause should apply current law to the termination of a lease entered into before the effective date.

The proposal would allow an adjustment to the basis of an asset to prevent the taxation of "gain" that is attributable to inflation and that does not reflect an increase in real value of the asset sold by the taxpayer. The inflation adjustment should be applied with respect to inflation occurring in taxable years after the effective date. Making such an adjustment retroactive would result in a substantial unanticipated gain for many asset holders.

Other Individual Income

Under the comprehensive income tax, several kinds of compensation and other items previously excluded would be included in gross income, and deductions for a number of expenditures that can be considered personal in nature would be disallowed.

Employee Compensation. Such items as earnings on pension plan reserves allocable to the employee, certain health and life insurance premiums paid by the employer, certain disability benefits, unemployment benefits, and subsidized compensation would be included in gross income.

It may be presumed that existing employment contracts were negotiated on the basis that such items (other than unemployment compensation) would be excluded from the employee's gross income, particularly in those cases where the exclusion reflects a policy of encouraging that particular type of compensation. In the absence of special transition rules, the inclusion of such items in income could create cash flow problems or other hardships for employees under such contracts. For example, a worker who is required to include in income the amount of his employer's health insurance plan contribution may have to pay the tax on this amount from what was previously "take home" pay if he cannot renegotiate his contract.

This problem can best be solved by an effective date provision that would apply the new rules to compensation paid in taxable years beginning after a period of time to allow employers and employees to adjust to the new rules. Thus, the tax-free status of items paid by employers on the date of enactment would continue for a specified period, such as 3 years. Alternatively, the inclusion of these items of income could be phased in over such a period, including one-third after 1 year, two-thirds after 2 years, and the full amount after the third year. Special rules for military personnel could be devised to grandfather servicemen through their current enlistment or term of service. Earnings of a qualified pension plan allocable to the employee that are attributable to periods before this delayed effective date would not be included in the gross income of the employee. However, earnings attributable to periods after that date (as extended with respect to binding contracts) would be included in gross income as accrued.

Generally, unemployment compensation, which would be included in taxable income under the proposal, would not represent a return of a tax-paid basis to the recipient, since the "premiums," or employer contributions, with respect to such compensation were not included in his gross income. Thus, the full amount of such compensation should be included in taxable income immediately after the general effective date.

Medical and Casualty Loss Deductions. Under the comprehensive income tax, certain nonbusiness expenditures, such as casualty losses, and medical and dental expenses would cease being deductible. Generally, the repeal of the deductibility of these expenses could be effective immediately. If the medical expense deduction is replaced by a catastrophic insurance program, or some other program to achieve the same ends, repeal of the deduction should coincide with the effective date of the substitute program.

Charitable Deductions. This provision should be phased in if the deductibility of charitable contributions is eliminated under the model comprehensive income tax. To the extent that direct public subsidies to the affected institutions do not replace the loss in private gifts from removal of the tax incentive for contributions, both employment in and services to beneficiaries of such institutions would decline greatly. A gradual phase-in would increase the extent to which employment losses occur through gradual attrition rather than layoffs and would aid in identifying the types of charitable recipients who might require greater direct public assistance when the deduction is completely ended. One possible method of phase-in would be to allow a declining fraction of contributions to be deductible in the first few years of the effective date.

Other Items Previously Excluded. The inclusion in gross income of scholarships, fellowships, and means-tested cash and in-kind government grants, would not appear to present any transition problems because, generally, the amounts of these items were not bargained for by the recipient and do not represent a return of a tax-paid basis.

Treatment of Retirement Benefits. Under the Comprehensive Income Tax, retirement benefits, including social security benefits and private pensions, will be included in the tax base, while contributions to private pension funds and to social security by both employees and employers will be exempted from any concurrent tax liability. A significant transition problem arises from this feature of the Comprehensive Income Tax. In the absence of special transition rules, currently retired persons would be required to pay tax on the returns of private pension contributions that had already been taxed. While the link between contributions and benefits is not so direct for social security, it still would be unfair to include social security benefits in the taxable income of persons who have been retired as of the effective date, again, because these taxpayers have paid tax on the part of income represented by employee social security contributions throughout their working years. Thus, persons retired as of the effective date should not have to pay tax on private retirement benefits which represent a return of contribution or on social security benefits. On the other hand, benefits paid by qualified pension plans that allowed deductibility of past contributions, should remain fully taxable, as under present law.

More complex provisions are required for retirement income of taxpayers who are in the middle of their working years as of the effective date. Such taxpayers will have been taxed on the employee portion of retirement contributions up to the effective date, but not afterwards. Thus, it seems fair that they should pay tax on a fraction of the retirement benefits which represent return of contribution, the fraction bearing some relation to the portion of the contributions that were excluded from taxable income. The general rule proposed is to include in the tax base a fraction of retirement income that represents return of contribution to an employee-funded pension plan. The fraction would depend on age at the effective date, ranging from 0 for taxpayers age 60 or over to 1 for taxpayers age 20 or under. A table could be provided in the tax form relating date of birth to the fraction of such income that is taxable. A similar treatment is proposed for social security benefits.

Treatment of Gifts and Transfers at Death as Recognition Events. Under the proposal, gifts and transfers at death would be treated as recognition events. Thus, in general, the excess of the fair market value of the asset transferred over its adjusted basis in the hands of the donor or decedent would be included in the gross income of the donor or decedent.

The portion of such gains attributable to the period before the effective date of any such recognition rule should be exempted. Provisions for such an exemption were made in the Tax Reform Act of 1976 in connection with the carryover basis at death rule. The gains deemed to have accrued after the effective date would be taxable on transfer at the same rates applying to other sources of income.

TRANSITION TO A CASH FLOW TAX SYSTEM

This section presents a proposal for transition from the current system to the model Cash Flow Tax proposed in chapter 4. The problems involved in a transition to the Cash Flow Tax would be considerable, and all of the alternative methods considered have major shortcomings. Presentation of this proposal includes discussion of administrative difficulties and some possible distributive inequities, and an explanation of why certain alternative plans were rejected.

In summary, the proposed transition plan would maintain the present tax alongside the Cash Flow Tax for 10 years before total conversion to the Cash Flow Tax. During the transition period, individuals would compute their tax liability under both systems and would be required to pay the higher of the two taxes. The corporate income tax would be retained for the interim and would be discontinued immediately at the end of the 10-year period. At that time, unrealized capital gains earned prior to full adoption of the Cash Flow Tax would be "flushed" out of the system through a recognition date, at which point they would be taxed at the current capital gains rates. Payment of taxes on past capital gains could be deferred, at a low interest charge, to prevent forced liquidation of small businesses.

The transition program outlined here would not fully realize the goals of transition presented below. It would, however, mitigate the redistribution of wealth that would result from immediate adoption of the cash flow tax and would simplify the tax system by eliminating, within a reasonable period of time, the need to keep the personal and business income tax records currently required.

Goals of Transition

The main objectives to be realized by the transition rules for the Cash Flow Tax are: (1) prevention of immediate or long-term redistribution of economic welfare, and (2) simplicity and administrative ease. Although some changes in consumption opportunities would be inevitable in a tax change as major as the one proposed, the proper transition program should be able to minimize large redistributions among taxpayers in ability to consume immediately and in the future. In particular, this program should prevent heavy additional tax liabilities (in present-value terms) for any clearly identifiable group of taxpayers. For purposes of simplicity, transition rules should eliminate the present tax system and its recordkeeping requirements promptly and, to the extent possible, avoid measuring current accumulated wealth and any annual changes in individuals' total wealth positions in the transition period, as well as afterward. After transition, the principal records for tax purposes would consist only of cash flow transactions for business activities, net deposits and withdrawals in qualified accounts, the usual wage and salary data, and transfer payments.

Distribution Issues

Two distribution issues are important in a transition in the Cash Flow Tax. (1) treatment of untaxed income before the effective date and (2) changes in the distribution of after-tax consumption.

Equitable treatment of income untaxed before the effective date would require that an individual who had unrealized capital gains at the time of adoption of the new system be treated in the same way as the individual who realized the capital gains before the effective date. The practical problems involved in achieving this goal influence the specifics of the transition proposal discussed below.

The treatment of past accumulated income that has been taxed poses a more difficult problem of equity. Because the Cash Flow Tax is, in an important sense, equivalent to exempting income from capital from tax, as outlined in chapter 4, a higher tax rate on current wages not saved would be required to maintain the same tax revenue. Thus, the short-term effect of a Cash Flow Tax would be a higher after-tax rate of return from ownership of monetary or physical assets regarded as tax prepaid and a lower after-tax wage rate. The distributive consequences of this change could be modified if some or all of accumulated wealth were to be treated as if already held in qualified accounts; i.e., subject to tax upon withdrawal for consumption.

For taxpayers making no gifts or bequests, if existing wealth were to be regarded as tax-prepaid under the new system, all future returns from such assets, as well as return of principal, would not be subject to tax. On the other hand, if existing wealth were to be regarded as receipts in the first year of the Cash Flow Tax, an equally logical approach, consumption of principal would be taxed, though the present value of tax liability would not increase as assets earned accrued interest, as it would under an income tax.

Table 1 illustrates the tax treatment, under a Comprehensive Income Tax and under the two alternative methods of transition to the Cash Flow Tax, of consumption out of $100 of past accumulated assets for different times at which wealth is withdrawn for consumption. A tax rate of 50 percent is assumed, assessed on annual interest earnings in the case of an income tax.

Table 1
Potential Consumption Out of Accumulated Wealth Under Different Tax Rules

Initial Wealth = $100
Assets Accumulate at 10 Percent Per Year If Untaxed;
5 Percent Per Year If Taxed

Years after effective date	Income tax	Cash Flow Tax; Asset tax-prepaid	Cash Flow Tax; Asset in initial receipts
0	$100	$100	$ 50
10	$163	$259	$130
20	$265	$673	$336

Under the Comprehensive Income Tax, the asset could be withdrawn and consumed tax-free, but future accumulation would be taxed.[9] Under the Cash Flow Tax, with the asset defined as tax-prepaid, returns from the asset would be allowed to accumulate tax-free and could also be withdrawn and consumed tax-free. Under the Cash Flow Tax, with the asset value initially included in the tax base, consumption from the asset would be taxed upon withdrawal, but the rate of accumulation of the asset would not be affected by the tax.

A transition to the Cash Flow Tax with assets initially defined as tax prepaid would increase the welfare of owners of assets. The after-tax consumption of these taxpayers would increase under the new system unless they consumed all of their wealth within the first year after the effective date, in which case consumption would be unchanged. If assets were initially included in the tax base, however, the after-tax consumption of owners of assets would decrease if they chose to consume a large portion of their wealth in the early years after the effective date. Inclusion of assets in the base would increase after-tax consumption relative to an income tax for asset-holders who deferred consumption out of accumulated wealth for a long period.[10]

As Table 1 illustrates, how past wealth is viewed would make a big difference in the present value of tax liabilities.

Inclusion of accumulated assets in the tax base would be unfair to older persons who are about to consume out of accumulated wealth during the retirement period, if the income from which this wealth was accumulated had been subject to tax during their working years. On the other hand, tax-prepaid designation would benefit owners of monetary and physical assets by eliminating tax on the post-transition returns from past accumulation. Thus, tax-prepaid treatment of capital assets for transition purposes may be viewed as inequitable.

The distribution problem caused by defining existing capital assets as prepaid would be reduced over time. The increased incentive to savings provided by the cash flow tax should raise the rate of capital formation, increasing the amount of investment and eventually lowering before-tax returns to capital and raising before-tax wages. However, in the first few years after transition, higher tax rates on current wages would not be matched by a corresponding increase in before-tax wages.

For certain types of assets, the appropriate rule for transition definition is clear. Under the present system, investments in owner-occupied houses and other consumer durables are treated very similarly to tax-prepaid investments, and they should be defined as prepaid assets for purposes of transition to a cash flow tax. The accrued value of employer-funded pension plans should be treated in the same manner as qualified accounts, because the contributions were exempt from tax under the old system and the receipts were fully taxable.

Designation of past accumulated assets as tax-prepaid assets would be the easier transition to administer. There would be no need to measure existing wealth. Tax-prepaid assets could be freely converted to qualified assets to enable the individual to average his tax base over time. An individual converting a tax-prepaid asset to a qualified asset would be able to take an immediate tax deduction, but would become liable for taxes upon withdrawal of principal and subsequent earnings from the qualified account.[11] If assets were defined initially to be part of an individual's tax base, it would be necessary to valuate them on the effective date. Individuals would have an incentive to understate their initial wealth holdings. Assets not initially accounted for could be deposited in qualified accounts in subsequent years, enabling an individual to take a deduction against other receipts.

A Preliminary Transition Proposal

Considering the objectives of basic reform (equity, simplicity, efficiency), it seems best to define all assets initially in transition to the Cash Flow Tax as prepaid assets. For a period of 10 years, the existing tax code would be maintained, with taxpayers filing returns for both tax systems and paying the higher of the two computed taxes.[12] For most taxpayers, the Cash Flow Tax would be higher. However, for persons with large amounts of income from assets relative to wages, the current tax would be probably higher.

The corporate income tax would be retained throughout the transition period. Theoretically, stockholders paying the Cash Flow Tax should receive their corporate earnings gross of corporate tax during the interim period. However, without full corporate integration, whereby all earnings would be attributed to individual stockholders, it would be practically impossible to determine what part of a corporation's earnings should be attributed to individuals paying the consumption tax and what part to individuals paying tax under the old law. It is likely that ownership of corporate shares would be concentrated among individuals who would be subject to the current tax during the interim period. For reasons of simplicity, therefore, the corporate tax would be retained for the transition period and would be eliminated immediately afterward.

All sales of corporate stock purchased before the beginning of the transition period by individuals paying under either tax base would be subject to a capital gains tax at the existing favorable rates. The reason for this provision is that capital gains which were accrued but not realized before the interim period should be taxed as if they were income realized at the effective date.[13] This is not administratively attractive, so for 10 years all capital gains would be taxed on realization, whichever tax base the individual was using.

A recognition date would be required at the end of the transition period to account for all remaining untaxed capital gains. Under the Cash Flow Tax with assets defined as prepaid and no records of current and past corporate earnings and profits kept, it would be impossible to distinguish between distributions that were dividends out of current income and distributions that were return of accumulated capital. The dividends would not be subject to tax under the new law. Distributing past earnings would be a way of returning to the individual tax-free, the capital gains which has arisen prior to the adoption of the Cash Flow Tax. To eliminate the need for permanent corporate records to capture this past income, it would be necessary to have a single day of recognition for past gains at the end of the transition period.

However, it would be possible to develop a method of allowing the final capital gains tax assessed on the recognition date to be paid over a long period at a low interest rate, to avoid forced liquidation of small firms with few owners.

The advantages of the transition proposal outlined here are the following:

1. It would enable all of the simplifying features of the Cash Flow Tax to be in full operation after 10 years, including elimination of tax records required under the present code, but not under the Cash Flow Tax.
2. It would allow consumption out of past accumulated earnings to be exactly the same as it would have been under the current tax during the first years after the effective date.
3. It would provide for appropriate and consistent taxation of income earned before the effective date.
4. Eliminating only on a gradual basis taxes on returns from past accumulated assets earned after the effective date would mitigate the redistribution of wealth to current asset owners that would occur after immediate full adoption of the Cash Flow Tax.

The major disadvantages of this transition program are that it would require a recognition date that would impose a large, one-time administrative cost on the system, and it would require some taxpayers to fill out two sets of tax forms for a period of 10 years, a *temporary* departure from the long-term goal of simplicity.

Alternative Transition Plans

One alternative plan would be to adopt the new tax system immediately, designating all assets as prepaid, without a recognition date to flush out past capital gains. Although this plan would be the simplest one, it would give too great an economic advantage to individuals with unrealized asset appreciation and would cause too large a transfer of future after-tax consumption to present asset owners.

Another transition plan would be to adopt the Cash Flow Tax immediately and designate all assets as receipts in the first year. This would require valuing all wealth on the effective date and imposing a one-time wealth tax. Such an approach would be harsh to older persons planning to live off accumulated wealth in the early years after the effective date.

A complicated variation on tax-prepaid treatment of assets would be one under which, in exchange for the elimination of taxes on consumption of assets defined as tax-prepaid, an initial wealth tax related to an individual's personal circumstances would be imposed. For example, the initial tax could be based on age and wealth, with higher rates for persons with more wealth and lower rates for older persons.[14] Although it might provide a transition program that approximates distributive neutrality, such a plan would be a significant departure from the goal of simplicity.

A third option would allow three types of assets: tax-prepaid, as defined above; qualified, as defined above; and a third type, which would treat assets as defined under the current system. In principle, it would be desirable for persons to be able to consume out of the third type of assets tax-free and to invest in prepaid and qualified assets only out of savings from current income. In effect, this plan would initiate the Cash Flow Tax on current earnings only and would treat pre-effective date earnings exactly as they are treated under the current system, including the same treatment of post-effective date capital accumulation from pre-effective date wealth. This plan would be extremely difficult to administer. Not only would individuals have to keep books for three types of assets, but total annual wealth changes also would have to be computed, in order to arrive at a measure of annual consumption. (Valuation of unsold assets would not be a problem because even if too high a value were imputed, raising both measured wealth and saving, consumption would remain unchanged.) Treatment of corporate income under this system also would be complicated, because some investments in corporate stock would come from all three types of assets.

Under this transition alternative, assets of the third type would be subject to a transfer tax and converted to prepaid assets at death. Eventually, these assets would disappear from the system, and the complete Cash Flow Tax would be in operation. Alternatively, all assets of the third type could be designated prepaid after a fixed number of years.

Although the three-asset plan has the advantage of treating owners of capital exactly as they would have been treated under the income tax, and would change the rules only for new wealth[15] its administrative complexity raises very severe problems.

Chapter Notes

CHAPTER 3

[1]The use of food stamps is restricted to a class of consumption items, but the range of choice allowed to recipients is sufficiently broad that the difference between the face value and the purchase price of the coupon may be regarded as a cash grant.

[2]This imputed income estimates the return to both equity and debt supplied during construction. To include interest paid in the calculation would count the debt portion twice.

[3]To be increased in increments to 12 months according to the Tax Reform Act of 1976.

[4]To be increased in increments to $3,000 according to the Tax Reform Act of 1976.

[5]A rule of thumb that is commonly suggested is that monthly rental is 1 percent of market value. However, as experience with local property taxes has shown, accurate periodic assessment is technically and politically difficult.

[6]This definition is based upon that of Galvin and Willis, "Reforming the Federal Tax Structure," p. 19.

CHAPTER 6

[1]The exact change in the rate of taxation on income earned in corporations for different taxpayers will depend on the fraction of corporate income currently paid out in dividends, the current average holding period of assets before realizing capital gains, and the taxpayer's rate bracket. While the current corporate income tax does not distinguish among owners in different tax brackets, integration, which would attribute all corporate earnings to the separate owners, would tax *all* earnings from corporate capital at each owner's marginal tax rate.

[2]The taxpayer could avoid this problem by selling his shares before the effective date at the current lower capital gains rate and then buying them back. However, one other objective of transition rules, discussed in the next section, should be to avoid encouraging market transactions just prior to the effective date.

[3]For example, workers damaged by employment reductions in industries with increasing imports due to liberalized trade policies are eligible for trade adjustment assistance.

[4]Note that it is not clear just what is meant by an "existing asset" in this context. For example, a building is greatly affected by maintenance and improvement expenditures over time.

[5]Appropriate depreciation schedules are those that conform most closely to the actual rate of decline in asset values.

[6]Section 1231 property is generally certain property used in the taxpayer's trade or business. If gains exceed losses for a taxable year, the net gains from section 1231 property are taxed at capital gains rates; if losses from section 1231 property exceed gains, the net losses are treated as ordinary losses.

[7]In the case of a subchapter S corporation, the character of net capital gains flows through to the shareholder. The character of tax-exempt interest does not.

[8]Expenditures made pursuant to binding contracts entered into before the effective date also should be grandfathered.

[9]The income tax computation assumes that all returns to investment would be taxed as accrued at full rates. Thus, the annual rate of percentage after-tax interest under the income tax would be cut in half. Under the present law, taxation of capital gains is deferred until realization and then taxed at only one-half the regular rate. For example, if the asset is sold after 20 years, potential after-tax consumption would be $530, which is computed by multiplying the long-term capital gain of $573 by .75 (the taxpayer is assumed to be in the 50 percent bracket) and adding the return of basis. It should be noted, however, that, if the asset is corporate stock, profits are also subject to an annual corporate tax. Combining the effects of corporate and personal taxes, the income of the asset holders may be taxed under current law at either a higher or lower rate than the rate on wage and salary income, depending on assumptions about the incidence of taxes.

[10]For example, if the before-tax interest rate were 10 percent, wealth would quadruple in 15 years. With the 50-percent tax rate used in Table 1, wealth holders would be better off under the consumption tax, even if their assets were initially included in receipts if they deferred consumption out of wealth for at least 15 years, obtaining a deduction against receipts in the first year by placing the asset in a qualified account.

[11]A wealthy person could appear to "shelter" his current consumption by converting prepaid assets into qualified assets, deducting the deposits in qualified assets from current wage and other receipts. However, this practice would not reduce the present value of his tax base, because he would have to pay a tax on the principal and accumulated interest whenever the qualified asset was withdrawn for consumption.

[12]It is possible that only wealthy persons should be required to fill out a return for the current personal income tax. The main reason for retaining the current tax would be to tax returns accumulated from past wealth for an interim period of time to mitigate the inequitable distribution effects of a transition to tax-prepaid treatment of assets. It is likely that only people with significant amounts of wealth would have a higher liability under the current tax. The requirement to file two income tax returns might be limited to taxpayers reporting an adjusted gross income above a certain minimum level (for example, $20,000 or more) in any of several years before the effective date.

[13]Technically speaking, individuals paying the Cash Flow Tax during the interim period should not have to pay capital gains tax between the first day of the interim period and the time an asset is sold. One way to avoid this would be to adjust the basis upward to conform to interest that would have been earned on a typical investment after the beginning of the interim period. By doing this, the present value of capital gains tax paid for assets growing at that interest rate would be the same as if the gain were realized on the effective date.

[14]Because the wealth of older persons might be subject to the accessions tax sooner, it might not be necessary for reasons of equity to tax it on the effective date.

[15]The three-asset plan can be viewed as a sophisticated form of "grandfathering."

Index

L

Life insurance, 40
  employer-paid premiums, 178
  term life, 55, 118
  whole life, 55, 118
Loan transactions, 111

M

Marriage penalty, 93, 153
  1976 law, table, 154
  Cash Flow Tax, table, 156
  Comprehensive Income Tax,
    table, 155
Marriage tax. *See* marriage penalty
Maximum tax, 5, 42, 70
Medicaid, 57
Medical catastrophe insurance, 83
Medical expense credit, 82
Medical expense deduction, 6,
  81, 105, 179
Medical insurance premiums, 81,
  105, 106, 178
Mineral deposits, 6
Minimum tax, 42, 70
Mortgage interest deduction, 6,
  77, 80, 120
Motor fuels taxes, 84, 86
Moving expenses, 51

O

Owner occupied housing, 6, 32
  imputed rental income, 77
  property tax deduction, 78, 105

P

Partnerships, 122
Payroll taxes, 56
Pension income, table, 140
Pension plans, 31, 118
  accrued earnings, 52
  benefits received, 52
  earnings on reserves, 178
  employer contributions, 52
  international considerations, 90
Pension rights, 40
Percentage depletion, 6
Personal exemption, adjustment
  for family size, 96
Personal exemption credit, 97
Phasing in, 168
Philanthropy. *See* charitable
  contributions

Pollution taxes, 86
Price changes, transition considera-
  tions, 159
Progressivity, 48, 139
  Cash Flow Tax, 122
Property tax deduction, 105
Public housing, 57
Public transfer payments, 56. *See
  also* government transfer
  payments

Q

Qualified accounts
  asset purchases, 110
  cash flow accounting, 102

R

Realization concept, capital gains
  and losses, 69
Recreational vehicles, 81
Retirement annuities, employer
  contributions, 10
Retirement benefits, 179
Retirement income, 7

S

Sales taxes, 7, 84, 85
Savings, 33, 46
  double taxation, 23, 37
Secondary workers, 94
Self-constructed assets, 61
Sewer assessments, 86
Simons, Henry, 22
Social security contributions, 118
Social security disability
  insurance, 55
Social security retirement
  benefits, 7, 54, 118
Standard deduction, 7
Standard-of-living approach, 30
  33, 38
State and local bond interest, 3,
  6, 76, 119
State and local property taxes, 77
State income tax deduction, 7, 83,
  84, 105
Subchapter S corporations, 63
Supplemental Security Income, 57

T

Tax Reduction Act of 1975, 97
Tax Reform Act of 1969, 1